D1002796

April 2013

Eleanor Parker

Woman of a Thousand Faces

a bio-bibliography and filmography

Doug McClelland

The Scarecrow Press, Inc.
Lanham, Maryland, and Oxford

SCARECROW PRESS, INC.

Published in the United States of America
by Scarecrow Press, Inc.
A Member of the Rowman & Littlefield Publishing Group
4501 Forbes Blvd., Suite 200, Lanham, MD 20706
www.scarecrowpress.com

PO Box 317
Oxford
OX2 9RU, UK

British Library Cataloguing in Publication Information Available

The hardback edition of this book was previously cataloged by the Library of
Congress as follows:

McClelland, Doug.
    Eleanor Parker : woman of a thousand faces : a bio-bibliography and
filmography / by Doug McClelland.
    p.   cm.
Includes index.
ISBN 0-8108-2242-3 (alk. paper)
1. Parker, Eleanor, 1922-   --Bibliography.   I. Title.
Z8660.62.M35   1989
[PN2287.P24]
016.79143'028'092—dc20   89-10292

⊖™ The paper used in this publication meets the minimum requirements of
American National Standard for Information Sciences—Permanence of
Paper for Printed Library Materials, ANSI/NISO Z39.48-1992.
Manufactured in the United States of America.

ISBN· 0-8108-4836-8   (paper)
ISBN: 978-0-8108-4836-8

This book is dedicated to

PAUL DAY CLEMENS

who proves that the fruit doesn't fall very far from the tree

CONTENTS

FOREWORD

We may as well face it. Someone, somewhere, is going to ask: Why another book about another movie star?

The answer is that there are two kinds of Hollywood stars and most of the books have been about one kind, the "personality" stars. Clark Gable was always Clark Gable, whether as the reporter in It Happened One Night or in Test Pilot. Even in Gone with the Wind, Gable did not become Rhett Butler, rather did Rhett Butler become Clark Gable. In Stagecoach and The Green Berets, John Wayne was John Wayne. Mind you, I loved them and admired them and so did audiences all over the world. That's why audiences went to their films, to see them rather than the character. That's why, during the vintage years of Hollywood, screenwriters mostly wrote "vehicles," stories tailored to showcase the personality of the star.

But there is another kind of star, quite different and, in my opinion, perhaps more worth our notice. Alec Guinness, for example. His The Lavender Hill Mob and The Bridge on the River Kwai gave us two vastly different creations, two distinct people, two submergings of the performer into the character.

That's why this book is different. It's about Eleanor Parker. You didn't go to her films to see Miss Parker being Miss Parker in a different dress or locale. You went to see what person she had created on film.

A star like that is a boon to a screenwriter. All of us, I suspect, indulge in dreams at one time or another. Screenwriters, by the very nature of their work, tend to dream more than most people. We dream that what we visualized and put on paper will come alive on the screen. This rarely ... very rarely ... happens.

It happened for me when I had the good fortune to have
Miss Eleanor Parker cast as the lead in Interrupted Melody.
I still believe that what helped our screenplay earn an Academy
Award was the quality and substance which she gave to the
starring role of Marjorie Lawrence. She, too, was nominated
as best actress, a distinction her performance richly deserved.
I felt then, and still do, that she should have won the Oscar.
What I have never been able to understand is why the studio,
M-G-M, gave no real support to her nomination, unlike producer Hal Wallis and Paramount Pictures, who mounted a
vigorous campaign for Anna Magnani in The Rose Tattoo,
which gained her the award. This was Miss Parker's third
nomination for best performance by an actress and it confirms
my view that even professionals tend quite often to remember
a personality more than a performance.

Miss Parker never gave a bad performance and always
revealed the person she portrayed rather than the actress
doing the portrayal. An undeviating perfectionist, a consum-
mate professional, she was one of the most technically accomplished, intensely hard-working and intelligently dedicated
artists I had ever been fortunate enough to have appear in
a script of mine ... and at that time I had been writing scripts
for some 20 years.

I've often wondered why she did not then and does
not now receive greater recognition. Two reasons occur to
me. She never played Eleanor Parker but was always the
character in the script. Audiences did not think of her but
thought of the character. The other reason, as I think about
it, is that she so thoroughly prepared a role that she made her
work look easy ... the way Fred Astaire made his dance
routines look easy. The sweat is never visible on the screen.
It comes in preparation, not in performance.

In The Odd Couple, Neil Simon has a scene in which
Jack Lemmon, who had asked Walter Matthau to watch a roast
Jack had been cooking on the stove, finds that Matthau had
forgotten to do so. The gravy has cooked away. Jack ex-
plodes. Matthau mumbles that he thought the gravy came
with the meat. Lemmon bitterly replies that gravy doesn't
come with the meat. You have to make the gravy.

With Eleanor Parker, the script provided the meat but
she always made the gravy. It's high time people knew it.

William Ludwig

*   *   *

Author's note: William Ludwig, who began as an attorney
in New York, joined M-G-M in the 1930s as a screenwriter
and stayed at "the Cadillac of Hollywood Studios" for 20 years.
The films he has written or co-written include several in the
Hardy family series, plus Journey for Margaret, The Human
Comedy (uncredited), An American Romance, Julia Misbehaves,
The Great Caruso, The Merry Widow (starring Lana Turner),
The Student Prince, Hit the Deck, Oklahoma!, Back Street
(starring Susan Hayward) and 1955's Interrupted Melody,
for which he and collaborator Sonya Levien received the best
story and screenplay Academy Award.

INTRODUCTION

Eleanor Parker was too good for her own good. Her versatility, her dazzling range as a film actress of unsurpassed gifts, has been both a blessing and a curse.

During the so-called Golden Age of Hollywood, when she was in her prime, personality generally counted for more than finished acting skills. If you were colorful enough, had specific qualities that set you apart from the run-of-the-mill, and of course were lucky enough to be given the opportunity to display them, you could become a major, possibly enduring star.

For instance: Ingrid Bergman was saintly, Claudette Colbert was charming, Jeanne Crain was virginal, Joan Crawford was poor, Bette Davis was neurotic, Irene Dunne was perfect, Joan Fontaine was shy, Greta Garbo was weary, Greer Garson was noble, Betty Grable was leggy, Susan Hayward was tough, Katharine Hepburn was haughty, Deborah Kerr was ladylike, Marilyn Monroe was sexy, Maria Montez was exotic, Barbara Stanwyck was dangerous, Elizabeth Taylor was beautiful, Mae West was raunchy and Esther Williams was wet.

But what--who--was Eleanor Parker?

At Warner Bros. Studios through the 1940s, then mainly M-G-M and 20th Century-Fox into the 1960s, Eleanor Parker was only colorful so far as the current role demanded. Despite a pronounced shyness off-camera (especially early in her career), she was different in every part, and the variety was remarkable. In films she has portrayed a would-be suicide; a war bride; a Cockney tart; an elegant Briton; a naive actress; a mental case and her identical, normal cousin; a prison inmate; an unwed mother; a detective's plain wife; a

xi

fiery, French redhead; the wife of the pilot who dropped the
first Atomic bomb; a Confederate spy; a backwoods hoyden;
an opera singer; a homicidal cripple; a girl with three personalities; a German baroness; and other roles. The Ohio native
was starred in remakes of vehicles played earlier by Sweden's
Greta Garbo and Massachusetts' Bette Davis. And she was
so completely, so convincingly all these diverse characters
that the moviegoing public, worshipping at the icon of personality, never quite knew where to light Eleanor Parker's candle.

There were newspaper and magazine articles about
her titled, "The Girl Nobody Knows," "Hollywood's Mystery
Girl," "Changeable Lady," "Please, Miss Parker: Look the
Same Girl--Just Once!" and "Eleanor Parker ... Girl of a
Thousand Faces." Columnist Sheilah Graham has written,
"Every time I see Eleanor I don't recognize her--she always
looks so different"; and a Sidney Skolsky "tintype" on the
actress was titled, "Hard to Recognize...."

None of this was lost on Parker, who nevertheless refused to take it to heart. "I don't always recognize myself
when I see my own (still) pictures," she admitted. "Even to
me, they look like Ingrid Bergman, Pat Neal, Myrna Loy,
Joan Fontaine and Eleanor Powell at various times. I never
look like me. Frankly, I think all this is wonderful. What
woman doesn't like a little mystery about herself?"[1]

Another time: "People still call me Eleanor Powell.
That will never stop. The studio [Warners] wanted me to
change my name to Eleanor Wiggins, but I refused. Sounded
too much like the cabbage patch."[2]

It remains extraordinary what passionate talent, attitude,
and sometimes a touch of make-up could mold out of Parker's
own strong, aristocratic countenance with its classically imposing profile.

A few years after she starred in Detective Story (1951)
for director William Wyler, winning an Academy Award nomination, she ran into him at a party. "Hello, Willie, how are
you?" she asked. He nodded coolly and walked away. Later,
he returned, contrite: "What have you done to yourself,
Eleanor? I didn't recognize you!" And she replied, "Just
a different hairdo. But don't let it bother you. It happens
all the time."

During the filming of <u>Scaramouche</u> (1952), she often came to the M-G-M commissary for lunch still wearing one of the elaborate red wigs required by the role. When she appeared one day in her own (then) blonde hair, Spencer Tracy. was lunching nearby with a friend. Exhibiting a male sexism that would have unhinged Katharine Hepburn in their 1949 women's rights comedy <u>Adam's Rib</u> (and probably elsewhere), Tracy remarked, "That simply <u>has</u> to have an accent." Only two days earlier Tracy had sat next to Parker at a luncheon in honor of the actress given by her producer, Carey Wilson, and director, George Sidney.

Perhaps the capper occurred during her marriage to producer Bert Friedlob. The Friedlobs were spotted at a Los Angeles theater by a Hollywood scribe who the next day in her column asked, "Who was that attractive girl with Eleanor Parker's husband last night?"

None of this kept Eleanor Parker from becoming a star-- talent and beauty of such high order will win out. Her leading men have included John Garfield, Errol Flynn, Ronald Reagan, Humphrey Bogart, Kirk Douglas, Robert Taylor, William Holden, Frank Sinatra, Clark Gable, Robert Mitchum, and Maurice Chevalier; her directors, Michael Curtiz, Delmer Daves, Edmund Goulding, John Cromwell, Robert Wise, William Wyler, Otto Preminger, Raoul Walsh, Ronald Neame, Frank Capra, and Vincente Minnelli. But superstardom and the kind of instant audience recognizability she deserved remained elusive. As the years passed and good film roles eventually became scarce, she turned almost completely to the stage and especially television. Today, except for movie buffs, older filmgoers, and scattered people close to the film business, when her name comes up she is still sometimes confused with the late M-G-M dancer Eleanor Powell.

In an article he once wrote for <u>The New York Times</u> waxing nostalgic about old movies, comedian Bob Newhart recalled when "Eleanor Powell or Parker, whichever one dances," tap-danced in Morse Code in a World War II spy movie. He was referring, of course, to Eleanor Powell. Early in 1988, syndicated columnist Jack O'Brian announced that this book was being written. He got the author's name correctly, ditto that of the actress-subject's helpful son, Paul Clemens. But he thought the book was about Eleanor Powell and proceeded to share his recollections of that terpsichorean star.

When his column was carried in a paper near this writer's
town, the headline read, "Area Writer Taps Life of Dancer."

To make matters worse, coincident with Parker's climb
to stardom there was an established actress busy in "B"
movies named Jean Parker--our heroine's whole name is Eleanor
Jean Parker, which she occasionally used when autographing
early Warner publicity portraits. Then there was a contemporary bit player named--Eleanor Parker! Fortunately, the
latter never rose above unnoticed, unbilled walk-ons in such
films as Republic Pictures' Atlantic City (1944), starring
Constance Moore.

Undeniably (and perhaps surprisingly, in view of certain
flamboyant characterizations), some of Parker's unheralded
stardom may have been due to her quiet personal life and
priorities: her family, including four children, has always
come first. True, there were also four husbands, but the
marriages (and three divorces) were accomplished with as
much discretion as is possible in Tinsel Town.

Alas, though, she didn't develop a set of distracting
mannerisms. She never "vanted" to be alone. She didn't
marry an older big star and ride in on his coattails. She
didn't have a long affair with a superstar that was divulged
after his death. She didn't marry a prince. She didn't cut
a wide swath through the popular watering holes of her heyday, such as Ciro's and Mocambo. She didn't kiss her leading
men, get kissed back, and immediately telephone Louella
Parsons. She didn't tyrannize "the little people" on her
sets. She didn't stand over a subway grating and let her
skirt blow up. She wasn't discovered sitting at a soda foun-
tain (though it was close). She didn't have a foreign accent.
She didn't insure her legs for a million dollars. She never
combed her hair over one eye. She never had a nervous
breakdown. She never made a glorious comeback. She didn't
die young.

In short, Eleanor Parker did few of the sensational,
publicity-grabbing, gimmicky things of which many folkloric
Hollywood careers have been made. Parker has said, "I've
prided myself on not dreaming up tales just to see my name
in print." What she did was act--in the grand manner, and
magnificently.

Certainly she did not lack influential advocates in the
film capital. As noted, she was not one to court publicity
and indeed could be reticent to the point of being uncom-
municative with some reporters, but major movieland chroniclers
Louella Parsons, Hedda Hopper, and Sidney Skolsky liked her.

Then there was British-born gossip writer Sheilah
Graham, who could not always suppress a tendency to be
snide. It all began in 1944 when Graham visited the set of
Warner Bros.' Of Human Bondage, the watershed Bette Davis
hit now being remade with relative newcomer Eleanor Parker.
Walking up to Parker, Graham practically snapped, "Young
lady, aren't you a bit presumptuous following Bette Davis in
the role she made famous?" Parker was struck almost speech-
less, but managed to explain that her interpretation of the
character would be different from Davis'. A few years later,
Graham wrote that she didn't like interviewing Eleanor Parker
because she didn't want to talk. Thereafter, while the
actress' name turned up frequently in her newspaper column,
Graham was fond of introducing a negative connotation--
bringing up her divorces, knocking a new Parker picture,
writing that she was feuding with a producer, or reporting
that she had "pulled a Marilyn Monroe" (when Parker was
out ill a few days during the filming of 1964's Panic Button).

The legendarily omnipotent (if reputedly unrestrained)
Louella Parsons, on the other hand, was a sincere fan and
friend. "Eleanor can play anything," she once wrote. On
another occasion: "She [Parker] is one of the most beautiful
women I have ever seen ... on screen or off." "The Gay
Illiterate," as Parsons called herself and her autobiography
with an understatement rare in "colossal" Hollywood, boosted
Parker often in her daily column (as did successor Dorothy
Manners). She wrote a number of newspaper interview pieces
on her (Parsons' movie magazine articles usually were saved
for the more sales- and blurb-oriented headline romances and
scandals of the day, which left Parker out). And in her
coveted Cosmopolitan magazine monthly "Movie Citations" of
the 1940s and 1950s, Parsons lauded almost every film of
Parker's that came along, giving her "best performance of
the month" citations as well.

"Hedda Hopper was entranced with Eleanor right from
the start," recalls Broadway actress Nancy Andrews, Parker's
roommate during two teen-age summers of stock at Martha's

Vineyard and then at the Pasadena Playhouse, where Parker
was discovered. "One day, soon after Eleanor had been
signed by Warner Brothers and I was working as a secretary
at the radio program Queen for a Day, we got together for
lunch in Hollywood. Hedda was there, too, the focus of all
eyes as she just got up and--one of those famous elaborate
hats of hers bobbing on her head--strode over to our table
and announced 'I must meet this lovely young woman'--
Eleanor."[3]

Years later, in one of the last columns she wrote before
her death in 1966, Hopper, revealing that Parker had been
cast in The Sound of Music, went on to complain, "Eleanor
Parker makes too few movies to suit me."

Sidney Skolsky's several newspaper "tintype" pieces
on her were full of such revelations as "She sleeps in pajamas,
always the trouser and jacket--very ladylike," but they were
positive and read.

The Hollywood Reporter, the widely read industry trade
paper published weekdays since 1930, stood staunchly behind
Parker, too, giving her some of the most glowing reviews any
actress ever received. Assessing an early starring performance in The Very Thought of You (1944), The Reporter wrote:

> Miss Parker will find her playing of the home girl
> who falls in love with the soldier a milestone on the
> road to success. She plays it with a warmth and
> understanding that have seldom been equalled. She
> is lovely, has a voice of splendid quality and a talent
> for tearing at the heartstrings that is as good as a
> ticket to the end of the rainbow.[4]

The next year, when she co-starred with John Garfield
in Pride of the Marines (1945), The Hollywood Reporter con-
tinued its support:

> Eleanor Parker is the first real acting find (and
> beautiful, too) for Warner Bros. since Bette Davis.
> She'll be a big star.[5]

On the occasion of Caged (1950), for which she was to
receive the first of three best actress Academy nominations,
The Reporter said:

Eleanor Parker gives the performance of her young
career. Her metamorphosis from a simple, not too
bright girl drawn innocently into a tragic situation
to an adult woman ready for the rocky road of prosti-
tution is an exceptionally complete characterization....
With this assignment the actress steps into the select
circle of great dramatic stars of the screen.[6]

Five years later, discussing Interrupted Melody (1955),
The Reporter was still trying to get the message across:

Eleanor Parker has now reached a point where she
must be recognized as one of the first women of the
theatre.[7]

And decades later, when subsequent looks at her work
reveal no loss of luster, this most complete record of her
career to date has been written in an effort to help Eleanor
Parker be recognized at last. In addition, as the only book
about her it should prove the definitive source for anyone
researching her career, as well as provide those interested
with insight into the rich Hollywood period in which Eleanor
Parker did most of her best work. It should also be helpful
to those seeking material on the sound era's outstanding
directors and male stars, many of whom were colleagues of
Parker. For general readers, this chronicle of an underrated
career could be informative and entertaining.

The writer is prepared, however, for the well-meaning
individual who, after publication, might rush up to offer con-
gratulations for his book on "Eleanor Powell." Or perhaps
even the review headline which could read, "Unsung Jean
Parker Finally Given Her Due in Book." Despite the pre-
cedent, few authors would be thrilled at this, while Eleanor
Parker fans have never suffered such ignorance lightly.
But the record suggests that the down-to-earth lady herself--
who always loved the work of acting but disdained the accou-
trements--might simply laugh and shrug it off one more time.

Not too many years ago, Eleanor Parker said:

Going unrecognized is more than just a blessing in
terms of one's private life. I revel in that, of course.
But it means something else to me, too--something even
more important. It means that I've been successful

in creating the characters that I've portrayed--that
I'm not just a personality who is seen in a variety
of roles. When I am spotted instantly somewhere it
means that my characterizations haven't covered up
Eleanor Parker, the person. I prefer it the other
way.[8]

*   *   *

Of the many who deserve thanks for their aid on Eleanor
Parker, Woman of a Thousand Faces, first mention must go
to Paul Clemens, Eleanor Parker's talented and devoted young
actor son, whom I interviewed for a previous book and am
proud to call friend. Although I did not ask his mother to
provide any direct assistance on the project (we all wanted
it to be wholly my vision), she did answer certain questions
of mine through Paul and gave permission for material from
some personal letters to be used. Paul was always helpful
and encouraging, cheerfully taking time over the months from
a burgeoning career to answer questions along with sending
me invaluable material from his own personal collection on his
mother.

But at no time was Paul more inspiring than when he
phoned to relate, after announcement of my signing to do the
book had appeared in a Hollywood trade paper, that not only
was he delighted about the undertaking but his mother had
told him, "If Doug McClelland is doing the book, I'm in good
hands!" It was flattering indeed to learn that the lady was
familiar with articles I had done on her from time to time,
as well as some of my books in which she was prominent. And
it was gratifying that my plans to do this book caused the very
private subject no displeasure.

Next, my deep gratitude to:

Kirk Crivello, who provided me with information from
files on a different coast, the Library at the University
of Southern California at Los Angeles (Leith Adams,
Warner Bros. Collection);

Jim Meyer, an admirer of Eleanor Parker's work for more
than four decades, who from 3,000 miles away very kindly and bravely mailed me two precious, useful scrapbooks on the star;

Bruce Yates, who many times went to the trouble of copying, and sending to me, numerous clippings from his collection.

Special thanks to Eleanor Parker's friends and colleagues for their exclusive comments: Nancy Andrews, Rosemary DeCamp, Dane Clark, Ronald Neame, George Sidney, Robert Wise, and particularly William Ludwig, who also wrote the foreword.

Other persons and organizations to whom I am much obliged are Peter Adamakos; Laurence Batsford, Canada; Robert Beliveau, Canada; William R. Boles, The Boston Globe; Paul Borseth, Wisconsin Center for Film and Theater Research at Madison; Eric Braun, England; Colin Briggs, Australia; Loraine Burdick; Neil Castanheiro, The Ontario Film Institute; John Cocchi; Rebecca Conlon; Mary Corliss, Museum of Modern Art, N.Y.: John Couch, Ralph Edwards Productions; Clive Denton, Canada; Denis F. De Wulf, Belgium; Maeve Druesne; Maxine Fleckner Ducey, Wisconsin Center for Film and Theater Research at Madison; Charlie Earle, Charlie Earle Public Relations, N.Y.; Vic Ghidalia, ABC Television, N.Y.; Allan Herzer; Mike Johnson; Robert L. Lindsey; Robin Little, Films in Review; Alvin H. Marill; David McGillivray, England; Johnnie Miller; Eduardo Moreno; The Movie/Entertainment Book Club; Apollinaris Mwila, Detroit Free Press; Susan Naulty, The Huntington Library, San Marino, Calif.; Gérard Neves, Ciné Revue, France; Eleanor O'Sullivan, The Asbury Park Press; James Robert Parish; Rasiel Pereira; Herb Pierson, The Washington Post; Michael R. Pitts; David S. Rode; Sharon L. Rowe; Ben Salecki; Andy Samet, Worldvision Enterprises, N.Y.; Charles Silver, Museum of Modern Art, N.Y.; Ken Slater, Canada; Charles Stumpf; Dorothy Swerdlove, Curator, and Staff, Theatre Research Library, Lincoln Center, N.Y.; Vincent Terrace; Lou Valentino; Jerry Vermilye; Ron Wright, England; and Mark Zak.

Most heartfelt thanks, though, belong to the matchless Eleanor Parker, whose brilliant career I have watched with intense, often awed esteem through the years, giving me pleasure unsurpassed. Ensconced on opposite coasts, we only crossed paths once, briefly, in July 1971, when she was starring in a Nyack, N.Y., summer theater production of Forty Carats. The manager there brought a friend and me backstage to meet her after a matinée. It was an unusually

steamy afternoon, and Parker had performed impeccably under
difficult circumstances: the house, minus air-conditioning,
was hot and humid. When we were introduced to her as
two writers from New York, she replied (with the same slightly
enigmatic, tantalizing half-smile that had melted "The King
of the Movies" plus a future President of the United States),
"Well, why don't you write something for me?"

Here it is, Miss Parker.

Doug McClelland
Bradley Beach, NJ
Spring, 1988

NOTES

1. Holland, Jack. "Hollywood's Mystery Girl." Screenland,
    July 1954.

2. Cedrone, Lou. "Miss Parker." The Baltimore Sun, July
    9, 1969.

3. Interview with author, 1987.

4. Hollywood Reporter, The. "W. B. 'Very Thought of
    You' Full of Heart and Charm." Oct. 16, 1944.

5. Hollywood Reporter, The. "'Pride of the Marines' Sets
    New Mark in Film Achievement." Aug. 7, 1945.

6. Hollywood Reporter, The. "'Caged' Grim Prison Drama;
    Parker Triumphs in Fine Wald Prod'n." May 2, 1950.

7. Moffitt, Jack. "'Interrupted Melody' Has Artistry, Big
    B.O. Appeal." The Hollywood Reporter, March 25, 1955.

8. Buffalo Courier-Express. "Don't Look Now, But--Eleanor
    Doesn't Stand Out in a Crowd." Feb. 21, 1965.

I. BIOGRAPHY

A Canadian friend of this writer and a long-time fan of
Eleanor Parker disputes the thesis of this book. "For years
I've heard that Eleanor Parker was neglected ... underrated,"
he says. "I don't agree with that. She has played every
sort of role and won three Academy Award nominations. I
think the lady has had exactly the career she wanted."

Certainly she wanted it early.

Eleanor Jean Parker was born June 26, 1922, on Miller
Street in Cedarville, Ohio, to mathematics teacher Lester Day
Parker, who was of English descent, and Lola Isett Parker,
of Pennsylvania-Dutch and Irish lineage. She was preceded
by brother John and sister Mildred. When Eleanor was two,
the family moved to the comfortable house in which she grew
up on Noble Road in Cleveland Heights. Her father taught
at Collinwood and Glenville high schools.

Although she came from a non-theatrical, middle-class
background of schoolteachers and farmers, Eleanor was be-
guiled by the shimmering Hollywood films of Greta Garbo,
Norma Shearer, Ann Harding, and her special favorite, Janet
Gaynor, on all of whom she kept scrapbooks. At age five
she decided to become a movie star herself. She went about
it with a single-mindedness and dedication far beyond her
years. No sooner had she entered Caledonia Elementary School
than her generally supportive parents permitted her to enroll
in the Tucker School of Expression. At age ten she joined
the Curtain Pullers, the children's acting group at Frederic
McConnell's Cleveland Playhouse, called the oldest resident
theater in the United States.

Only once did the Parkers demur. When Eleanor asked
for dancing lessons, her parents refused because they thought
she was too young. The child saved her lunch money, then
when it seemed that she had accumulated enough for a lesson,

she took a streetcar to the Cleveland studio of dancing teacher
Leo Fredericks. Eleanor told her mother and father what
she had done, and they decided that if she wanted dancing
lessons that much, she would have them.

When she found the time, she also played "dress-up"
in the attic and starred in basement and backyard productions
which she also wrote, charging two cents admission.

Decades later, the actress remembered those years for
columnist Sheilah Graham:

> I always did character parts. I've played men, I've
> played witches. I was never the heroine until I hit
> Hollywood. Even in The Three Bears, when I was
> five, I was the mother bear, not Goldilocks. In
> Pinocchio I was the scrubwoman.[1]

As a precursor to multifaceted characterizations she
would one day give on the screen, she also portrayed a
caterpillar who crawled along the floor in an outfit her mother
had made from a burlap bag, in the end emerging as a beautifully costumed butterfly.

Eleanor still found time for "normal" mid-Western childhood activities. A tomboy, she played baseball and football
with the boys, climbed trees and monkey bars, cracked a
tooth doing so, and also feels her later trademark husky
voice came from all the yelling she did while at play as a
youngster. She has said, "I was a demon on wheels as a kid,
a real menace," refusing to share her toys with other children,
taunting her brother and sister, and "cooking up trouble
for my friends. I was the little girl who was always daring
them to do something awful, but always very careful to stay
out of trouble myself."

By the time she had entered Kirk Junior High and then
Shaw High School, the insecurities of young womanhood had
brought forth a more reserved, shy Eleanor. Nevertheless,
a rangy five-foot-six, 118-lb. brownette with long-lashed,
blue-green eyes, she was popular, dated, and unsurprisingly,
acted in school plays, eventually being voted President of
the Dramatic Club and her sorority. At 15 she convinced her
parents to allow her to spend her summer vacation studying
at the Rice Summer Theater on Martha's Vineyard, Mass.

In 1953, Parker told Howard Thompson in The New York
Times:

> At Martha's Vineyard, where I studied stage acting
> for two summers, I earned my keep by [ushering]
> and waiting on tables. They finally let me appear
> in one play, a bit in What a Life! [2]

A visiting talent scout from 20th Century-Fox Studios
offered her a screen test, but this time it was she herself
who thought she was too young; Eleanor opted to finish high
school first. Upon graduation, she pondered attending either
the American Academy of Dramatic Art in New York City or
Gilmor Brown's Pasadena Community Playhouse in California.
Nancy Andrews, the would-be actress friend from Beverly
Hills with whom she had shared attic digs during her Martha's
Vineyard summers, convinced her that the Pasadena Playhouse,
patrolled by studio talent scouts, would be a speedier entree
into films, Eleanor's real goal. She wrote the Playhouse and
was accepted.

In the January 1946 issue of Movie Show magazine,
Parker informed interviewer John Hammond:

> I wasn't the least worried about coming to California.
> I knew I'd get in pictures. I wasn't even afraid of
> all the tough luck stories I'd heard about other girls
> who had gone to Hollywood but hadn't conquered. I
> knew that if I trained myself properly, I'd be ready
> for the break when it came. [3]

Eleanor drove to Southern California with the aunt and
uncle of one of her boyfriends. For a time, she lived with
Nancy and her family. "I took the usual course at Pasadena,"
she later said, "but never got on a stage. New students
aren't allowed to appear in plays until after the first year."
In February of her first semester, Eleanor, formally attired
per the custom there for such occasions, attended a performance at the Playbox, an intimate Little Theater connected with
the Pasadena complex. As she was filing out, Irving Kumin,
the assistant casting director at Warner Bros. Studio, approached her about a screen test. Eleanor said she'd prefer
to finish her first year at the Playhouse; he told her to call
him when she was ready. She phoned in June. At Warners
she prepared two scenes from the plays Claudia and The

Animal Kingdom with studio drama coach Sophie Rosenstein.
She tested on June 24, 1941, two days before her 19th birthday; was told she had passed the following day; and on her
birthday, June 26, was signed to a Warner Bros. contract
at $75 a week.

She took a small room with a tiny kitchenette near the
Burbank studio.

Parker's progress was slow and often frustrating at
Warners, a lot known for its gritty, hard-edged product
which nevertheless, in its acting roll call, boasted Hollywood's
most sizzling sisterhood.   When Parker arrived, grappling for
parts there were Bette Davis, Olivia de Havilland, Ann
Sheridan, Ida Lupino, Jane Wyman, Mary Astor, Joan Leslie,
Priscilla Lane, Geraldine Fitzgerald, Betty Field, Alexis Smith,
Brenda Marshall, Nancy Coleman, Susan Peters, Faye Emerson,
and Eve Arden; coming soon, Joan Crawford, Barbara Stanwyck,
Lauren Bacall, Doris Day, Patricia Neal, Ruth Roman, Dorothy
Malone, Viveca Lindfors, Virginia Mayo, Joyce Reynolds, Julie
Bishop, Irene Manning, Janis Paige, Joan Lorring, Andrea
King, Martha Vickers, Geraldine Brooks, Dolores Moran, and
Jean Sullivan.

Parker's debut before cameras seemed promising, on
paper.   Under the veteran Raoul Walsh's direction, she was
given a brief scene in They Died with Their Boots On (1942),
starring Errol Flynn and Olivia de Havilland, in which she
said goodbye with a kiss to Army lieutenant Gig Young (at
that early stage of his career working under the name Byron
Barr).   But the film ran well over two hours, much too
long for the double feature bills of the day, so when editing
was completed Parker was entirely cut out.

During her first year-and-a-half at Warners, she spent
only four weeks on camera.   Mostly, she assisted other people
in tests.   As one fan magazine writer put it, "She had her back
to the camera more often than her face."   She posed for
publicity photos.   Coach Sophie Rosenstein was a tower of
strength and encouragement to Parker during this period.

Parker's first certifiable half-dozen associations with
film seemed hardly likely to advance a career.   World War II
recently had begun, and she finally got on screen in a Technicolor defense short subject entitled, Soldiers in White

(1942), playing a nurse. Next, she was an off-stage voice
in a Humphrey Bogart vehicle, The Big Shot (1942); a flyer's
wife in a second propagandistic color two-reeler, Men of the
Sky (1942); and had a bit in the short Vaudeville Days
(1942). She made her feature debut in the "B" film Busses
Roar (1942), supporting as a counter girl. Another short,
We're with the Army Now (1943), about the Women's Army
Corps, followed.

Discussing this period in a January 1945 Movieland
magazine article called "Nice Girl," she confessed to Marion
Cooper, "I was such a nice, quiet little thing that no one
would give me a chance to play anything else on the screen....
Hollywood might have been kinder, had I been a sophisticate."
Another time she would say, "Those early jobs were all good
preparation for me. They taught me what not to do.... I
wanted to be a real actress, rather than a personality star."

When she was given the ingenue lead in the important
Mission to Moscow (1943), directed by Michael Curtiz who had
just done Casablanca (1942), her prospects brightened--on
screen and off. In November 1942 tall, fair, and handsome
Lieut. Fred L. Losee of the Navy Medical Corps visited the
set. Parker once related:

> His medical studies had centered around plastic sur-
> gery. One day he came to the studio to see how they
> make those plastic masks worn by actors in weird
> make-ups, and someone introduced us. [4]
>
> He came back soon afterward ostensibly to show me
> some photos he had taken during his visit. [5]
>
> I've always wanted to marry a doctor or a lawyer
> and we both knew immediately that this was "it."
> He was stationed at Tia Juana, so we were married
> there (on March 21, 1943). [6]

Losee became an oral surgeon attached to the Marines in the
South Pacific. The couple didn't see each other for more
than a year.

For actress Parker, there were more "B" pictures, such
as The Mysterious Doctor (1943), as the English heroine,
plus another unbilled voice-only stint in Destination Tokyo
(1944), starring Cary Grant and directed by Delmer Daves,

whose personal interest in Parker soon would help her attain
stardom.   She was starred for the first time in an "A" film,
Between Two Worlds (1944), with John Garfield and Paul
Henreid, then graced her final "B"s: Crime by Night and The
Last Ride (both 1944).   Delmer Daves presently used her in
three popular productions: The Very Thought of You (1944),
depicting a soldier's bride; the all-star Hollywood Canteen
(1944), as herself; and Pride of the Marines (1945), the acclaimed true story of a blinded war hero and his loyal sweetheart (John Garfield, Parker).

     Dane Clark, then an up-and-coming Warner Bros. con-
tract player who appeared in all the Parker-Delmer Daves
films, and who would guest-star in her 1969 television series
Bracken's World, today says:

> Eleanor Parker was a lovely, lovely lady and a superb
> actress.   She didn't work at being an actress--didn't
> come with drama school pedigrees and a copy of Stanis-
> lavsky under her arm.   She simply was an actress and
> played the truth.   You could not fault her, on screen
> or off.   She was always pleasant on the set.   There
> was never any temperament or animosity around the
> girl, as there were with some others I saw in pictures
> then.   She was exceptional in appearance, too, sort
> of statuesque and regal with a fresh, un-Hollywood
> beauty.   From time to time through the years we've
> run into each other, and it's always given me a warm
> feeling.[7]

     Character actress Rosemary DeCamp had one of her
best parts as the Red Cross worker who helped the wounded
John Garfield in Pride of the Marines.   She comments:

> Eleanor Parker is a charming subject for a book--
> so beautiful and a very good actress.   I did not know
> her more than to say "Good morning."   We had no
> scenes together in Pride of the Marines, but I saw
> the film many times and found her heartbreakingly
> real and loving.   As a person, she was rather remote,
> didn't chat up the crew or hairdressers.   The cast
> in Pride was aware of Delmer Daves' adoration of
> Eleanor.   He was a fine director, a witty, outgoing
> Irishman who managed to win all-out efforts from every
> actor.   For instance, if you had a sad scene to do he

would sit under the camera with a box of tissues and
weep on every take! Lovely for us; made us give
every nuance and throb we could produce. As for
his romance with Eleanor, perhaps he always fell in
love with his star, I don't know. Lots of directors
do that--consciously to get a better performance, or
unconsciously because they get caught in the magic
web they are weaving. At any rate, there was no
breath of this affair in the press. They were both
married, I believe, and respected by the people they
worked with. In any event, it certainly put a glow in
Eleanor's work for that film. And of course it may
not have been an affair at all, but just an assumption
by those of us who watched. [8]

In his 1975 biography Body and Soul: The Story of
John Garfield, author Larry Swindell claimed that the late
Garfield also was infatuated with Parker and requested she
be his leading lady in Pride of the Marines. Of Garfield,
Parker will recall only:

When I first acted with John Garfield, I thought,
"He's not doing anything." He was a big star but
I couldn't help wondering, "Can he really act?" He
seemed so ordinary while we were doing the scenes.
Then when I saw the rushes I realized that the camera
loved him: he had a quality, a wonderful power that
really only seemed to come across on screen. [9]

With loans from her father, Parker bought a 1942 Chevy
and a two-bedroom bungalow in the Toluca Lake section of
Los Angeles. Not long after, when her father retired, she
gave the house to her parents. Around that time she revealed to Inez Wallace of The Cleveland News:

I'm in this spot because I gave up everything else
to get here. But at that, I never could have made
it without Daddy. Somebody has to believe in you
enough to pay the bills.... You must remember that
Daddy is a schoolteacher, not a millionaire, and my
tuition for one year (at Pasadena) was $600. My
room and board, without lunch, was $40 a month.
But it was worth it. [10]

Parker divorced Fred Losee on December 5, 1944,

testifying that he had embarrassed her by telling houseguests
he had never seen any of her films and "wasn't interested"
in her career. She admitted to a reporter that she had
realized the marriage was a mistake before he went overseas,
but hadn't thought it right to divorce a serviceman leaving
for war. Privately, she told a friend, "Fred was not in love
with the truth."

Her growing reputation as a rising young star was aug-
mented by a number of particularly positive articles about her
then appearing in magazines and newspapers. Among them:
"Eleanor Parker is the Favorite Girl of Movie Directors,"
by Myrtle Gebhart, Boston Sunday Post, July 16, 1944; "Bound
for Glory ... The Girl," by John Franchey, Screen Stars
magazine, November 1944; "The Voice You Love to Hear,"
by Gloria Brent, Motion Picture magazine, November, 1944;
and "Director Labels Eleanor Parker 'Best Actress Since
Greta Garbo'," by Louella O. Parsons, The Miami Herald,
Oct. 21, 1945. The last piece alluded to director Edmund
Goulding's remarks about working with Parker in Of Human
Bondage (1946), Warners' remake of Bette Davis' star-making
1934 success. On the first day that Parker filmed, she received a large bowl of gardenias with a note that read: "I
hope that Mildred will do as much for your career as she did
for mine. In your hands I know she will. Bette Davis."
As the Cockney slattern Mildred Rogers, Parker had her most
formidable role to date, coming away from the project with,
as Bette Davis predicted, a new respect for her versatility
from the Hollywood and critical contingents, as well as the
general public.

She was rewarded with leads opposite the studio's rakish
superstar, Errol Flynn, in Never Say Goodbye (1946), a
comedy, and Escape Me Never (1947), a drama. She remembers:

> I guess I was a little old-fashioned for Errol. He
> used to call me Grandma. Once, while we were waiting
> for a scene to be set up, he was holding a glass of
> what looked like milk. I was thirsty from rehearsing
> and asked for a sip. I nearly choked! The drink
> was mostly gin. But I liked Errol. He treated you
> the way you wanted to be treated. He was always a
> gentleman with me.[11]

On January 5, 1946, Eleanor Parker married husky Bert
Friedlob, a wholesale liquor dealer and fast-talking, colorful
member of the Hollywood scene for years who was not above
an occasional nightclub row. "He's made fortunes and lost
them," his bride said at the time, allegedly one of his solvent
periods. Director Tay Garnett, in his 1973 autobiography
Light Your Torches and Pull Up Your Tights, wrote of his one-
time friend and associate: "In 1935 [Bert Friedlob] had lammed
out of Hollywood 1½ jumps ahead of the collectors for a gamb-
ling syndicate. Bert admitted blithely that he was a sucker
for trying to fill an inside straight." His first wife was
Harriet Annenberg, daughter of publisher M.L. (Moe) Annenberg, and his second, the actress Jeanette Loff, whose
1920s-30s films included King of Jazz (1930). On August
5, 1942, at age 36, Loff died after swallowing a bottle of
ammonia. Friedlob's brother Fred also had married a Warner
actress, June Travis, who then moved with him to Chicago.
Soon after his marriage to Parker, Bert Friedlob became owner
of the International Roller Speedway, a roller derby type of
operation.

Parker told Sheilah Graham:

> We met on a double date. Bert had a girl of his
> own and I was going with Norman Millen [a local press
> agent]. Then, I went for a year with Joe Kirkwood,
> Jr. [who would soon star in the Joe Palooka film
> series]; everyone had us getting married every few
> days. Joe and I broke off and wasn't it lucky be-
> cause a few days afterward Bert called me. He had
> broken with his girl. It was New Year's Eve, 1946,
> at the Beverly Hills Club. We were in a party and
> Bert took me aside and said, "Here's a ring that is
> inscribed and everything." It was a five-carat
> diamond! I was amazed because I never thought of
> getting married to Bert. [12]

They eloped to Las Vegas, bringing along their mutual
friend Alfred Bloomingdale. They decided to keep it a secret
for a while, but as Parker explained to Modern Screen
magazine's John Maynard in the 1951 article, "They Took
Their Love to Las Vegas":

> Two weeks later--two o'clock one Saturday morning--
> Louella Parsons called and said the jig was up. She'd

identified Eleanor Jean Losee, the girl who was married
in Vegas, and was going to break the story. So we
rushed over to her house, drank to our marriage in
champagne ... and have lived happily ever since.[13]

Parker then won the part of the young actress in The
Voice of the Turtle (1947), the sought-after feminine lead
in the film version of John van Druten's long-running Broadway
comedy. Her co-star was Ronald Reagan. Years later, during
his early months as President of the United States, she ap-
prised the National Enquirer, "I think [Ronald Reagan's]
doing great. I think he's doing fine. I hope everything goes
great for him." Things didn't go too well for her at the
beginning of Turtle. As she informed an interviewer: "I
got me a shingle bob and a nervous stomach from the first
two weeks' shooting. Irving Rapper, the director, and I had
a head-on blow-up. Then we were good friends." Subsequently, Rapper even wrote a highly complimentary article
about her for the March 1948 issue of Screen Guide magazine,
"Director's Pet ... Eleanor Parker."

Her next assignment, the dual role of identical cousins
in the melodramatic The Woman in White (1948), was a challenge; but except for a bit as herself in the star-filled It's
a Great Feeling (1949), Parker did not make another film
until the airplane drama Chain Lightning (1950), teaming her
with Humphrey Bogart.

Now settled into an opulent Colonial mansion on Beverly
Drive in Beverly Hills, the Friedlobs welcomed their first
child, Susan Eleanor, on March 7, 1948. Parker put her career
on hold while she cared for her infant and traveled abroad
with her husband. Over the years, Parker was often to state
that while she loved acting, her family came first and that if
her work ever interfered with her private life she would quit
performing and never look back.

Caged (1950), directed by John Cromwell, afforded
Parker her greatest acting opportunity thus far. As a vul-
nerable teen-aged convict corrupted after abuse by 225-
pound, six-foot-two matron Hope Emerson, Parker was voted
the world's best actress at the Venice Film Festival and received her first best actress Academy Award nomination.
In a letter a few years ago to Paul Clemens, Oscar-winning
actress Ellen Burstyn wrote: "I love your mother's work.

Her film Caged was one of the first films I ever saw where I understood the transformation of character that is possible for an actress in a film." Discussing her nemesis in Caged, Parker says, "Hope Emerson was just the opposite of the woman she played in Caged. She was a sweet, gentle lady who played the piano for us between scenes and was very worried about her sick mother."

Parker, who once said that she wanted "scads of children," gave birth to her second child, Sharon Ann, on April 18, 1950. That year Eleanor Parker was voted Mother of the Year by the Society of American Florists.

Ironically, Three Secrets (1950) found her impersonating a girl who gives up her illegitimate baby for adoption. It concluded her Warner Bros. contract. They wanted her to re-sign, but Parker, although grateful to Warners, had been suspended many times for refusing roles she felt were unsuitable; she decided to see what the other studios had to offer. In addition, as she explained then to John L. Scott in the Los Angeles Times: "I have two children and I must have some time with them. When you're under exclusive, long-term contract, you jump when the studio calls."

Robert Wise, her director on Three Secrets and 1965's The Sound of Music, shares his recollections:

> After several years at RKO (where I started as a cutter), I had just escaped when I did Three Secrets for Warners. (I say "escaped" because Howard Hughes had just bought RKO and I had a feeling which proved justified that it was not going to be run too well.) I signed a non-exclusive contract with 20th Century-Fox, but before going there my agent submitted the script for Three Secrets. I think Warners was already tailoring it for three of their contract actresses: Eleanor Parker, Patricia Neal, and Ruth Roman. I signed to direct it, and although we had to do some rewriting the shooting generally went smoothly. Certainly the women were fine in their roles. Fifteen years later, we were casting the baroness in The Sound of Music and looking for an aristocratic beauty with some name value who could also act and look well with Julie Andrews. I thought of Eleanor Parker, with whom I had loved working in

Three Secrets. She fit the bill perfectly. We engaged her and she was wonderful in the part, a sort
of light "heavy" who was also ultimately quite touching.
I have great admiration for Eleanor Parker, an artist
of the first rank.[14]

Parker's first film after leaving Warners was Columbia
Pictures' Valentino (1951), a fictionalized biography of the
silent screen star with newcomer Anthony Dexter as Valentino
and Parker as his "composite" move queen girlfriend.

Meanwhile, Bert Friedlob had become an independent
producer releasing through 20th Century-Fox. Among his
films: The Fireball (1950), with Mickey Rooney and a nascent
Marilyn Monroe; The Steel Trap (1952), with Joseph Cotten
and Teresa Wright; The Star (1952), which earned Bette Davis
a best actress Academy Award nomination; and one of particu-
lar moment here, A Millionaire for Christy (1951), a screwball
farce starring Fred MacMurray and Mrs. Friedlob (Eleanor
Parker), who enjoyed this rare foray into Carole Lombard
country.

Although she has always said she preferred playing
drama to comedy, there is evidently another side to Parker
personally. "She had the most delightfully wicked sense of
humor," wrote Patricia Neal, her It's a Great Feeling/Three
Secrets colleague, in her autobiography, As I Am. "No one
made me laugh the way Eleanor could."

Parker went to Paramount Pictures for the dramatic
Detective Story (1951), evolved via producer-director William
Wyler from Sidney Kingsley's Broadway success. As the falli-
ble wife of rigid policeman Kirk Douglas, she won her second
best-actress Oscar nomination.

If the illustrious Wyler had wanted Parker, that was
good enough for Metro-Goldwyn-Mayer, which signed her
to a contract that also allowed her to make one film a year
elsewhere. Dore Schary now ran the studio. In 1951, he had
deposed Louis B. Mayer, under whose nearly three-decade
rule the Culver City operation had become the industry's
most capitalistic, glamour-oriented studio. According to recent
observations by M-G-M's swimming luminary Esther Williams,
the politically liberal, proletariat minded Schary "didn't know
what to do with movie stars. He was only interested in

featured players. People like Nancy Davis." Nevertheless, while such M-G-M mainstays as Clark Gable, Greer Garson, Lana Turner, and even Esther Williams were driven from the lot during this period by poor films, Eleanor Parker's star sparkled brightly throughout Schary's five-year reign.

She commenced her M-G-M epoch with a winner opposite Stewart Granger, Scaramouche (1952), a lavish swashbuckler. For the past few films the normally brown-haired Parker had been a blonde, but in Scaramouche she was adorned by long red wigs; the effect was spectacular. In this writer's 1987 book StarSpeak: Hollywood on Everything, director George Sidney remembered:

> Actresses. When I was preparing to direct Scara-mouche, I asked our leading lady, Eleanor Parker, who was to play a fiery actress, to dye her hair red for the role. But she said, "I'm a blonde and I'm going to stay that way." So we had these elaborate, costly red wigs made for her, and they gave us plenty of problems during the shooting. A couple of weeks after we wrapped the picture I ran into Eleanor in a restaurant--and she was now a redhead! I said, "What happened to your hair?" And she replied, "Oh, I thought I looked so good in the red wigs that I decided to become a redhead!" [15]

From then on, unless a role required otherwise, she remained, professionally and personally, a redhead (although in varying degrees of brightness). One exception was the momentous factual drama Above and Beyond (1953), wherein she represented the blonde wife of the pilot (Robert Taylor) who led the atomic bombing of Hiroshima.

Parker also was performing on radio, her vehicles including several dramatizations of her films: Pride of the Marines (The Lux Radio Theatre, December 31, 1945); Caged (Screen Directors Playhouse, August 2, 1951); and Detective Story (The Lux Radio Theatre, April 26, 1954).

Her first son, Richard Parker Friedlob, was born on October 8, 1952. The marriage, however, was going sour, and on November 10, 1953, she divorced Bert Friedlob, charging "grievous mental suffering." She testified that he had made fun of her while she was expecting their third child,

belittled her in front of friends and would not let her have
any say in her own career.   There were rumors that her suffering was also physical, that Friedlob had been abusive;
and that he had been involved with New York model Dorian
Leigh.   Parker remained mum, telling Louella Parsons, the
columnist friend with whom they had celebrated their elope-
ment, "Only the two of us know the real reason back of our
separation. I have never discussed it." Friedlob died at 49
on October 7, 1956, losing a five-month bout with cancer.

At M-G-M, Parker enacted a spy in Escape from Fort
Bravo (1953), a Western co-starring William Holden; and at
Paramount, a mail-order bride in The Naked Jungle (1954),
science fiction about man-eating ants also starring Charlton
Heston.   Then two more with Robert Taylor: Valley of the
Kings (1954), shot mostly in Egypt; and Many Rivers to Cross
(1955), a pioneer farce with Parker at her liveliest as a man-
chasing, gun-toting backwoods belle.   Perhaps because Parker
and Taylor were such a frequent and felicitous screen team,
there were whispers that they had become a romantic item
away from cameras as well.   In a May 1953 issue of Silver
Screen magazine, she had admitted to writer Helen Hendricks:

> There isn't one of my leading men I haven't gotten
> a kick out of, but Bob's my favorite!   Such a com-
> pletely nice, sweet guy.   To use a quaint old term--
> such a gentleman.   I felt real good working with
> him.[16]

Two days after her divorce from Friedlob, Parker had
left for Egypt to begin Valley of the Kings, and back home
after its completion she swore to Jack Holland in Screenland
magazine for July 1954:

> Bob [Taylor] and I both expected there would be
> romance talk--Egypt is supposed to be a romance
> background--and we were only surprised it didn't
> start sooner.   But this time the old bromide is truly
> true--I assure you we're just good friends.   We don't
> date at all.   Bob dates Ursula Thiess and I go out
> with several different friends.[17]

One of these "friends" was the dryly humorous, pro-
fessorial-looking Paul Clemens, noted celebrity portrait painter.
In an article she wrote for Motion Picture in October 1955,
entitled "Love Walked In," Parker recounted:

Paul actually came into my life, I guess, when I
worked with Bill Holden in Escape from Fort Bravo.
Between shots, Bill talked about the Clemens portrait
of his wife and children. "It is so beautiful and life-
like," Bill said. Then another time, when we were
discussing people in general, Paul's name came up
again.... We finished the picture and I didn't see
Bill until two and a half months later. This time I
was making The Naked Jungle, and one day we ran
into each other on the Paramount lot. Paul Clemens
was coming over, he told me, and asked if·I would
like to join them for lunch. The result of that luncheon? On my first day off, I went over to Paul's
studio to pose for my portrait. During one of the
sittings, the Holdens called to invite Paul to an im-
promptu barbecue. He told them I was there and they
asked him to bring me along. By the time the portrait
was finished, we had had several quiet dates. [18]

Parker and Clemens, who had a teen-aged daughter from
a previous marriage, were married on November 25, 1954,
in the First Methodist Church of Hollywood. In 1957, when
Parker learned she was pregnant, Clemens legally adopted
her three children by the late Bert Friedlob. "It was better
that way," she explained to Louella Parsons in 1961. "Now
they all have the same name." Her last child, a son named
Paul Day Clemens, was born on January 7, 1958.

She almost didn't get Interrupted Melody (1955), the
true story of polio-stricken opera star Marjorie Lawrence and
usually cited by Parker as her favorite film; it earned her a
third, final best-actress nomination from the film Academy.
The producer, Jack Cummings, aware that Parker's family-
oriented lifestyle ran more to blue jeans and cheeseburgers
than the hautes couture and cuisine, initially felt that she had
the wrong temperament to portray a prima donna. And although indeed she normally was not one to pursue roles ag-
gressively, she recognized the exceptional dramatic possibilities
of this one. She stormed into Cummings' office, accused him
of disliking her and flamboyantly proceeded to show and tell
him how she would play the opera singer. Cummings advised
her that if she were given the part she would play it the way
instructed. Suddenly he realized she was purposely displaying
exactly the temperament needed for Marjorie Lawrence. She
was hired. Later, her co-star, Glenn Ford, would declare,

"Eleanor Parker is the most untemperamental girl in Hollywood."

Curtis Bernhardt was signed to direct the screenplay by
William Ludwig and Sonya Levien, soprano Eileen Farrell to
sing the many operatic and popular selections Parker would
pantomime. According to scenarist Ludwig:

> Marjorie Lawrence was supposed to do the singing in
> Interrupted Melody, but the abdominal muscles were
> gone and the repertoire too gruelling. MGM approached
> Eileen Farrell, who was married to a New York police-
> man and had refused to join the Met because she didn't
> want to leave her husband and children. She agreed
> to do the singing for Eleanor Parker as Marjorie
> Lawrence on the condition that she get no publicity,
> because Lawrence was planning some concert tours
> and Eileen didn't want to hurt Lawrence's business by
> letting it be known that she wasn't able to sing for
> her own life story. It was one of the most unselfish
> things I've ever seen in this business. Later, Law-
> rence herself spilled the beans when she sued MGM
> over not being allowed to sing in the film.

Ludwig continues:

> I remember watching them shoot the very dramatic
> scene in which Eleanor, as the now crippled Lawrence,
> crawls across a room to knock over a record player
> playing one of her old recordings. Eleanor gave it
> everything she had, which was plenty; her knees
> were bleeding when the director yelled "Cut!" Looking
> at the rushes afterward, some technician noticed that
> an overhead microphone was dimly visible in the
> scene. They were going to shoot it again, but I
> said, "Look, there's no way Eleanor can possibly
> top what she's done in this scene. And if people are
> looking toward the ceiling while she's crawling along
> the floor, then we don't have a scene to begin with."
> The mike was left in, and to my knowledge not one
> person or critic ever noticed it. [19]

Parker threw herself into the demanding role of Marjorie
Lawrence with such ardor that one day she collapsed on the
set from overwork and was taken to the hospital for a brief
rest. Later, she recalled:

I don't have an opera voice and I don't speak all those
foreign languages--what a challenge. I secluded myself in a mountain cabin at Lake Arrowhead [Califor-
nia] for 10 days and listened to records day and night,
learning 22 arias. For good measure, I had six lessons from MGM's voice coach to help with my lip
synchronization.

I drove to work in the morning with the score propped
up on the steering wheel of my car, and I woke up
at night to find I'd been repeating the songs in my
sleep.[21]

In a 1967 Esquire magazine article entitled "ME? A
movie about me? Manny, it's a natural," in which celebrities
chose the film stars they wanted to portray them on the
screen, Parker received a unique encomium from much-publicized, ex-GI, transsexual Christine Jorgensen. "A movie of
my life story would require an actress with great talent and
courage. Eleanor Parker possesses both of these qualities,"
selected Jorgensen, probably remembering the vivid, vital
characterization of the real-life, strife-torn Marjorie Lawrence.

United Artists released her next two: the controversial
The Man with the Golden Arm (1955), produced and directed
by Otto Preminger, with Parker as the wife of a drug addict
(Frank Sinatra); and The King and Four Queens (1956), a
Western co-starring Clark Gable. In 1969, she discussed
Sinatra with Lou Cedrone of the Baltimore Sun: "He can be
a bad boy, but he does it charmingly. He is always a gentleman." The same year she told Bettelou Peterson of the
Detroit Free Press that the Gable film was one of the few she
was ever really anxious to do, confessing, "It was not a good
movie, but I wanted to work with Clark Gable. I was a real
fan of his."

Parker returned to M-G-M for a pair of 1957 releases:
Lizzie, as a girl with three personalities (she is the rare
star to have enacted both a dual role and a triple
role on screen); and The Seventh Sin, a troubled remake with
Parker as an adulteress. Director's credit on Sin went to
England's Ronald Neame. He explains:

The Seventh Sin was my first Hollywood film. It
was from an old Somerset Maugham story called "The

Painted Veil" which in 1934 had been a vehicle for
Garbo. I don't think it was the ideal property with
which to launch a career in America in the fifties,
but I was anxious to make a film here and the script
was sent to me. I worked with Eleanor Parker on it
for five or six weeks, then there was a change of
management at M-G-M. The new regime didn't seem
to be interested in the project and I became unhappy
and resigned. Vincente Minnelli completed the picture.
As for Eleanor, she was a fine actress as well as a
beautiful one. We got on very well during our few
weeks together. The thing I remember most about
her is rather frivolous: she made a superb, very dry
martini with little onions instead of olives. During the
early days of preparation, we would meet at her house
and consume great quantities. I saw her several
times over the years after I left the production, and
we both agreed that The Seventh Sin wasn't the
happiest of experiences for either of us. [22]

She played a lonely widow in United Artists' A Hole in
the Head (1959), a comedy reuniting her with Frank Sinatra
for producer-director Frank Capra; then an unforgiving wife
in M-G-M's Home from the Hill (1960), opposite Robert Mitchum
and directed by Vincente Minnelli. Around this time the
Clemenses sold their Bel Air residence and moved to a seven-
bedroom house in Lido Isle, a beach community about 55 miles
from Los Angeles then popular with film people. They remained there for a few years.

On May 19, 1960, Eleanor Parker made her dramatic
television debut as an Irish nun in a 90-minute CBS Buick
Electra Playhouse tape dramatization of Ernest Hemingway's
short story "The Gambler, The Nun and the Radio." She
became very active in the medium, emoting in more than 30
TV productions. Outstanding have been The Eleventh Hour
(Feb. 6, 1963), wherein she portrayed a woman whose fear
of men drove her to drink and hallucination, winning an Emmy
Award nomination for Outstanding Single Performance by an
Actress in a Leading Role; Bob Hope Presents the Chrysler
Theatre (Oct. 18, 1963); a two-part The Man from U.N.C.L.E.
(Jan. 8, 1968/Jan. 15, 1968); Hans Brinker (Dec. 13, 1969);
the two-part, four-hour Vanished (March 8, 1971/March 9,
1971), at that time the longest film yet made for TV; Home
for the Holidays (Nov. 28, 1972); The Great American Beauty

Contest (Feb. 13, 1973); Fantasy Island (Jan. 14, 1977);
The Love Boat (Sept. 15, 1979); She's Dressed to Kill (Dec.
10, 1979); Vega$ (Dec. 3, 1980); Madame X (March 16, 1981);
and Hotel (Dec. 7, 1983).

NBC's Bracken's World, the weekly dramatic hour with
Eleanor Parker at the top of the cast as a movie mogul's
secretary, premiered on September 19, 1969. After filming 16
episodes, she quit the show, explaining to Bob Freund in the
Fort Lauderdale News:

> It was supposed to be a repertory show, with just
> the contracted players appearing every week. But
> then, to bolster it, they used guest stars. That
> left me answering telephones and scolding the "child-
> ren." This was not the concept I had accepted when
> I signed for it.[23]

Parker did not forsake the big screen. In the early
sixties, she did two films back to back at 20th Century-Fox:
Return to Peyton Place (1961), the sequel to the 1957 hit;
and Madison Avenue (1962), opposite Dana Andrews, who called
Parker "the least-heralded great actress." In the former, she
succeeded Lana Turner as the small-town mother and in the
latter essayed an advertising executive.

With good roles in Hollywood features becoming increasingly scarce for mature women, and "runaway production"
at a peak, Parker soon found herself in Italy making the
Yankee-Gorton Associates English language comedy Panic
Button (1964), with Maurice Chevalier; and in Austria playing
the baroness in the 20th Century-Fox boxoffice sensation The
Sound of Music (1965), produced and directed by Robert Wise
and voted the year's best film by the Motion Picture Academy.

On March 9, 1965, charging "extreme cruelty and mental
suffering," Parker divorced Paul Clemens. "My husband took
less and less interest in our home and marriage," she asserted.
Clemens had painted a dozen or more portraits of his wife,
including one of her pregnant with their son Paul. She still
has several of them.

Although it won no Oscars, Embassy Pictures' The Oscar
(1966), co-starring Parker as a Hollywood talent scout, will
always be special to her. In 1966, while visiting friends and

relatives in Boston where she was promoting The Oscar, she
met Raymond N. Hirsch, a dark, presentable widower with
two teen-aged daughters. An extra man was needed to complete a dinner party Parker was to attend, and Hirsch, in
town on business and acquainted with the same circle, was
elected. He had always been a fan of Eleanor Parker's, and
the courtship began. A third generation member of a family
in theater production and management for 65 years, he opened
the first music tent in Chicago in 1950 and was treasurer
with the Shubert theatrical organization in that city for 20
years. A short time later, while visiting at the Hollywood
home of Bill Schiffrin, then Parker's agent, she and Hirsch
decided to get married, flying to Las Vegas for a civil ceremony on April 17, 1966. Parker relocated with her family
to Chicago, where her husband was employed, but after two
years they all returned to California and a new home in the
Hollywood hills. Hirsch became managing director of the
Shubert Theater in Los Angeles. Later, they moved to an
apartment in Beverly Hills.

Raised a Protestant, Parker converted to Judaism, her
husband's religion, telling New York Daily News columnist
Kay Gardella in August 1969: "I think we're all Jews at
heart. I know I've always felt more Jewish than anything
else. I wanted to convert for a long time."

The same summer she informed Boston Globe writer
Percy Shain that her daughter Susan was about to marry a
young Israeli named Dan Levron, who lived on an agricultural
kibbutz, further revealing:

> Although her father was Jewish, Susan was not brought
> up as a Jew. But after trying out college at U.S.C.
> and Wisconsin, she became enamored of the idea of
> living in a kibbutz in Israel.... From the start
> she threw herself into the life of Israel. She studied
> Hebrew, picked fruit, and did all that was expected
> of her with enthusiasm, living in a kibbutz between
> Tel Aviv and Haifa. She got along on the skimpiest
> of pin money, yet she never asked us for a cent.[24]

Parker's next two film jobs were "cameos": a rich bitch
in Warner Bros.' An American Dream (1966) and a merry widow
in Paramount's Warning Shot (1967). She returned to Italy
to make, in English, Embassy's The Tiger and the Pussycat

(1967), as Vittorio Gassman's neglected spouse. In the Universal thriller Eye of the Cat (1969), she was an invalid aunt; and in her last film so far, Paramount's Sunburn (1979), with Farrah Fawcett-Majors, she had the small part of a former Nazi's wife.

Parker has never been as interested in the stage as in the screen and did not get around to working in the theater professionally until late in her career. Despite excellent personal reviews, thus far she has starred in only five plays, starting with Forty Carats, Jay Allen's romantic comedy in which Parker, as a middle-aged woman in love with a younger man, toured Eastern seaboard theaters in 1970-71. Her husband, Raymond Hirsch, appeared as her ex-husband in the production, his first acting since college. To prepare for her second stage role, Parker studied singing with popular voice teacher David Craig. Beginning in June 1972, she took over for original star Lauren Bacall as the volatile actress in the national touring company of Broadway's Applause, the musical version of the 1950 Bette Davis film, All About Eve. The music and lyrics were by Charles Strouse and Lee Adams, respectively, and the book by Betty Comden and Adolph Green. As the summer wore on, however, business fell off and the costly tour was forced to shut down prematurely. Parker's son, actor Paul Clemens, also advises:

> Not far into the run of Applause, my mother tore
> ligaments in her ankle during one of the dance num-
> bers. She was in great pain; the ankle had to be
> frozen with an antiseptic spray for performances.
> Miraculously, she was able to keep it from affecting
> her once the curtain rose, although sometimes she
> had to be carried off stage. The show closed in
> Washington, D.C., for financial reasons--the production
> was just too expensive to keep going. Afterward,
> a doctor told my mother that if she had continued to
> work then with her injured ankle it might have been
> permanently impaired. [25]

The ankle healed; she reprised her portrayal in Dallas, Texas, during the summer of 1973.

Then came Finishing Touches, the family comedy by Jean Kerr with Parker as a professor's wife, joined in the cast by her husband and three of her children (Sharon,

Richard, and Paul), at the Pheasant Run Playhouse, St.
Charles, Illinois, in late 1974; The Night of the Iguana, by
Tennessee Williams, presenting Parker as the bawdy hotel
proprietress at the Ahmanson Theatre, Los Angeles, in late
1975-early 1976; and Pal Joey, the Richard Rodgers-Lorenz
Hart musical revival which, during previews at Circle in the
Square, New York, in late May-early June 1976, starred
Parker as the earthy matron who was "bewitched, bothered
and bewildered." Due to "artistic differences" with Circle
in the Square principals, Parker, co-star Edward Villella, and
other members of the Pal Joey company left the show before
it officially opened on June 27, then starring Joan Copeland
and Christopher Chadman. It ran for 73 performances.

Parker's two sons, Richard Parker (who does not use
the adopted surname of Clemens professionally) and Paul
Clemens are both full-time actors. Now divorced, Richard
received his B.A. in Theater at Ripon College, Wisconsin,
and has performed in several plays and films; among the
latter, Punchline (1988), starring Sally Field and Tom Hanks.
Paul, acting since adolescence, has guested on the television
series Quincy and Murder, She Wrote, co-starred in the TV
movie The Family Man and, as a real-life teen-ager indicted
for matricide, starred in the 1978 CBS docudrama A Death
in Canaan. Reviewing young Clemens in this, John J.
O'Connor in The New York Times wrote: "With Paul Clemens
delivering an impressively sensitive performance as Peter Reilly,
the bulk of A Death in Canaan is a powerful commentary."
His youth, vulnerability and persuasiveness in a jail setting
recalled his mother's big screen incarceration 28 years before
in Caged. Clemens' theater films have included The Passage
(1978), Promises in the Dark (1979), The Beast Within (1982)
and All's Fair (1989). He is currently writing and will star
in a one-man play about Edgar Allan Poe.

Parker's daughter Susan lives on a kibbutz in Israel,
where she and her husband have three children. Sharon,
who once studied acting at New York's Actors Studio, has
married for the second time and has one child. She lately
owned and operated a video shop in Camarillo, California.

Eleanor Parker's last acting assignment to date was a
guest star role as an alcoholic actress on the December 14,
1986, segment of TV's Murder, She Wrote. It marked the
45th anniversary of her professional career. Since 1976, she

has lived at her house in Palm Springs, California. She and husband Raymond Hirsch are homebodies, preferring backgammon, golf, tennis, and swimming to Hollywood nightlife. In 1980, when Canadian columnist George Gamester asked why she was seen so rarely on screen anymore, she replied:

> Because I don't care for most of today's films, with their nudity, explicit sex, and low moral tone. If I were a young girl again, trying to break into movies now, I'm afraid I wouldn't have a career.[26]

For a number of years recently, Parker's "hobby" was transcribing books into Braille. She bought her own machine with which to do it, often toiling four or five hours a day at it. "This work is more rewarding than a bunch of Oscars," said Eleanor Parker, who, despite a glorious compulsion to act, has always had her priorities straight.

NOTES

1. Graham, Sheilah. "Babies Play Key Part in Eleanor Parker's Career, Private Life." The Indianapolis Star, Feb. 24, 1952.

2. Thompson, Howard. "Miss Parker Plots a Placid Career." The New York Times, Jan. 11, 1953.

3. Hammond, John. "Never a Dull Moment." Movie Show, Jan. 1946.

4. Gebhart, Myrtle. "Eleanor Parker Is the Favorite Girl of Movie Directors." Boston Sunday Post, July 16, 1944.

5. Cooper, Marion. "Nice Girl." Movieland, Jan. 1945.

6. Wallace, Inez. "Cleveland's Eleanor Parker Gave 'Everything' to Films." The Cleveland News, June 4, 1944.

7. Interview with author, 1987.

8. Interview with author, 1987.

9. Comments to son, Paul Clemens, 1987.

10. Wallace, Inez. "Cleveland's Eleanor Parker Gave 'Every-
    thing' to Films." The Cleveland News, June 4, 1944.

11. Comments to son, Paul Clemens, 1987.

12. Graham, Sheilah. "Marriage, House Make Eleanor Parker
    Happy." North American Newspaper Alliance, Jan. 9,
    1947.

13. Maynard, John. "They Took Their Love to Las Vegas."
    Modern Screen, April 1951.

14. Interview with author, 1987.

15. McClelland, Doug. StarSpeak: Hollywood on Everything.
    Winchester, Mass.: Faber & Faber, 1987, pp. 65-66,
    74-75, 241.

16. Hendricks, Helen. "My 3 Great Desires." Silver Screen,
    May 1953.

17. Holland, Jack. "Hollywood's Mystery Girl." Screenland,
    July 1954.

18. Parker, Eleanor. "Love Walked In." Motion Picture,
    Oct. 1955.

19. Interview with author, 1987.

20. ABC Television press release. "Eleanor Parker Eyes
    Broadway." Nov. 16, 1972.

21. Downing, Hyatt. "Changeable Lady." Photoplay, April
    1955.

22. Interview with author, 1987.

23. Freund, Bob. Cover: "Show Time" section/"Stage At-
    tracts Movie Superstar." Fort Lauderdale News, March
    27, 1970.

24. Shain, Percy. "Night Watch: Eleanor's Daughter to Wed
    Israeli." The Boston Globe, July 7, 1969.

25.   Interview with author, 1987.

26.   Gamester, George.   "Names in the News."   <u>Toronto Star</u>
      (Canada), May 14, 1980.

A. Theater Films

1. SOLDIERS IN WHITE. Warner Bros. 1942. Technicolor.
    20 Mins.

Produced in cooperation with the U.S. Army; supervisor, Gordon
Hollingshead; director, B. Reeves Eason; screenplay, Owen Crump.

Cast: WILLIAM T. ORR, JOHN LITEL, ELEANOR PARKER, Ray
Montgomery, Michael Ames/Tod Andrews, Jeanette Starke.

Filmed at the Medical Division at Fort Sam Houston, Texas, the
story focuses on a rebellious young intern (William T. Orr) drafted
into the Army Medical Corps. Eleanor Parker has the feminine lead,
a nurse. The purpose of this defense featurette is to show the great
contributions being made to the war effort and medical science by
Army doctors. Also highlighted are Army Medical Corps training and
maneuvers. According to "Wear." in the trade paper Variety, "Perfect color, snug direction and superb performances all contribute
to the excellence of this film."

2. THE BIG SHOT. Warner Bros. 1942. 82 Mins.

Producer, Walter MacEwen; director, Lewis Seiler; original screen-
play, Bertram Millhauser, Abem Finkel, Daniel Fuchs; camera, Sid
Hickox; music, Adolph Deutsch; editor, Jack Killifer; dialogue direct-
or, Harold Winston; assistant director, Art Lueker; art director, John
Hughes; gowns, Milo Anderson; make-up, Perc Westmore; sound,
Stanley Jones; orchestrations, Jerome Moross.

Cast: HUMPHREY BOGART (Duke Berne); IRENE MANNING (Lorna
Fleming); Richard Travis (George Anderson); Susan Peters (Ruth
Carter); Stanley Ridges (Martin Fleming); Minor Watson (Warden
Booth); Chick Chandler (Dancer); Joseph Downing (Frenchy); Howard
da Silva (Sandor); Murray Alper (Quinto); Roland Drew (Faye);
John Ridgely (Tim); Joseph King (Toohey); John Hamilton (Judge);
Virginia Brissac (Mrs. Booth); William Edmunds (Sarto); Virginia
Sale (Mrs. Miggs); Ken Christy (Kat); Wallace Scott (Rusty); Eleanor
Parker (Telephone Operator's Voice).

Near the end, unbilled Eleanor Parker has a few brief lines as
the voice of an unseen operator during a telephone conversation
between escaped convict Humphrey Bogart and warden Minor Watson.

3. MEN OF THE SKY. Warner Bros. 1942. Technicolor. 20 Mins.

Produced in cooperation with the U.S. Army Air Forces; producer,
Gordon Hollingshead; director, B. Reeves Eason; original screenplay,
Owen Crump; camera, Charles Boyle; music, Howard Jackson, William
Lava.

Cast: MICHAEL AMES (Frank Bickley); ELEANOR PARKER (Jane
Bickley); Don DeFore (Dick Matthews); Ray Montgomery (Jim Morgan);
Ruth Ford (Bob's Girl); David Willock (Bob "Sir Galahad" Gladdens);
Harry Harvey, Jr. (Jim Morgan as a Boy); William Lechner (Little
Brother); Jack Mower (Mr. Morgan); Frank Mayo (Mr. Matthews);
Inez Gay (Mrs. Matthews); Jack L. Warner (Himself); Owen Crump
(Narrator).

This wartime propaganda featurette dramatizes the stories of
four Air Force fighter pilots. One flashback episode tells of young
Michael Ames, a bank employee married to Eleanor Parker. Despite
a recent promotion, Ames wants to join the Air Force. Parker dis-
courages him until the daily newspaper arrives with the headline
"Japs Bayonet Innocent Prisoners." Much of the production was shot
at Hamilton Field, San Francisco; Merced Field, Merced, California;
and Raukin Nautical Academy, Tulare, California.

4. VAUDEVILLE DAYS. Warner Bros. 1942. 20 Mins.

Producer, Gordon Hollingshead; director, LeRoy Prinz; original
screenplay, George Beatty; music, M. K. Jerome, Jack Scholl.

Cast: Eddie Garr, the Whirling Camerons, the Duffins, the Rio
Brothers, Leo White, Eleanor Parker, Juanita Stark, Harriett Hadden,
Elaine Francis, Doris Canfield, John Boyle, Jim O'Brien, Harriet
Olson, Dorothy Dayton, Dorothy Schoemer, Janet Barrett, Lucille
LaMarr, Mary Landa, Joy Barlow, Nancy Worth, Sylvia Opert, Eleanor
Troy, Kay Gordon, Billie Lane, Rosemary Wilson, June Earle, Betty
Gordon, Lynne Baggett, Paul A. Speer, Lorraine Kreuger, Johnny
Berkes, Dolores Moran, Diane Mumby.

For this short subject cavalcade of vaudeville skits and musical
numbers, Eleanor Parker did one day's filming at the studio.

5. BUSSES ROAR. Warner Bros. 1942. 59 Mins.

Associate producer, William Jacobs; director, D. Ross Lederman;

screenplay, George R. Bilson, Anthony Coldeway; original story, Coldeway; camera, James Van Trees; editor, James Gibbons; special effects, Edwin A. DuPar; dialogue director, Harry Seymour; assistant director, Bill Kissell.

Cast: RICHARD TRAVIS (Sgt. Ryan); JULIE BISHOP (Reba); CHARLES DRAKE (Eddie); Eleanor Parker (Norma); Elizabeth Fraser (Betty); Richard Fraser (Dick); Peter Whitney (Hoff); Frank Wilcox (Detective Quinn); Willie Best (Porter); Rex Williams (Silva); Harry Lewis (Danny); Bill Kennedy (Moocher); George Meeker (Nick Stoddard); Vera Lewis (Mrs. Dipper); Harry C. Bradley (Mr. Dipper); Lottie Williams (First Old Maid); Leah Baird (Second Old Maid); Chester Gan (Yaminto); Henry Blair (Billy); Inez Gay (Billy's Mother); Beal Wong (Radio Operator); Rolf Lindau (German Spy); Creighton Hale (Ticket Agent); Bill Hopper, Bill Edwards (Sailors); Bruce Wong (Japanese Officer); Paul Fung (Japanese Sub Captain); George Lee (Japanese Radio Operator).

Despite (or maybe because of) its minimal budget, Busses Roar offers a tight, timely 59 minutes of suspense with a personable troupe of players, among them Eleanor Parker in her first feature appearance. The plot hinges on Axis saboteurs who plant a bomb on a San Francisco-bound bus to explode as it passes vital oil fields. Although most of the film concerns bus station preliminaries, there is no dearth of action and intrigue, hence Busses Roar achieves its unpretentious aims with all-around competence. Taking the leads, Richard Travis, Bette Davis' love interest in The Man Who Came to Dinner (1941), appears as a Marine; Julie Bishop, who had acted in thirties films as Jacqueline Wells, as a stranded passenger; and Peter Whitney as a Nazi, with Parker lending capable support as the candy girl at the terminal.

6. WE'RE WITH THE ARMY NOW. Warner Bros. 1943. 20 Mins.

Supervisor, Gordon Hollingshead; director, Jean Negulesco.

Cast: Marjorie Hoshelle, Betty Hopkins, Faye Emerson, Eleanor Parker, Nina Foch, Ann Shoemaker, Josephine Gilbert, Peggy Carson, Frank Mayo, Francis Morris, Jack Mower.

Eleanor Parker is a WAC in this Women's Army Corps training short.

7. MISSION TO MOSCOW. Warner Bros. 1943. 112 Mins.

Producer, Robert Buckner; director, Michael Curtiz; based on the book by Joseph E. Davies; screenplay, Howard Koch; art director, Carl Jules Heyl; choreography, LeRoy Prinz; technical advisor, Jay Leyda; montages, Don Siegel; camera, Bert Glennon; editor, Owen Marks; music, Max Steiner; wardrobe, Orry-Kelly, Leah Rhodes.

Cast: WALTER HUSTON (Joseph E. Davies); ANN HARDING (Mrs.
Davies); Oscar Homolka (Litvinov); George Tobias (Freddie); Gene
Lockhart (Molotov); Eleanor Parker (Emlen Davies); Richard Travis
(Paul); Helmut Dantine (Maj. Kamenev); Victor Francen (Vyshinsky);
Henry Daniell (Minister Von Ribbentrop); Barbara Everest (Mrs.
Litvinov); Dudley Field Malone (Prime Minister Churchill); Roman
Bohnen (Krestinsky); Maria Palmer (Tanya Litvinov); Moroni Olson
(Col. Faymonville); Minor Watson (Loy Henderson); Maurice Schwartz
(Dr. Potkin); Jerome Cowan (Spendler); Konstantin Shayne (Bukharin);
Manart Kippen (Stalin); Kathleen Lockhart (Lady Chilston); Kurt
Katch (Timoshenko); Felix Basch (Dr. Hjalmar Schact); Frank Puglia
(Judge Ulrich); John Abbott (Grinko); Olaf Hytten (Parliament Mem-
ber); Art Gilmore (Commentator); Leigh Whipper (Haile Selassie);
Georges Renavent (President Paul Van Zeeland); Don Clayton (Vin-
cent Massey); Clive Morgan (Anthony Eden); Duncan Renaldo, Nino
Bellini (Italian Reports); Ferd Schumann-Heink, Rolf Lindau, Peter
Michael (German Reporters); George Davis, Jean Del Val (French
Reporters); Alex Chirva (Pierre Laval); Emory Parnell (Speaker of
House); Pat O'Malley (Irish-American); Mark Strong (Englishman);
Albert d'Arno (Frenchman); Rudolf Steinbeck (German); Gino Corrado
(Italian); Glenn Strange (Southerner); Frank Faylen, Joseph Crehan
(Reporters); Isabel Withers (Woman); Edward Van Sloan (German Dip-
lomat); Tanya Somova (Flower Girl); Pierre Watkin (Naval Attaché);
Elizabeth Archer (Elderly Woman); Lumsden Hare (Lord Chilston);
Robert C. Fischer (Von Schulenberg); Alex Caze (Coulendre); Leonid
Snegoff (Kommodov); Edgar Licho (Bookseller); Victor Wong, Luke
Chan, Allen Jung (Japanese Diplomats); Frank Ferguson, Billy Ken-
nedy, Louis Jean Heydt, John Hamilton, William Forrest (American
Newsmen); Tamara Shayne (Russian Nurse); Alexander Granach
(Russian Air Force Officer); Francis Pierlot (Doctor); Forbes Murray,
Edward Keane, William Gould (Isolationists); Harry Cording (Black-
smith); Mike Mazurki (Workman); Lionel Royce (Dr. Schmitt); Tom
Tully (Engineer); Hooper Atchley (Father); Betty Roadman (Mother);
Eugene Eberly (Son); Arthur Loft (Man with Microphone); Eugene
Borden (French Minister); Oliver Blake, Monte Blue, Edmund Cobb,
Ernie Adams, Eddie Kane, Howard Mitchell, Frank Wayne, Jack Kenny,
Ben Erway, Mauritz Hugo (Hecklers); Al Kunde (Father); Evelynne
Smith (Daughter); Frank Hemphill (Grandfather); Lily Norwood/Cyd
Charisse, Michael Panaieff (Specialty Dancers); Gene Gary (Russian
Foreman).

Based on the best-selling book by American Ambassador Joseph
E. Davies sympathetically recounting his adventures in the Soviet
Union, Mission to Moscow--before cameras from November 1942 through
February 1943--is lavishly produced with one of the largest casts of
the sound epoch thus far. But it is dull and naive, as well as the
rosiest view of the Reds ever to come from Hollywood. With the
possible exception of the musical genre, it has less plot than any
film of its time and definitely set the record for speeches made in a
single movie. Joyce Reynolds was originally cast as Emlen, daughter
of Ambassador and Mrs. Davies (Walter Huston, Ann Harding) who

accompanies them on a pre-war mission to Moscow. At the last minute
it was decided that Reynolds looked too young to represent a college
graduate, and Parker, who'd been assisting on some tests, was asked
by director Michael Curtiz, "Can you be ready to start tomorrow?"
The nascent Parker stepped in to play the vivacious ingenue lead
who, once in Russia, becomes the belle of the Bolsheviks, courted
most heatedly by Russian officer Helmut Dantine and American engineer Richard Travis. She draws the film's most ludicrous line when,
at the Russian Ballet (danced by Cyd Charisse in her second movie),
she explains that it is "just like the Ballet Russe back home." She is
quietly informed that this is the real Ballet Russe. Furthermore,
Parker makes an unexplained disappearance sometime before the end,
leaving the incorrect impression that the ambassador, returning to
the states, has left his daughter behind in Russia. Still, it was
Parker's most important film to date, and under the direction of the
prolific Curtiz, she was noticed favorably, her probably fictional
didoes a welcome relief from the political palaver. "Eleanor Parker
[is] delightful," wrote The Hollywood Reporter. In his autobiography,
As Time Goes By, screenwriter Howard Koch opined that director
Curtiz, however, was wrongly "cast," calling him a director of action
epics not in tune with conversational films, quickly forgetting, apparently, that Casablanca--which Koch himself co-wrote and Curtiz
directed just before Mission to Moscow--is all talk. Koch further
recalled that Warner Bros. made the film at the urging of President
Roosevelt, who wanted the American public to have a better understanding of our then-allies, the Soviets, and that he had to be coaxed
into adapting Davies' book for the screen. When the film opened,
right-wing extremists picketed some of the theaters that played
Mission to Moscow. It really fell into disrepute, though, as the
1950s approached and the House Un-American Activities Committee
was reactivated to investigate alleged Communist subversion in the
film industry. The glowing portrait of the Soviet Union in Moscow
went under fire, studio chief Jack Warner testifying that he had had
to fire writer Koch for "slipping Communist propaganda in their films."
Observed Koch (soon blacklisted in Hollywood), "This had a special
irony since it was at Warner's urgent request that I wrote the
screenplay for Mission to Moscow."

8. THE MYSTERIOUS DOCTOR. Warner Bros. 1943. 57 Mins.

Associate producer, William Jacobs; director, Ben Stoloff; screenplay,
Richard Weil; from a story by Weil; camera, Henry Sharp; editor,
Clarence Kolster; art director, Charles Novi; set decorator, Casey
Roberts; assistant director, Wilbur McGaugh; sound, Charles Lang.

Cast: JOHN LODER (Harry Leland); ELEANOR PARKER (Letty);
Bruce Lester (Lt. Christopher Hilton); Lester Mathews (Dr. Holmes);
Forrester Harvey (Hugh); Matt Willis (Bart Redmond); Art Foster
(Saul Bevan); Clyde Cooke (Herbert); Creighton Hale (Luke); Phyllis
Barry (Ruby); David Clyde (Tom Andrews); Crawford Kent

(Commandant); Stuart Holmes (Peter); Harold de Becker (Peddler);
Frank Mayo (Simon); Hank Mann (Roger); DeWolf Hopper (Orderly);
Jack Mower (Watson); Leo White (Headless Man).

One of Eleanor Parker's more interesting "B" melodramas during
the early Warner years, The Mysterious Doctor, although burdened
with a silly potboiler plot, has the virtues of respectable production
values, eerie atmosphere, and an efficient cast. The contemporary
story is set in the rocky, remote Cornwall town of Morgan's Head,
where locals believe an abandoned tin mine is haunted by the be-
headed pirate who gave the community its name and who has now
come back to look for his head. In reality, a plan to sabotage the
British war effort is afoot--the dénouement reveals the villain to be
a Nazi spy. Considering the circumstances, heroine Parker displays
notable charm and poise as benefactress to the village idiot (Matt
Willis) and fiancée of the Army investigator (Bruce Lester). The
film, while scarcely important enough to be designated controversial,
nevertheless succeeded in dividing the two most prestigious Manhattan
dailies. In The New York Times, Thomas M. Pryor found the proceedings "completely suspenseless"; while, surprisingly, The New
York Herald Tribune's Otis L. Guernsey, Jr. was more beneficent
to this lower-case entry than to some of Parker's major later productions, writing:

> For thriller fans the new co-feature at the Palace ... is a
> satisfying bit of film fare.... Those who like their murder
> mysteries combined with the supernatural should find The
> Mysterious Doctor entertaining. John Loder, Matt Willis,
> Eleanor Parker and others play their parts for all the excite-
> ment that this fantastic tale is worth.

9. DESTINATION TOKYO. Warner Bros. 1944. 135 Mins.

Producer, Jerry Wald; director, Delmer Daves; screenplay, Daves,
Albert Maltz; story, Steve Fisher; art director, Leo E. Kuter; set
decorator, Walter Tilford; technical advisor, Lieut. Com. Phillip Compton; music, Franz Waxman; music director, Leo F. Forbstein; orchestrator, Leon Raab; assistant director, Art Leuker; sound, Robert B.
Lee; special effects, Lawrence Butler, Willard Van Enger; camera,
Bert Glennon; editor, Christian Nyby.

Cast: CARY GRANT (Capt. Cassidy); JOHN GARFIELD (Wolf);
Alan Hale (Cookie); John Ridgely (Reserve Officer Raymond); Dane
Clark (Tin Can); Warner Anderson (Executive Officer Andy); William
Prince (Pills); Robert Hutton (Tommy); Tom Tully (Mike); Faye
Emerson (Mrs. Cassidy); Peter Whitney (Dakota); Warren Douglas
(Larry); John Forsythe (Sparks); John Alvin (Sound Man); Bill
Kennedy (Pete, the Gunnery Officer); William Challee (Quartermaster);
Whit Bissell (Yo Yo), John Whitney (Communications Officer); George
Lloyd (Chief of Boat); Maurice Murphy (Toscanini); John Hudson

(Radio Man); Paul Langton (Barber); Joy Barlowe (Wolf's Girl); Bill
Hunter (Market St. "Commando"); Hugh Prosser (Pilot); Frank Tang
(Japanese Pilot); Angel Cruz (Japanese Bombardier); Benson Fong,
James B. Leong (Japanese Men); Pierre Watkin (Admiral); Kirby
Grant (Captain at Briefing); Lane Chandler (C.P.O.); Mary Landa
(Tin Can's Girl); Warren Ashe (Major); Lou Marcelle (Narrator);
Eleanor Parker (Voice of Mike's Wife).

After submarine crewman Tom Tully is knifed to death trying
to help a downed Japanese flyer, his buddies play a recording made
back home by his wife of ten years. For a minute, only the unbilled
Eleanor Parker's voice is heard declaring her devotion with touching
simplicity:

> Hello, honey. I hope you play this record.... The kids
> miss you and make believe you're at the table each night....
> I hope I've made you happy.... I love you with every bit
> of my heart.

10. BETWEEN TWO WORLDS. Warner Bros. 1944. 112 Mins.

Producer, Mark Hellinger; director, Edward A. Blatt; screenplay,
Daniel Fuchs; from the play Outward Bound by Sutton Vane; camera,
Carl Guthrie; music, Erich Wolfgang Korngold; editor, Rudi Fehr;
dialogue director, Frederick de Cordova; gowns, Leah Rhodes.

Cast: JOHN GARFIELD (Tom Prior); PAUL HENREID (Henry); SYD-
NEY GREENSTREET (Thompson); ELEANOR PARKER (Ann); Edmund
Gwenn (Scrubby); George Tobias (Pete Musick); George Coulouris
(Lingley); Faye Emerson (Maxine); Sara Allgood (Mrs. Midget); Den-
nis King (Rev. William Duke); Isobel Elsom (Mrs. Cliveden-Banks);
Gilbert Emery (Cliveden-Banks); Lester Mathews (Dispatcher); Pat
O'Moore (Clerk).

In time of war, when death and destruction are never far from
people's minds, not to mention their thresholds, it is not really surprising that Hollywood should become intrigued by stories of after-
life. During World War II, Heaven and Hell and inhabitants thereof
were featured in a number of major films, among them Topper Returns,
All That Money Can Buy, and Here Comes Mr. Jordan (which actually
opened on the eve of war), plus I Married an Angel, The Remarkable
Andrew, Cabin in the Sky, Heaven Can Wait, I Married a Witch,
Happy Land, The Human Comedy, A Guy Named Joe, The Uninvited,
The Curse of the Cat People, The Canterville Ghost, The Horn Blows
at Midnight, and That's the Spirit. Most haunting and bizarre of all,
perhaps, is Between Two Worlds, despite the fact that its source was
already vintage: the 1924 Sutton Vane play Outward Bound and the
same-titled 1930 film version. The remake also marks the first starring role in an "A" film for Eleanor Parker, who substitutes for
Joan Leslie, detained overtime filming Rhapsody in Blue.

It opens in an English seaport town in 1944. Parker, a Briton,
is married to Paul Henreid, a jobless Viennese concert pianist whose
hands were injured when he fought with the Free French. Refused
an exit visa for the United States, he seals the windows in their
shabby flat and turns on the gas. Parker rushes in, pleading to
die with him as the gas hisses. A breath later, they find themselves on a mysterious, sparsely populated steamship liner where
Parker recognizes the people in the ballroom as the small group of
travelers she had seen struck by a bomb in the street earlier.
Miraculously, Henreid finds he is able to play the piano again. The
others are introduced: John Garfield, "a broken-down newspaperman
who drinks too much"; Faye Emerson, Garfield's flashy, sometime
girlfriend, a failed American actress ("I got Ann Sheridan sitting up
nights worrying her head off about me"); George Coulouris, an arro-
gantly wealthy, disreputable businessman; Sara Allgood, a poor,
elderly woman who dreams of having a cottage by the sea; George
Tobias, a Merchant Marine with a new baby back in the states;
Dennis King, a sheltered minister; Isobel Elsom, a rude, snobbish
English dowager; and Gilbert Emery, her hectored husband.

Since Henreid and Parker are suicides, they realize immediately
that everyone aboard is dead. "Where are we sailing for?" she asks
the one crew member in sight, steward Edmund Gwenn. "To Heaven
... and to Hell," he replies. The still unknowing Emerson, meanwhile,
has decided to accept Coulouris' offer to become his mistress. When
Garfield overhears Henreid and Parker discussing their plight, he
realizes they are all dead and informs the others. A shaken Henreid
takes in the passengers' horror at losing the life he threw away. On
Judgment Day, Sydney Greenstreet, as the Examiner, comes aboard
to sort things out. After gently dispatching King and Tobias, he
accuses Coulouris of "organized thuggery," ordering him to the launch
outside. Elsom then approaches Greenstreet: "I'll be brief. What I
want is a villa...." She is quickly promised a castle, but because
she had married for money and position and been selfish all her life,
she is condemned to live alone in it forevermore. Her husband chooses
not to go with her. As she exits for the launch, still trying to keep
up appearances she airily bids a "Goodbye, everybody," turning at
last to exclaim, "You swine!" Emerson, who had refused to appear
before the Examiner, shows up finally in a stark ensemble: plain
black dress, severe coiffure, little make-up. Greenstreet tells her
there is still hope as she grimly departs. He promises Allgood her
long dreamed-of cottage, but she prefers to go with wastrel Garfield
as his housekeeper even though his road, warns Greenstreet, will
be hard. It is learned she is Garfield's mother, who had abandoned
him in childhood. Greenstreet will allow Parker to go ashore with
him, but Henreid, because he is the real suicide, must be doomed to
sail back and forth on a ship like steward Gwenn, also a suicide.
She tells Greenstreet, "What ever happens to him, the same thing
must happen to me." She stays behind on the liner. Soon Henreid
begins hearing glass breaking somewhere. Then he disappears, and
Gwenn explains, "He lives again." A frantic Parker searches in vain
for her husband on deck. All of a sudden, Parker and Henreid

regain consciousness back in their flat: a German bomb has shat-
tered the window, letting in fresh air.   They are alive after all, and
happy at last to be.

In his autobiography, Ladies' Man, Paul Henreid wrote:

> Between Two Worlds was received very well by the critics
> and public, although the attempt to update it in a prologue,
> which had all the other passengers on the boat killed by a
> bomb, took away from the eerie quality of the play.   The
> play's slowly unfolding realization that these people are all
> dead didn't work in the version we did.   The audience knew
> it, and the suspense was gone.   The reviews picked this up,
> and though they praised our performances, they weren't hap-
> py about the script.

The offbeat film, which even 20 years after its Broadway beginning was called "artistic" and "experimental," is nevertheless a
stirring experience.   Its impact across the proscenium arch in the
early twenties must have been tremendous.   Although Daniel Fuchs'
screenplay is often overwritten, verbosely florid and pretentious in
its verse-like rhythms, with characters occasionally more sociological
symbols than flesh-and-blood, Between Two Worlds is cumulatively
effective, imaginative story-telling.   Obviously, director Edward A.
Blatt and cinematographer Carl Guthrie believed in the project;
their sincere dedication is usually forefront; the dramatic entrances
and exits, though limited in space, are fluently visualized.   Contri-
buting, too, is the prismatic score of Erich Wolfgang Korngold, rather
surprisingly said to be the personal favorite of the distinguished
Viennese composer whose almost two dozen film scores included the
grandiose but monumental music for The Adventures of Robin Hood
(1938), The Sea Hawk (1940) and Kings Row (1941).   Korngold
himself dubbed the piano playing for Paul Henreid.

The company is well chosen.   Henreid, in a part initiated on
both stage and screen by Leslie Howard, is earnest as the sensitive,
maimed, despondent musician, while Garfield is vigorous as the gar-
rulous, cynical, dissolute journalist.   Portraying the loving young
wife created on stage by Margalo Gillmore and in the first film version
by Helen Chandler, Eleanor Parker (notwithstanding a wardrobe con-
sisting of the same simple skirt and blouse) is inexorably every inch
a star.   The ensemble ebb and flow of character and plot relegate
her to the sidelines from time to time, but when she takes center
stage--as in her moodily photographed, tearfully frenzied, semi-
conscious search for Henreid on deck near the end--she fully justifies
Warner Bros.' faith in her.   She is an incandescent, graceful artist
ready for great roles.   Critics agreed, among them Screen Stars
magazine which wrote: "Special praise for Eleanor Parker's portrayal
of the girl who won't be separated from her husband."   The mammoth
Greenstreet makes a choice Examiner, cordial but all-knowing, fair
but firm--with just the faintest suggestion of the sinister.   Gwenn is
his usual loveable, accomplished self, the slightest smug, I-know-
something-you-don't-know glint creeping into the little steward's

otherwise kindly eyes early in the proceedings. Emerson has one of
her meatiest roles as the two-bit actress making a last-ditch grab
for security with the rich but odious Coulouris, whose one note of
angry imperialism might have been varied to more palatable effect.
Elsom, regally beautiful in her middle years, is an especially credible
haughty socialite, with Emery touching as her weary, finally freed
spouse. Allgood likewise is very moving as the unsuspecting Garfield's simple little mother whose cry as she leaves to accompany her
son of "Heaven, that's what it is. Heaven!" even causes the Examiner
to blow his nose.

Between Two Worlds was an auspicious entry into big-budget
stardom for Eleanor Parker, as well as one of Hollywood's more serious,
literate and stylish forays into the realm of fantasy. And, its age
aside, the story took on a peculiar timeliness during wartime. To
embarking servicemen, as well as the thousands at home losing sweet-
hearts, husbands, children, it was subliminally comforting to be told
there was a just after-life that would reward sacrifice.

11. CRIME BY NIGHT. Warner Bros. 1944. 72 Mins.

Associate producer, William Jacobs; director, William Clemens; screenplay, Richard Weil, Joel Malone; from the novel Forty Whacks by
Geoffrey Homes; camera, Henry Sharp; editor, Doug Gould.

Cast: JANE WYMAN (Robbie Vance); JEROME COWAN (Sam Camp-
bell); Faye Emerson (Ann Marlowe); Eleanor Parker (Irene Carr);
Charles Lang (Paul Goff); Stuart Crawford (Larry Borden); Cy
Kendall (Sheriff Max Ambers); Charles C. Wilson (D. A. Hyatt);
Juanita Stark (Maisie, switchboard Operator); Creighton Hale (Horace
Grayson); George Guhl (Harry, Jailer); Hank Mann (Mr. Dinwiddie);
Bill Kennedy (Hospital Attendant); Dick Rich (Fred, Chauffeur); Fred
Kelsey (Dad Martin); Bud Messinger (Bellboy); Jack Mower (Tenant);
Roy Brant (Waiter); Jack Cheatham, Eddie Parker, Jack Stoney,
Frank Mayo (Deputies).

Crime by Night was made with more finesse than most Warner
"B" products and is longer, but the real reason this gabby little
detective whodunnit is worth noting today is that it features three
budding contract actresses: Jane Wyman, Eleanor Parker, and Faye
Emerson. Forsaking the supporting ranks for a rare leading role,
Jerome Cowan is the sleuth in question investigating axe murders at
a lakeside resort. As the daughter of a millionaire victim and ex-
wife of suspect Stuart Crawford, Parker meanders in and out but
has little opportunity to display her beauty and ability. Wyman, as
Cowan's wise-cracking secretary, and Emerson, ultimately exposed as
the spy-murderess, have more colorful roles and make the most of
them.

12. THE LAST RIDE. Warner Bros. 1944. 56 Mins.

Associate producer, William Jacobs; director, D. Ross Lederman;
original screenplay, Raymond L. Schrock; camera, James Van Trees;
editor, Harold McLernon; art director, Leo E. Kuter; dialogue director, Jack Lucas; sound, Francis J. Scheid; set decorator, Walter
F. Tilford; gowns, Milo Anderson; make-up, Perc Westmore.

Cast: RICHARD TRAVIS (Pat Harrington); CHARLES LANG (Mike
Harrington); ELEANOR PARKER (Kitty Kelly); Jack LaRue (Joe
Genna); Cy Kendall (Capt. Butler); Wade Boteler (Delaney); Mary
Gordon (Mrs. Kelly); Harry Lewis (Harry Bronson); Michael Ames
(Fritz Hummel); Virginia Patton (Hazel Dale); Ross Ford (Joe Taylor);
Jack Mower (Shannon); Frank Mayo (Walters); Stuart Holmes (Maltby);
Leah Baird (Mrs. Bronson); Dolores Moran (Bomb Victim).

The title The Last Ride was doubly prophetic. Eleanor Parker's
last "quickie" at Warners also marked the studio's cessation of "B"
production for the duration. The piece is a fast-paced urban crime
drama souped up to feature the wartime black market in tires, but with
a basic plot that had been worn bald. As "Jona." in Variety pointed
out, screenwriter Raymond L. Schrock "dug deep in the trunk to come
up with Last Ride, which concerns such vintage characters as the
n'er-do-well gangster and his detective brother, both in love with
the same girl. End runs true to form, the hoodlum dying in his
brother's arms after being drilled by fellow racketeers." Richard
Travis is the good brother, Charles Lang the bad, with Eleanor
Parker as the pretty feminine focus of the triangle. Echoing Variety
and most audiences, Wanda Hale in the New York Daily News:

> The story is well presented by director D. Ross Lederman and
> the acting is good, but we are so familiar with the cops and
> racketeer technique that the picture holds little suspense for
> us. There are few moves in this melodrama that we cannot
> anticipate.

13. THE VERY THOUGHT OF YOU. Warner Bros. 1944. 99 Mins.

Producer, Jerry Wald; director, Delmer Daves; screenplay, Alvah
Bessie, Daves; original story, Lionel Wiggam; camera, Bert Glennon;
editor, Alan Crosland; special effects, Warren Lynch; assistant director, Art Lueker; music, Franz Waxman; art director, Leo Kuter;
set decoration, Fred MacLean; gowns, Milo Anderson; make-up, Perc
Westmore.

Cast: DENNIS MORGAN (Dave); ELEANOR PARKER (Janet); DANE
CLARK ("Fixit"); Faye Emerson (Cora); Beulah Bondi (Mrs. Wheeler);
Henry Travers (Pop Wheeler); William Prince (Fred); Andrea King
(Molly); John Alvin (Cal); Marianne O'Brien (Bernice); Georgia Lee
Settle (Ellie); Dick Erdman (Soda Jerk); Francis Pierlot (Minister);

Colleen Townsend (Young Bride); Royne O'Neil (Bridegroom); John
Roy (Soldier); Bob Gary (Young Soldier); Jim O'Gatty (Driver);
Doria Caron (Cal Tech Girl); Edward Fielding (Prof. Cathcart); Al
Woods (Man on Bus); Jack Mower (Drug Store Manager); Sybil Lewis
(Hope); Wally Walker (Marine); Victoria Vinton (Marine's Bride);
Jay Ward (Bell Hop); Philip Van Zandt (Assistant Clerk); Henry
Sharp (Chief Clerk); Eddie Kane (Hotel Clerk); Charles Marsh (Apart-
ment Clerk); Dick Bartell (Trailer Camp Manager); Angela Greene
(Nurse); Sam McDaniel (Porter); Barbara Brown (Mrs. Burns--cut
from film).

    Although by and large an engaging entertainment, The Very
Thought of You is significant for solidifying Eleanor Parker's position
as a new star at Warner Bros. A last-minute replacement for ailing
Ida Lupino in the female lead, Parker also chalks up her third appearance in an "A" production, each of the three roles having come
to her when the actress originally slated became unavailable.
    The newest film concerns the American homefront during World
War II as observed by two GIs (Dennis Morgan, Dane Clark) on leave
after two years in the Aleutian Islands. Neither as heartwarming and
expansive as David O. Selznick's superproduction sanctifying hearth-
side fortitude, Since You Went Away (1944), nor as moving and
thoughtful as William Wyler's resonant drama of returning war veterans, The Best Years of Our Lives (1946), it is a smoothly produced
program film with two main distinguishing factors: a rapturously
beautiful Eleanor Parker in full youthful bloom, photographed with a
care bestowed upon few other starlets before or since, and, on occasion, a startlingly dark portrait of stateside family life during war.
A number of reviewers were alienated by the latter grim turn, feeling
the film's makers were unpatriotic. They concluded that the home
should have been made as inviting and steadfast as possible to keep
up the fighting spirit and morale of our men overseas and that the
family should have been a model for other families. Of course, they
were the same critics who had just repudiated the homefront delineation in Since You Went Away as too idealized!
    In Very Thought of You, Dennis Morgan picks up parachute
factory employee Eleanor Parker on a Pasadena, California, bus
and is taken home for Thanksgiving dinner with her nagging mother
(Beulah Bondi), rude 4-F brother (John Alvin), and promiscuous
sister (Andrea King), who steps out on her absent sailor husband
(William Prince). To the charming romantic strains of the old Ray
Noble title song, Morgan and the sweet Parker court and marry, are
separated by war, have a baby, and are reunited after Morgan is
wounded in action. Meanwhile, his buddy, the girl-crazy Dane Clark
("Long time no she!"), is playing wolf-and-mouse with Parker's
worldlier factory friend (Faye Emerson).
    The screenplay credit goes to Delmer Daves, who also directed,
and Alvah Bessie, one of the infamous "Hollywood 10" jailed for a
year in the early fifties for refusing to testify before the House Un-
American Activities Committee, then investigating alleged Communist
subversion in the American film industry. In his memoir of those

days entitled, Inquisition in Eden, Bessie said that producer Jerry
Wald asked him to write some social significance into the "light and
frivolous" original story, so he created a subplot involving a black
girl with a serviceman husband who worked with Parker in the parachute factory. But, claimed Bessie, director Daves surreptitiously
re-wrote Bessie's script, removing all but a quick, somewhat puzzling
flash of the black girl (Sybil Lewis) and inserting off-color gags.
Daves then took co-screenwriter credit with Bessie.

A total cast casualty was the character actress Barbara Brown,
who had filmed her scene as Dennis Morgan's mother whom he and
Dane Clark visited upon returning from overseas. Deciding that the
segment served only to delay the men's meeting with Eleanor Parker
and Faye Emerson, Daves cut it prior to release. The resulting film
is still extremely likable, the kind of romantic, occasionally humorous,
battle-free fare that went over especially well with the girls left
behind during the second World War. ("WANT TO SEE ONE GREAT
BIG HONEY OF A PICTURE ABOUT ROOKIES AND THEIR COOKIES?"
asked the redoubtable Warner advertising department.) And there
are some unexpectedly perceptive moments, notably the oddly poignant,
quiet little scene in which nostalgic soldier Morgan re-visits his
college alma mater after several years, encountering a favorite professor (Edward Fielding) who is now older and, isolated by the walls
of academe, unaware that his former student has even been away.

The popular Morgan is a personable hero, Clark and Emerson
make a winning second team, and newcomer King leaves an impression
(despite, at last, an abrupt about-face in her wartime wanton). But
it is Parker's picture. Few adult actresses even back in 1944 could
put on a hair ribbon and get away with it, but she does. "Miss
Parker turns in a beautiful performance.... We could see [The Very
Thought of You] again," said Photoplay: "Eleanor Parker is just the
kind of sight any GI would be grateful for even without spending
two years in the Aleutians," said Thomas M. Pryor in The New York
Times. Lovingly photographed by Bert Glennon (at the instruction,
no doubt, of director Daves, who was personally smitten with Parker
and must have ordered her many ravishing, sunny close-ups), Parker
was the idealized embodiment of every faithful homefront sweetheart
during the war. Ida Lupino's undeniable talent aside, it is almost
impossible to imagine that tougher, older, British actress in this
quintessentially all-American girl role.

14. HOLLYWOOD CANTEEN. Warner Bros. 1944. 124 Mins.

Producer, Alex Gottlieb; director-scenarist, Delmer Daves; musical
numbers, LeRoy Prinz; art director, Leo Kuter; musical director,
Leo F. Forbstein; music adaptation, Ray Heindorf; camera, Bert
Glennon; editor, Christian Nyby; sets, Casey Roberts; assistant
director, Art Leuker; make-up, Perc Westmore; wardrobe, Milo Anderson; unit manager, Chuck Hansen; sound, Oliver S. Garretson,
Charles David Forrest.

Cast: JOAN LESLIE (Herself); ROBERT HUTTON (Slim); DANE CLARK
(Sergeant); JANIS PAIGE (Angela); Jonathan Hale (Mr. Brodel);
Barbara Brown (Mrs. Brodel); Betty Brodel (Herself); Steve
Richards/Mark Stevens, Dick Erdman (Soldiers on Deck); James Flavin
(Marine Sergeant); Eddie Marr (Dance Director); Theodore von Eltz
(Director); Ray Teal (Captain); Rudolph Friml, Jr. (Orchestra Lead-
er); Betty Bryson, Willard Van Simons, William Alcorn, Jack Mattis,
Jack Coffey (Dance Specialty); George Turner (Tough Marine); Robin
Raymond (Blonde on Street); John Dehner, Robin Short, Lang Page,
Byron Nelson (Allied Servicemen); Marilyn Hare, Phyllis Stewart
(Canteen Hostesses); Jan Wiley, Virginia Carroll (Waitresses); the
Andrews Sisters, Jack Benny, Joe E. Brown, Eddie Cantor, Kitty
Carlisle, Jack Carson, Joan Crawford, Helmut Dantine, Bette Davis,
Faye Emerson, Victor Francen, John Garfield, Sydney Greenstreet,
Alan Hale, Paul Henreid, Andrea King, Peter Lorre, Ida Lupino,
Irene Manning, Nora Martin, Joan McCracken, Dolores Moran, Dennis
Morgan, Eleanor Parker, William Prince, Joyce Reynolds, John Ridgely,
Roy Rogers and Trigger, S. Z. Sakall, Alexis Smith, Zachary Scott,
Barbara Stanwyck, Craig Stevens, Joseph Szigeti, Donald Woods,
Jane Wyman, Jimmy Dorsey and His Band, Carmen Cavallaro and His
Orchestra, the Golden Gate Quartet, Rosario and Antonio, the Sons
of the Pioneers, Virginia Patton, Lynne Baggett, Betty Alexander,
Julie Bishop, Robert Shayne, Johnny Mitchell, John Sheridan, Colleen
Townsend, Angela Greene, Paul Brooke, Marianne O'Brien, Dorothy
Malone, Bill Kennedy, Mary Gordon, Chef Joseph Milani (Themselves).

Hollywood Canteen is an enjoyable, name-filled tribute to that
estimable World War II servicemen's haven where, if one believed
this Warner Bros. film, only stars from that studio donated their
talent and time. The wafer-thin plot concerns naive young soldier
Robert Hutton's crush on movie star Joan Leslie. At the canteen
(simulated on the Warner lot), where most of the action takes place,
Barbara Stanwyck feeds the boys while Joan Crawford dances with
them and Sydney Greenstreet and Peter Lorre frighten them. Bette
Davis and John Garfield, co-founders of the establishment, are in
evidence. Astride Trigger, Roy Rogers sings Cole Porter's great
popular hit of the day, "Don't Fence Me In," followed immediately
by another complete rendition by the Andrews Sisters. A highlight,
too, is the sprightly, unpretentious song-and-dance to "What Are
You Doin' the Rest of My Life?" performed by Jack Carson and Jane
Wyman (who refuses to play up to a soldier saying, "Not me. I've
been Reaganized!").

        Eleanor Parker has a couple of scenes as herself: first, as one
of several Warner contract actresses helping at the canteen, then
coming out of a Hollywood nightclub with Helmut Dantine. And the
Warner publicity mill churned on. According to a news release when
the film opened, servicemen at the canteen voted Parker "Miss Hollywood Canteen" for her frequent visits there to dance with the boys.
One of the major attributes of Hollywood Canteen (profits from which
went to war charities) is Robert Hutton's disarmingly understated,
attractive performance in the central role. It should have made him

a major star, but somehow did not--although he did have a vocal
bobbysox following for a time and was a favorite of Hollywood glamour
girls on the Ciro's circuit.

15. PRIDE OF THE MARINES. Warner Bros. 1945. 119 Mins.

Producer, Jerry Wald; director, Delmer Daves; screenplay, Albert
Maltz; adaptation, Marvin Borowsky; from a book by Roger Butter-
field; music, Franz Waxman; camera, Peverell Marley; art director,
Leo Kuter; editor, Owen Marks; sound, Stanley Jones; set decorations,
Walter F. Tilford; special effects, L. Robert Burks; technical ad-
visors, Maj. Louis Aronson, USMC, Maj. Gordon Warner, USMC,
Ret.; wardrobe, Milo Anderson; make-up, Perc Westmore; orchestral
arrangements, Leonid Raab; musical director, Leo F. Forbstein;
assistant director, Art Lueker.

Cast: JOHN GARFIELD (Al Schmid); ELEANOR PARKER (Ruth
Hartley); DANE CLARK (Lee Diamond); John Ridgely (Jim Merchant);
Rosemary DeCamp (Virginia Pfeiffer); Ann Doran (Ella Merchant);
Ann Todd (Lucy Merchant); Warren Douglas (Kebabian); Don McGuire
(Irish); Tom D'Andrea (Tom); Rory Mallinson (Doctor); Stephen
Richards/Mark Stevens (Ainslee); Anthony Caruso (Johnny Rivers);
Moroni Olsdon (Capt. Burroughs); Dave Willock (Red); John Sheridan
(Second Marine); John Miles (Lieutenant); John Compton (Corporal);
Lennie Bremen (Lenny); Michael Brown (Corpsman); Harry Shannon
(Uncle Ralph).

     War films proliferated during World War II, some of them ad-
mirable but too often with mere hints of plot staggering under repeated special effects blitzkriegs. Pride of the Marines, begun in
late 1944 while the war was still raging and released nationally the
week it ended, is different. It is a true story: the personal, human,
uplifting drama of "an ordinary guy" named Al Schmid who joined
the Marines in 1941 and, after killing 200 Japanese while defending
his Guadalcanal machine gun post, was blinded. There are a couple
of effectively noir battle scenes, but the timely focus is on the despairing Schmid's battle with himself. Since he left a pretty, loyal
girl back home, it is also a tender love story. (The real-life Schmid
was present as advisor during much of the filming.) As the leads,
John Garfield, in probably the most substantial role he had in seven
years at Warner Bros., and Eleanor Parker are brilliantly affecting.
Said Photoplay:

          Pride of Hollywood could well be the title of this enormously
          enthralling film.... John Garfield ... gives just about the
          best performance of his career ... Coming into her own is
          Eleanor Parker, who delivers a sensitive, restrained and
          beautifully etched performance.

     Much of the film was shot on location in Al Schmid's hometown,

West Philadelphia, where his character is introduced as a happy-go-
lucky "confirmed" bachelor who works in a foundry and boards with
married friends (Ann Doran, John Ridgely). Against his wishes,
Doran keeps arranging blind dates for him, praising the latest (Parker) as "a good bowler." Although they dislike each other at first,
Garfield and Parker soon go hunting and spend New Year's Eve
together. After Pearl Harbor, he joins the Marines, asking Parker
if she'll wait for him. "You'll have to pry me loose. I'm the sticking
kind, Al," she answers. After he has wiped out the Japanese assault
troops, one of their wounded manages to throw a grenade in his
face, blinding him. He is sent to the Naval hospital at San Diego,
where sympathetic Red Cross worker Rosemary DeCamp writes his
letters to Parker. Embittered when he learns he may never see again,
he instructs DeCamp to write Parker that he is never coming home,
that they are through--"I won't have her being a seeing-eye dog for
me!" He is forced to return, however, when the Navy Cross is presented to him there. He and his girl meet at Doran and Ridgely's
on Christmas Eve, where Parker angrily tells him, "You want to be
lonely! You want to feel sorry for yourself! You want to be help-
less!" When he accidentally knocks over the Christmas tree, she
becomes more impassioned in her attempts to make him realize that he
can still lead a happy, productive life, that he can eventually even
have his old job back--"I need you, Al. Sure, you need me, too.
But what's wrong with that? Why shouldn't two people need each
other?" He receives his medal, and taking a taxi home with Parker
is able to see--albeit fuzzily--the red roof on the cab.

The gifted John Garfield, born on New York's lower East Side,
died at 39 in 1952 after a year of intensive scrutiny during the Communist investigations of the time. Too rarely did he have the dimensional opportunity afforded him in Pride of the Marines, a project
he had helped initiate and which might not have been realized without
his persistence. An actor of tremendous intensity and vitality, he
graphically conveys every facet of Al Schmid, from light-hearted
"average Joe" ("Where's Pearl Harbor?"), meeting the latest in a
string of set-up dates ("I feel as if I met her dozens of times"),
to enraged, courageous combatant ("You ring-tails!"), through despondent casualty ("Why don't God strike me dead?") and acceptance
("Home," he tells the cabbie who picks Parker and him up after the
Navy Cross ceremony). He is aided by the inventive direction and
photography of, respectively, Delmer Daves and Peverell Marley, who
light the blinded Garfield's eyes in eerily effective dark shadows.
Daves and Marley also use chiaroscuro imaginatively for a nightmare
scene of Garfield's: turning the film partially into a negative, they
show Garfield reliving the Guadalcanal battle and then, on a train
platform, embracing Parker while a blind man with a tin cup comes
closer and closer--until he is revealed to be Garfield. Eleanor Parker
plays his determined sweetheart with charm as well as spunk, proving
a worthy adversary for the early iconoclastic Garfield/Schmid character.
She is not just "the girl" in a war movie, but a living, breathing per-
son--and, with that strategically placed lock on her left forehead,
a mighty fetching one. Dane Clark, too, scores as Garfield's Marine

buddy, also wounded in the Solomon Islands. Possessed with an
energy similar to Garfield's, he has his most searing scene on the
train as he accompanies his protesting blind friend home for the Navy
Cross. Trying to bolster his confidence, Clark says, "Sure, there'll
be guys who won't hire you even when they know you can handle the
job. There's guys who won't hire me because my name is Diamond
instead of Jones. Because I celebrate Passover instead of Easter."
Reliable Rosemary DeCamp has one of her better roles as Garfield's
concerned Red Cross worker--so concerned is she, in fact, that one
wonders if she isn't slightly in love with him. DeCamp's face and
voice radiate emotion. John Ridgely and Ann Doran, two work-horse
utility players of the era, are pleasant as Garfield's married chums,
while young Ann Todd, who enacts their daughter with a teen-age
crush on Garfield, is good company, too.

   Pride of the Marines travels with considerable grace and power
to its moving, satisfying conclusion. There is only one scene which
jars: the plopped-down polemic in the San Diego hospital ward where
several of the wounded worry at length about whether the society for
which they have just fought will have post-war jobs for them. "Don't
tell me we can't make it work in peace like we do in war," Clark
finally interjects. "Don't tell me we can't pull together." The words
of these men are no doubt thoughtful and timely, but as self-conscious-
ly presented they smack of preachment and politics, and seem out of
place, certainly plot-halting, in a straightforward personal story.
They were written by scenarist Albert Maltz, radical playwright of the
thirties and long-time Garfield associate who a few years after was
jailed as one of the "Hollywood 10." Pride of the Marines brought
Maltz a best-screenplay Academy Award nomination, on the whole
richly deserved. In The New York Times (which would select the
film one of 1945's ten best), Bosley Crowther wrote:

> To say that this picture is entertaining to a truly surprising
> degree is an inadequate recommendation. It is inspiring and
> eloquent of a quality of human courage that millions must try
> to generate today.

16. OF HUMAN BONDAGE. Warner Bros. 1946. 105 Mins.

Producer, Henry Blanke; director, Edmund Goulding; screenplay,
Catherine Turney; based on the novel by W. Somerset Maugham;
camera, Peverell Marley; music, Erich Wolfgang Korngold; art directors, Hugh Reticker, Harry Kelso; editor, Clarence Kolster; sound,
Stanley Jones; special effects, Warren Lynch; set decoration, George
James Hopkins; wardrobe, Milo Anderson; make-up, Perc Westmore;
musical director, Leo F. Forbstein; assistant director, James McMahon.

Cast: PAUL HENREID (Philip Carey); ELEANOR PARKER (Mildred
Rogers); ALEXIS SMITH (Nora Nesbit); Edmund Gwenn (Athelny);
Janis Paige (Sally Athelny); Patric Knowles (Griffiths); Henry
Stephenson (Dr. Tyrell); Marten Lamont (Dunsford); Isobel Elsom

(Mrs. Athelny); Una O'Connor (Mrs. Foreman); Eva Moore (Mrs. Gray); Richard Nugent (Emil Miller); Doris Lloyd (Landlady); Bill Kennedy (Flannagan); Jacqueline Milo, Marla Thunis, Yolanda Lacca, Jeanne Grandel, Rita Pike, Nina Bara, Christine Gordon, Kerry Vaughn, Gloria Stratton, Vivien Mason, Marilyn Buferd, Mikki Saunders, Betty Price, Betty Dunston (Models); Charles André, Armand Roland, Alphonse Martel, Jacques Lory, Mayo Newhall, George Bruggeman, Gary Leonoff, Georges Renavent, Jean de Briac, George Davis (Artists); Joan Winfield (Waitress); Bobby Hyatt (Boy); Connie Leon (Nurse); Jane Blanton (Jane Athelny); Jo Ann Marlowe, Richard Glyn, Gregory Muradian (Athelny Children); Betty Fairfax (Cockney); Matthew Boulton (Mr. Foreman); Donald Dewar (Thorpe Athelny).

In 1934, Warner Bros. loaned Bette Davis to RKO to play the Cockney guttersnipe in the first film version of W. Somerset Maugham's celebrated novel Of Human Bondage, and she came back a star. She had allowed herself to be photographed in joltingly un- flattering make-up and attitudes, something few, if any, Hollywood leading ladies had dared before Davis. By the 1940s, both Davis and her vehicle had become legends. In 1944, when Ohio's Eleanor Parker, becoming known for her warm, loving characters, was men- tioned by Warners to play this unpleasant role, moviegoers were in- credulous, and so was the remake's proposed director, London-born Edmund Goulding. At the request of Jack Warner, Goulding visited the set of The Very Thought of You to observe Parker at work. "She's lovely and obviously a fine young actress," he reported to Warner, "but to follow Bette Davis?! As Mildred Rogers?!" Ida Lupino, also under contract at Warners, was more to his liking and he said so. She was talented, too, but like Mildred came from a genuine Cockney background and had proved her worth in a similar role in The Light That Failed (1939). Lupino, however, hoping to assimilate into American roles of which there was greater number in her adopted country, was not up for another British part. At first, even Parker, then 22, thought her boss was crazy to want her for Mildred. Warner suggested that Goulding at least test Parker, the proviso being that if she proved inadequate he could find another Mildred. It was decided she would make three tests for the role. To prepare, she read and re-read Maugham's novel, studied a book on the Cockney dialect and took lessons in the ac- cent from English character actress Doris Lloyd (also set for a landlady bit in the film). After doing two of the tests, Goulding said, "Never mind the third. You're my girl. I wouldn't do the picture now without you." It was the wisest decision made in con- nection with his Of Human Bondage.
    Parker gives a bravura, unforgettable depiction of evil incar- nate in a production that would have foundered completely without her. Unlike the Davis version, which was contemporary, the remake is set in the earlier period Maugham intended--all to the good. It starts in the Parisian Latin Quarter late in the nineteenth century. Failed painter Paul Henreid--who, despite a clubfoot, declares he is

"in love with love"--has decided to return to London and become
a doctor. There, fellow medical student Marten Lamont introduces
him to Parker, an insolent, coarse tea shop waitress with whom he
has become infatuated; Henreid immediately becomes even more
ardent. He takes her to the theater, where she gulps down champagne during intermission, and continues his pursuit. She, however,
prefers fun-loving Richard Nugent, a businessman from Birmingham
for whom she soon breaks a date with Henreid. When he confronts
her in an alley, she screams, "You dirty cad! I thought you was
a gentleman!" And he jealously snaps, "Do you think a gentleman
would be likely to take an interest in you?" She runs away with
Nugent; Henreid's studies suffer. After a while, he begins a romance with novelist Alexis Smith, confessing to student friends Lamont and Patric Knowles that Parker was "an obsession, a bondage."
Parker returns, pregnant and abandoned. Henreid finds her a
flat and breaks off with Smith, whereupon Parker takes up with
Knowles--"I never liked you, not from the beginning!", she rails
at Henreid. He becomes a frequent guest at the warm home of im-
pecunious but hearty Edmund Gwenn, a middle-aged man with nine
children, the oldest of whom, nubile teen-ager Janis Paige, he continually throws at Henreid. After encountering Parker soliciting on
Piccadilly Circus, he moves her and her baby into his flat. Re-
pulsed by the life she has been leading, he insists the arrangement
be platonic. She continually makes advances, though, and following
a particularly heavy campaign one Christmas Eve, he exclaims, "You
disgust me!" The floodgates open; Parker roars into her big, final
renunciation scene, shrieking after the hastily departing Henreid:

> You slimy, sneakin' swine! ... You mug! I never cared
> for you!... We used to laugh and laugh at you!... I let
> you kiss me for the money! I had to wipe my mouth!... It
> makes me sick to the stomach to think I ever let myself be
> mauled about by a cripple! Yes, that's what you are, a
> dirty cripple! Cripple! Cripple!

Using a poker, she smashes his belongings, burns his medical school
tuition money and leaves. Months later, he tells Knowles, "It's
because of the suffering she caused me that I'll never be quite
free of her." Knowles and Lamont then take him to the contagious
ward of the hospital, where he observes a dying, still Parker. Her
child preceded her by a month. Extricated from his bondage at
last, Henreid proposes to Paige.
       Edmund Goulding's Of Human Bondage is no slavish imitation
of the earlier incarnation directed by John Cromwell. Although the
basic story remains the same, there are many differences. The
first telling, for one thing, made much more of the hero's clubfoot,
with lengthy shots of his feet as he limped along. Star Leslie
Howard's medical student, in addition, was considerably more anguished about his deformity which eventually was corrected by an
operation that has no facsimile in the remake. The 1934 version,
featuring dream sequences in which Howard idealized Bette Davis'

little strumpet, was more brightly lit and romantic than the forties-
noir, constricted vision of Edmund Goulding, with its dank alleys,
dim, gusty streets and sudden rainstorms. There was a suggestion
of sympathy for Davis' blonde Mildred, who sometimes seemed the
victim rather than the victimizer, more possessed by ill temper and
ignorance than the unmitigated malevolence at the core of her successor's unsoftened virago.

Parker's no-holds-barred job must have stunned even her advocates. Deprived of all glamour trappings, she looks even crummier
than Davis. She is cannily assisted by the make-up and wardrobe
departments: a dollop of sweat; a frizzy clump of mousy brown hair;
tacky, feathered outfits; and dangling, cheap jewelry giving the
star a remarkable "period" appearance. She looks to have stepped
from a turn-of-the-century daguerreotype. Over the years in films,
many performers have played parts calling for ensembles of another
period or epoch, but none have done so with more credibility than
Eleanor Parker as Mildred Rogers. And it is not all make-up and
wardrobe (which, afterward, Parker said came from "what the studio
calls the rag bag"). Parker even altered her walk to play the character, slithering around rooms and slinking deep into chairs like a
cobra returning to its lair. Her voice, too, normally so melting,
here has an appropriate shrill quality, and her Cockney accent on
such lines as Mildred's favorite expression, "I don't mind," sounds
extraordinarily right. According to writer Mary Benedetta in a 1950
article on Parker in the British magazine Picturegoer, "When the
picture came to London the critics were startled by the genuineness
of her Cockney performance." Parker has said, "I wrote every
word out phonetically and memorized the role that way." Her restless,
raging Mildred is a conscienceless animal who, almost mouth-water-
ingly, has found her prey. Certain close-ups are unsettling in the
extreme, as when we see the light come into her eyes at the first
sniff of her swain's vulnerability, or go out of them when her baby
cries and she shouts, "Ah shut up, you!"

Author Maugham, who based his cathartic "autobiographical
novel" (as he termed it) on his own youthful experiences, had his
Mildred contract syphilis. In Davis' film version, it was changed to
consumption. In Parker's, her fatal malady is not named, although
a scene shot but later cut showed the debauched Parker coughing
severely while streetwalking, so the original plan must have been
to have her die of consumption as well. Syphilis was not a word
or disease used on the silver screen of the thirties and forties.
Davis got to deteriorate on screen, but, after the evidently still
hale Parker routs Henreid in a fit of invective on Christmas Eve,
we do not see her again except for a brief, unidentifiable shot of
her motionless back (or somebody's back) in the hospital near the
end. Parker has said, however, that she did shoot a death scene
showing her ravaged by illness, but the powers-that-be thought the
make-up and performance too graphic and disturbing, casting a pall
over the upcoming Henreid proposal to Paige. It was cut before
release. She didn't need it: her every appearance is an electric
prod to a piece in danger of going numb from inertia.

In connection with this role, one of her favorites, Parker received tremendous newspaper and magazine publicity, including spreads in Life and Look. Her personal reviews for the film, though, were controversial. Some, like the New York paper PM (headline: "Lightning Only Strikes Once"), compared her unfavorably to rose-colored memories of Bette Davis' performance, which today comes out a trifle overcooked. And it probably would have done so even in 1946, if television, VCRs, and revival theaters had been available so critics could have re-evaluated Davis' 12-year-old characterization. Withal, many did recognize the value in Parker's delineation. In The New Yorker, John McCarten wrote: "Miss Parker seemed to me a lot more plausible than Miss Davis as Mildred, possibly because she indulges less frequently in hyperthyroid hysterics." Newsweek's opinion:

> Top acting honors go to Eleanor Parker, who draws every last drop out of the part of Mildred Rogers ... Her final scene, when even Carey will have nothing more to do with her and she rips his apartment to shreds, is a superb example of the old "Hell hath no fury" axiom.

Said Philip K. Scheuer in the Los Angeles Times: "Her tantrums are something to behold." In its regular feature called "Screen Album's Oscar To...," Screen Album magazine honored "Eleanor Parker for overcoming her jitters and turning out a bright new interpretation of the Bette Davis role in Of Human Bondage."

Paul Henreid, despite an extra layer of pancake make-up and a blond toupée, is too old and too Viennese for the young London medical student, although he explains that while his father was English, his mother was Viennese. Probably to convince viewers, characters keep calling him "My young friend"/"The young doctor"/ "My nice young friend," but this only serves to point up the fact that the glum Henreid looks old enough to be Parker's father. Free of his "bondage" rather speedily, he fails to convey the obsessive sexual attraction Parker holds for him, a near-fatal flaw in the story. The scenario as it plays may be at fault to an extent. In his autobiography, Henreid said screenwriter Catherine Turney originally turned in a "fine screenplay," but that director Goulding had damaged it by rewriting as they went along and shooting many long, static "takes"; the result was "boring." After principal photography was completed in October 1944, the studio embarked on extensive cutting which, by the time of release almost two years later, Henreid claimed added some vitality to the continuity. But not quite enough--a new choppiness in the drama seemed to cancel out these late efforts. Too many people and events are discussed but not shown. Among the entire scenes cut was a much-publicized sidewalk argument between Parker, Henreid, and Richard Nugent.

None of the other actors come near Parker's achievement, either. Curiously, the decorous Alexis Smith, though starred with Henreid and Parker and playing mostly leads at the time, is eliminated after only a handful of early scenes. An episode that would have

strengthened and resolved her character, wherein Henreid returns
to resume their relationship and finds her now married, was completely cut. Edmund Gwenn, always polished, and who next year
would win the supporting Oscar as Santa Claus in Miracle on 34th
Street, is sorely tried as the relentlessly cheerful "neo-Bob Crachit"
(Bosley Crowther, The New York Times). An exception is his
unfathomable introductory scene in a hospital bed, suffering the
pain of gout while Henreid, doctors, and nurses chuckle and smile
at his discomfort! Janis Paige is winsome as his helpful daughter,
silently in love with Henreid--though it is not easy to swallow this
zoftig exponent of breezy Americanism as a 16-year-old English
virgin!

        Erich Wolfgang Korngold's music tends to attempt to act for
the cast, but often succeeds only in being intrusive, though his
theme for Alexis Smith is charming. For some reason, Edmund
Goulding, director of such revered films as Grand Hotel, Dark Victory,
The Old Maid, The Constant Nymph, The Razor's Edge and Nightmare
Alley, was not entirely able to pull this one off. Perhaps he was
too totally concentrated on working with the crucial Eleanor Parker,
who, praising his understanding of women, spoke very highly of
him at the time. As he did of her: during production he told
Louella Parsons, "She's the best actress we've had since Garbo."
His interesting but rather lumbering Of Human Bondage--not shown
since original 1946 release, after which the rights probably reverted
to the Maugham estate--could lay no claim to being the definitive
screen version of the 1915 novel, but Eleanor Parker's indelible
Mildred Rogers is unlikely to be bettered. Certainly Kim Novak's
Cockney catamount in the even more troubled 1964 film version
finished out of the money.

17. NEVER SAY GOODBYE. Warner Bros. 1946. 97 Mins.

Producer, William Jacobs; director, James V. Kern; screenplay,
I.A.L. Diamond, Kern; adaptation, Lewis R. Foster; based on an
original story by Ben, Norma Barzman; music, Frederick Hollander;
camera, Arthur Edeson; dialogue director, Robert Stevens; editor,
Folmar Blangsted; art director, Anton Grot; set decorator, Budd
Friend; sound, Stanley Jones; wardrobe, Leah Rhodes; make-up,
Perc Westmore; special effects, William McGann, Willard Van Enger;
orchestrations, Leonid Raab; assistant director, Phil Quinn; paintings,
sketches by Zoe Mozert.

Cast: ERROL FLYNN (Phil Gayley); ELEANOR PARKER (Ellen Gay-
ley); Lucile Watson (Mrs. Hamilton); S. Z. "Cuddles" Sakall (Luigi);
Forrest Tucker (Cpl. Fenwick Lonkowski); Donald Woods (Rex
DeVallon); Peggy Knudsen (Nancy Graham); Tom D'Andrea (Jack
Gordon); Hattie McDaniel (Cozy); Patti Brady (Phillippa "Flip"
Gayley); Helen Pender (Louise); William Benedict (Messenger);
Charles Coleman (Withers), Arthur Shields (McCarthy); Doris Fulton
(Hat-check Girl); Tom Tyler, Monte Blue (Policemen); Sam McDaniel
(Porter); Roy Gordon (Detective).

Never Say Goodbye may not have been among the biggest or
best films of 1946 (sometimes called the last great year for the
Hollywood movie, in terms of quality and attendance), but one thing
is certain: as lensed by Casablanca cinematographer Arthur Edeson,
there was no more handsome couple seen that year than co-stars
Errol Flynn and Eleanor Parker. Their vehicle is a frothy romantic
farce about a recently divorced but still in love pair (Flynn, Parker)
whose small daughter (Patti Brady) desperately wants them to re-
marry. She spends six months with her father, then six months with
her mother, whom she is joining as the story begins. To assuage
her loneliness, the youngster has invented two imaginary little
brothers whom she calls Nicodemus and Ebeneezer. Furthermore,
using some rather provocative letters from a book on how to write
to servicemen, she also corresponds regularly with an overseas
Marine (Forrest Tucker), but encloses a photo of her mother--a
device lifted from the 1944 Norman Krasna stage success Dear Ruth.
Flynn, as a well known commercial artist whose eye for women is not
confined to his "Gayley Girl" pin-ups, wants to return to his wife
and daughter, and Parker still loves him, too, but various complications keep them apart. These include the arrival home of his
daughter's bruiser Marine pen pal, who proceeds to court Parker.
At the end, when their daughter briefly runs away, Parker and
Flynn are reunited.
        Most of the film's gags and situations were wheezy even in
1946, but one of the screenwriters is I.A.L. Diamond, later collaborator with Billy Wilder on a number of that eminent writer-director's
most successful comedies, so the clichés were touched up by experts.
The characters, additionally, are etched with sprightly abandon by
an able cast. Although more associated with adventure films, the
debonair Flynn kept a wink in his eye even in those and was a
natural light comedian. Never Say Goodbye gives him one of his
better chances to show it. Whether rushing back and forth between
the two unknowing women he has quartered in the same restaurant,
gamboling throughout his ex-wife's house on Christmas Eve disguised
as Santa Claus, or masquerading as a trench-coated tough from whom
emanates the actual soundtrack voice of fellow Warner player Humphrey Bogart, Flynn proves a far more gifted actor than was thought
at the time. Parker is chic in elaborate hairdos and one of her
dressiest modern wardrobes designed by Leah Rhodes to make the
early-20's actress look sophisticated enough to have been through
the marriage mill with Errol Flynn and have a seven-year-old daughter.
While not given the same farcical opportunities as her co-star, she
is still a perfect partner--lovely, lively, and no slouch with a comic
riposte herself. When she visits her ex-husband's bachelor quarters
and comments that they could use a woman's touch, Flynn airily
replies, "I have a girl who comes in every now and then and does
things around the house." Taunts Parker, "That's not what I
meant." Roly-poly, jowl-jiggling S. Z. "Cuddles" Sakall (his actual
billing), one of the great character actor scene-thieves of the era,
accounts for a large share of the laughs as owner of the restaurant
where Flynn originally proposed to Parker, then his model. The

Hungarian Sakall continues to wrest maximum amusement from his
shrewd massacre of the English language (he refers to Patti Brady's
imaginary brothers as "Niconeezer" and "Epidemic"). He also has
some of the best lines. When told at his restaurant that he is looking
great, he shrugs, "Why not? I've been eating across the street."
Another time, when artist Flynn is trying to evade his persistent,
volatile model (Peggy Knudsen) who has been "inspiring" him for
months, Sakall asides, "You take a girl out to dinner two or three
hundred times and right away she thinks you're interested in her."
Playing the cast-off girlfriend, Knudsen raises the dust attractively,
while that formidable dowager Lucile Watson, as Parker's interfering
mother, doffs her dignity with style. Forrest Tucker is well cast
as the musclebound suitor; reliable Hattie McDaniel, perfection as
the fanciful Patti Brady's realistic nurse. "Introduced" in a large,
demanding part, little Miss Brady is the roll's one sour note.
Obviously someone's pet, she is indulged with almost as many close-
ups as the two stars, which only serve to magnify her shortcomings.
She is an affected, plain child with terminal "cutes." Flynn and
Parker should have divorced her.

18. ESCAPE ME NEVER. Warner Bros. 1947. 104 Mins.

Producer, Henry Blanke; director, Peter Godfrey; based on the
novel The Fool of the Family and the play Escape Me Never by
Margaret Kennedy; screenplay, Thomas Williamson; assistant director,
Claude Archer; dialogue director, Robert Stevens; music, Erich
Wolfgang Korngold; orchestrators, Hugo Friedhofer, Ray Heindorf;
ballet sequences, LeRoy Prinz; art director, Carl Jules Weyl; set
decorator, Fred M. MacLean; ballet costumes, Travilla; wardrobe,
Bernard Newman; make-up, Perc Westmore; sound, Dolph Thomas;
special effects, Harry Barndollar, Willard Van Enger; camera, Sol
Polito; editor, Clarence Kolster.

Cast: ERROL FLYNN (Sebastian Dubrok); IDA LUPINO (Gemma
Smith); ELEANOR PARKER (Fenella MacLean); Gig Young (Caryl
Dubrok); Reginald Denny (Ivor MacLean); Isobel Elsom (Mrs. Mac-
Lean); Albert Basserman (Prof. Heinrich); Ludwig Stossel (Steinach);
Milada Mladova, George Zoritch and the Corps de Ballet (Ballet
Sequence); Frank Puglia (Guide); Hector Sarno (Waiter); Alfredo
Sabato, Mario Siletti (Gondoliers); Helene Thimig (Tyrol Landlady);
Ivan Triesault (Choreographer); Doris Lloyd (Mrs. Cooper); Anthony
Caruso (Dino); Frank Reicher (Minister); Jack Ford (Double for
Albert Basserman).

    Escape Me Never (from Margaret Kennedy's 1928 novel, The
Fool of the Family), which became a 1930s British play and a film
starring Germany's Elisabeth Bergner, was surely a bit dog-eared
even in February 1946, when the Hollywood version was completed.
And being kept on the shelf for almost two years before it was
finally released did not help things. In spite of this, the Warner

Bros. telling was redeemed by earnest acting, Erich Wolfgang Korn-
gold's richly melodious score, and the direction of Britain's Peter
Godfrey, who captained many not-quite but atmospheric features at the
Burbank studio.

Following the adventures of two brothers from the large, ec-
centric musical family introduced in the earlier Kennedy novel,
The Constant Nymph (released as a film by Warners in 1943), Escape
Me Never opens in Venice, 1900, where waif-like Ida Lupino (in the
Bergner role) and her infant move in with struggling composer Errol
Flynn. Traveling to the Dolomites, they perform at an inn where
Flynn is "inspired" to write a ballet (titled Primavera) by the beautiful Eleanor Parker, an aristocratic, restless Englishwoman with a
weakness for impoverished musical geniuses. Unfortunately, Parker
is engaged to Gig Young, Flynn's brother and a musician-turned-
businessman. They all troupe to London, where Lupino's baby dies,
Parker and Young finally get married, and Flynn, realizing he loves
the devoted Lupino, rededicates his ballet to her.

Lupino is the cynosure, and she runs an unusually demanding
gamut: from food-thief in schoolgirl drag to café entertainer, jilted
lover to bereaved mother. That she is both convincing and appealing
is a testament to the considerable ability she possessed and which
Warners, glutted by Hollywood's most formidable stable of female
stars, never adequately exploited. As Fenella MacLean, the untaxed
Parker projects stately allure in her starched shirtwaists and elegant gowns and coats. "Feneller," says Lupino in her only slightly
refined Cockney, "is the type who is always taking cold bawths."
In the Los Angeles Times, reviewer Edwin Schallert saw it this way:
"Miss Parker has the native loveliness to make a trouble-maker in-
gratiating." Flynn may have seemed obvious casting because of his
character's roving eye--"He was the kind of liar you almost believed
... nearly forgave ... completely loved!" tooted the advertising.
But with Lupino and Parker confronting each other over their off-
stage genius, the ever-jaunty actor suggests nothing so much, or
so thankless, as George Brent caught between Bette Davis and Mary
Astor.

19. THE VOICE OF THE TURTLE (re-titled ONE FOR THE BOOK
     on TV). Warner Bros. 1947. 103 Mins.

Producer, Charles Hoffman; director, Irving Rapper; based on the
play by John van Druten; screenplay, van Druten; additional dialogue, Hoffman; art director, Robert Haas, set decorator, William
Kuehl; music, Max Steiner; orchestrator, Murray Cutter; music
director, Leo F. Forbstein; assistant director, Lee Guthrie; sound,
Stanley Jones; special effects, Harry Barndollar, Edwin DuPar; montages, James Leicester; camera, Sol Polito; editor, Rudi Fehr; wardrobe, Leah Rhodes.

Cast: RONALD REAGAN (Sgt. Bill Page); ELEANOR PARKER (Sally
Middleton); Eve Arden (Olive Lashbrooke); Wayne Morris (Commander

Ned Burling); Kent Smith (Kenneth Bartlett); John Emery (George
Harrington); Erskine Sanford (Storekeeper); John Holland (Henry
Atherton); Nino Pepitone (Headwaiter); Helen Wallace, Sarah Edwards
(Women); William Gould (Man); Frank Wilcox (Stanley Blake); Ross
Ford (Soda Clerk); Bunny Cutler (Girl at Telephone); Dick Bartell
(Ticket Agent); Jack Lee (Director); Doris Kemper (Woman in
Delicatessen); Nicodemus Stewart (Elevator Boy); Janet Warren,
Tristram Coffin, Lois Austin (Theater Party); Philip Morris (Door-
man); Alan Foster (Vendor); Brian O'Hara (Boxoffice Clerk); Joan
Lawrence (Bill's Ex-girlfriend); Ernest Anderson (Elevator Man);
Peter Camlin, Suzanne Dulier (French-speaking Couple); Bernard
DeRoux (French-speaking Waiter); Noel Delorme (French Hat-check
Girl); Douglas Kennedy (Naval Officer); Robert Spencer (Boy).

   The Voice of the Turtle was probably Eleanor Parker's most
prestigious coup to date. The role of Sally Middleton, the heart-
on-her-sleeve scatterbrain, had been a personal triumph for Margaret
Sullavan in 1943 on the New York stage where John van Druten's
then somewhat risqué romantic comedy ran for five years (and was
still playing when the film opened). Upon purchasing it for the
screen, Warners immediately saw the young soldier lead as ideal
for their contract star of the past ten years, Ronald Reagan, recently
returned from World War II service. And while every ingenue in
town saw herself in the feminine lead, as did some rather past that
age bracket (such as Olivia de Havilland, Jean Arthur, and Vivien
Leigh), Warners eventually gave it to their burgeoning young star
Eleanor Parker. Ads for the picture called the new team "A woo-
some two-some!" In his autobiography, Where's the Rest of Me?,
Reagan wrote:

      The girl the soldier inevitably meets and romances was
      played by Eleanor Parker.... A number of new performers
      had come along while I was flying my air force desk and she
      was one of them. To me she was unknown, and I wanted
      the studio to borrow June Allyson from MGM. It took only
      one scene with Eleanor for me to realize I'd be lucky if I
      could stay even. She is one of the truly fine actresses in
      motion pictures.

   The somewhat laundered film version opens on a snowy December
evening in 1944 as Broadway producer Kent Smith is ending his
affair with struggling young actress Parker because she has grown
too serious--"I thought we could keep it gay," he tells her. "You're
the kind who can't sew a button on a man without thinking it's for
life," admonishes her sophisticated friend Eve Arden, also an actress
but one whose main career seems to be men. That rainy spring,
when Arden breaks a date with Reagan, a sergeant on a weekend
pass, to go out with old Naval commander boyfriend Wayne Morris,
Parker dates the soldier. And despite her vow never to become
involved again, she and Reagan fall in love. That's about all there
is to the story, but there are many warm comic touches heightened

by Parker's endearing work as the quirky, slightly goofy heroine--
surprise casting in a coveted role that helped earn the actress some
of the most extensive publicity of her career.

Although required for no good reason to wear Margaret Sullavan's trademark bangs (in a particularly mop-like facsimile) and
possessing a similar naturally throaty voice, Parker's performance
is no imitation of her predecessor. In fact, she had not seen Sullavan
in the part. And Thomas M. Pryor in his New York Times review
perceived that "Miss Parker is altogether winning.... Miss Parker
brings to [the role] the innocence and bewilderment of youth that
is so essential and in this respect she is even more successful than
was Miss Sullavan." While Newsweek chorused that "Eleanor Parker
brings a delightful spontaneity to the role of Sally Middleton."
Movie Stars Parade magazine awarded her their "Performance of the
Month" page, the film itself picking up "Movie of the Week" spreads
in Parade and the New York Sunday Mirror magazines as well as
"Movie of the Month" honors from Movieland and Motion Picture.
Frightened of egg-beaters, horrified when a radio is left on in a
vacant apartment to play "all by itself," our fey miss has a particularly delicious few minutes of pantomime as she prepares for Reagan
to sleep over on a daybed. Emptying ashtrays with an oblivious,
jolting bang, quickly covering a spot on the furniture, methodically
punching the centers of couch pillows. folding a large bedspread
by falling headlong into each fold, Parker displays a pronounced
flair for physical comedy.

Eve Arden, in the part originated on Broadway by Vicki
Cummings, steals every scene she's in. per usual, her timing and
reaction shots providing some of the film's lustiest laughs. Asked
if she wants a drink, Arden requests a soft one, confessing, "Hard
drinks make me weak. I'm saving my weaker moments." In a lunch
counter discussion of a recent romantic fling, she floridly calls it
"One of those lovely things that isn't meant to last," whereat a
waiter yells, "One ham on!" And her body language can be priceless,
too: after ringing Parker's doorbell insistently for minutes while
Reagan is hastily being hidden within. Parker finally throws open
the door to reveal a slumping Arden, weary, suspicious and funny
on sight.

The film also is one of the affable Reagan's better credits.
Created on stage by Elliott Nugent, his role is the perfect one for
a future President of the United States: a GI who is earnest, nice,
and sensible--healthy but proper. His character is so proper that
after he kisses Parker, there is a fast, gratuitous shot of him leaving
her building to go to a hotel for the night. Arden and Parker have
most of the good dialogue and business, but Reagan does get off
one line that today might prompt chuckles when considering the ex-
actor: "I'm afraid the only talent I ever had was a talent for
appreciation." He solves the mystery of the title when he recites
the biblical words, "The winter is past and the voice of the turtle
is heard in our land"--he quickly explains, "Turtle doves."

The production has one of the most serenely charming endings

of the day as Reagan and Parker sit down to lunch by a sunny
spring apartment window, hands clasped across the small table while
Max Steiner's music tinkles gently on the soundtrack. In fact, the
overall enduring appeal of Voice of the Turtle is helped inestimably
by the perky, tuneful score of the fecund Steiner, about whom
Bette Davis once said, "Max knew more about drama than any of us."
Applause is also due the tasteful work of two other veterans of the
Bette Davis Wars: Irving Rapper, director, too, of Davis' 1942
romantic classic, Now, Voyager, and that film's cinematographer,
Sol Polito, one of Davis' favorite cameramen.

20.   THE WOMAN IN WHITE. Warner Bros. 1948. 109 Mins.

Producer, Henry Blanke; director, Peter Godfrey; screenplay,
Stephen Morehouse Avery; based on the novel by Wilkie Collins;
camera, Carl Guthrie; art director, Stanley Fleischer; editor,
Clarence Kolster; sound, Charles Lang; dialogue director. Herschel
Daugherty; set decorations, George Southam; special effects, William
McGann, Robert Burks; wardrobe, Bernard Newman; Alexis Smith's
gowns, Milo Anderson; make-up, Perc Westmore; music, Max Steiner;
assistant director, Claude Archer.

Cast: ALEXIS SMITH (Marian Holcombe); ELEANOR PARKER (Laura
Fairlie/Ann Catherick); SYDNEY GREENSTREET (Count Fosco); GIG
YOUNG (Walter Hartright); Agnes Moorehead (Countess Fosco);
John Abbott (Frederick Fairlie); John Emery (Sir Percival Glyde);
Curt Bois (Louis); Emma Dunn (Mrs. Vesey); Matthew Boulton (Dr.
Nevin); Anita Sharp-Bolster (Mrs. Todd); Clifford Brooke (Jepson);
Barry Bernard (Dimmock).

    Inveighing against decreasing attendance for the weighty cos-
tume epics of the twenties and thirties, one motion picture exhibitor
cried, "Don't give us any more movies where the hero writes with
a feather!" And Hollywood listened. Consequently, The Woman in
White was generally under-appreciated in 1948, a period, plotty melodrama anomaly at a time when cinematic attention was going to the
more contemporary tolerance tracts, institutional exposés, psychological
explorations, postwar problem dramas and "semi-documentaries"
(true stories shot away from the studios on actual locations). The
one popular gimmick of Woman in White is the dual role that fell
to one of its stars, Eleanor Parker. Many of the decade's most
dynamic screen actresses had played double or multiple parts. Judy
Garland was both mother and daughter in Little Nellie Kelly (1940),
as was Valerie Hobson in Great Expectations (1947), while Jeanette
MacDonald appeared as aunt and niece in Smilin' Through (1941);
Lucille Ball as Madame Du Barry and nightclub singer in Du Barry
Was a Lady (1943); Rita Hayworth as grandmother and granddaughter
in Cover Girl (1944); Deborah Kerr as three unrelated characters
in Colonel Blimp (1945); Joan Leslie and June Haver as various
characters through history in Where Do We Go from Here? (1945);

Diana Lynn as two unrelated characters in Ruthless (1948); Betty
Grable as countess and great-great-grandmother in That Lady in
Ermine (1948); and Rhonda Fleming as King Arthur's niece and
great-great-grandniece in A Connecticut Yankee in King Arthur's
Court (1949). Most noticeable, though, were stars as identical
twins: Martha Raye in Keep 'Em Flying (1941); Claudette Colbert
in The Palm Beach Story (1942); Maria Montez in Cobra Woman
(1944); Betty Hutton in Here Come the Waves (1944); Bette Davis
in A Stolen Life (1946); Olivia de Havilland in The Dark Mirror
(1946); and Bonita Granville in The Guilty (1947).

Now it was Eleanor Parker's turn, only in yet another twist
she doesn't play twins or any of the previously cited variations:
she plays identical first cousins. Her vehicle is based on Wilkie
Collins' book, published in England in 1859 and, many feel, the model
for the modern mystery novel. It had been filmed a half-dozen
times before, but probably never with the literacy, atmospheric
production values, and stellar casting with which this gripping
Warner Bros. production is blessed. The insidious mood is perfectly
established at the beginning as painter Walter Hartright (Gig Young)
detrains at an English country village, seemingly alone in the night
except for wisps of train smoke and Max Steiner's ambient music
score of madrigal-type themes. The time is 1851 and Hartright
is en route to Limmeridge House, where he is to teach drawing to
its mistress, Laura Fairlie (Parker I). Walking there, he is suddenly
accosted by a strange and terrified woman in white (Parker II),
who, as a carriage approaches, disappears just as quickly. At
Limmeridge, Hartright meets Laura, a beautiful and charming young
woman with an uncanny resemblance to his apparition of the road;
her devoted cousin/companion, Marian Holcombe (Alexis Smith);
Count Fosco (Sydney Greenstreet), the gluttonous, sinister "critic
and scientist"; Fosco's near-catatonic, browbeaten wife (Agnes
Moorehead); Sir Percival Glyde (John Emery), the mayhem-minded
fiancé of Laura; and Frederick Fairlie (John Abbott), neurotic,
reclusive lord of the manor and Laura and Marian's uncle who is
being blackmailed by Fosco and Glyde because of a scandalous family
secret. The stage is set for the most dastardly deeds as the woman
in white, now known to be an Ann Catherick, reappears to Hartright
and reveals that she has escaped from a mental asylum where Fosco
and Glyde have kept her. She tells him further that Laura is in
great danger and must not marry Glyde. They wed, however, and
soon the weak-hearted Ann is frightened to death by Fosco and Glyde
who then inter her as Laura. The latter, meanwhile, has been incarcerated in the same asylum from which her lookalike cousin had
fled. There, Fosco and Glyde, having appropriated Laura's fortune,
try to brainwash the now pregnant young woman into thinking she
really is Ann Catherick. She escapes, and in the street encounters
Hartright and Glyde who is killed in the ensuing melee. Later, after
Countess Fosco has been uncovered as the sister of Frederick Fairlie
and mother of the illegitimate Ann Catherick, the countess stabs
Fosco to death. Hartright marries Marian.

The genealogy is sometimes a bit dense, but to the committed

it is all sorted out satisfactorily by the finish. The important
thing is that the most has been made of a still arresting Victorian
thriller, in no small measure due to its vivid mummery. Parker,
second-billed on screen to Alexis Smith but appearing first in all
the advertising, is compelling as both Laura and Ann. As the former,
she is at first lovely in dainty curls and opulent frocks of the day,
as well as accomplished, trusting--"an angel," one character calls
her. But during her ordeal, she becomes haggard, resourceful,
and courageous, a quick flash of the actress' expressive face before
the dying Fosco showing that the angel also has learned how to hate.
Parker's Ann Catherick is a pathetic, mentally and physically de-
bilitated creature, stringy-haired, wasting, and black under the
eyes throughout. Whisking on and off in her constant white dress
and cloak, she is the more haunting of the two women with her
tragic aura and steadfast loyalty to her cousin Laura, with whom
as a child she had stayed for a happy while. (It was then, as
explained, that Laura's kind late mother had given Ann a white
dress she loved--"I will wear white as long as I live," she vowed.)

Like most of her sisters in duality, Parker has a couple of
scenes in which split-screen photography allows her to play to herself. Wrote Newsweek: "Miss Parker performs her tricky dual
role with considerable distinction and gets excellent support."
Alexis Smith, so often the ice queen in early Warner roles, has
warmth and gumption as the loving cousin who near the end is
willing to go away with the lecherous Fosco to free Laura. Corpulent,
irreplaceable Greenstreet, his flowery verbiage unable to conceal
eyes that dart like some predatory animal, is, as the Photoplay
reviewer put it, a "mountain of menace." Moorehead's small part
is almost silent, but her pantomime and presence are striking.
Though he might have sketched his stalwart with a tad more color,
the eternally supporting Young is acceptable in a rare hero's role.
In truth, though, the script doesn't ask too much of him, and his
sudden choice of Marian for a wife is curious, since it is Laura he
has been courting up to then. But bug-eyed John Abbott is capital
as the wildly eccentric, nervous-wreck uncle who quivers and gasps
at the slightest noise or excitement: "Oh, no violence, please.
Police, bodies--my nerves could never stand it."

The language in Stephen Morehouse Avery's generally well-
constructed screenplay seems to approximate that of its proper era,
while Peter Godfrey's direction moves the melodrama about the spacious
main-set mansion and grounds, through dark nights and even darker
doings with a dignified stealth that does not obfuscate the chills
inherent in this superior The Woman in White.

21. IT'S A GREAT FEELING. Warner Bros. 1949. Technicolor.
     84 Mins.

Producer, Alex Gottlieb; director, David Butler; story, I.A.L.
Diamond; screenplay, Jack Rose, Melville Shavelson; art director,
Stanley Fleischer; set decorator, Lyle B. Reifsnider; music director,

Ray Heindorf; orchestrators, Sidney Cutter, Leo Shuken; choreography, LeRoy Prinz; songs, Jule Styne, Sammy Cahn, Technicolor
consultant, Mitchell Kovaleski; make-up, Perc Westmore; wardrobe,
Milo Anderson; sound, Dolph Thomas, Charles David Forrest; special
effects, William McGann, H. F. Koenekamp; camera, Wilfrid M. Cline;
editor, Irene Morra.

Cast: DENNIS MORGAN (Himself); DORIS DAY (Judy Ames); JACK
CARSON (Himself); Bill Goodwin (Arthur Trent); Irving Bacon (In-
formation Clerk); Claire Carleton (Grace); Harlan Warde (Publicity
Man); Jacqueline de Wit (Trent's Secretary); Wilfred Lucas (Mr.
Adams); Pat Flaherty (Gate Guard); Wendy Lee (Manicurist); Sue
Casey, Nita Talbot, Eve Whitney, Carol Brewster, Joan Vohs (Models);
Lois Austin (Saleslady); Tom Dugan (Wrestling Fan); James Holden
(Soda Jerk); Jean Andren (Head Waitress); Dudley Dickerson (Por-
ter); Sandra Gould (Train Passenger): Shirley Ballard (Girl on Bike);
Errol Flynn (Jeffrey Bushdinkel); Gary Cooper, Joan Crawford, Syd-
ney Greenstreet, Danny Kaye, Mazzone-Abbott Dancers, Patricia
Neal, Eleanor Parker, Maureen Reagan, Ronald Reagan, Edward G.
Robinson, Jane Wyman, David Butler, Michael Curtiz, King Vidor,
Raoul Walsh (Themselves).

Despite the today startling all-star cast of legendary, mainly
Warner players (Crawford, Flynn, Wyman, Reagan, Robinson, Cooper,
etc., as themselves), the modest, unstructured wackiness of It's
a Great Feeling earned little attention in 1949. Now, when audiences
are not so besieged by stars of this caliber and have come to accept nonlinear entertainments more freely, the Technicolor musical
spoof of movieland appears a surprisingly lively, even interesting
lark--if still sometimes silly and pointlessly slapstick. The story
concerns the efforts of Dennis Morgan and Jack Carson (cast as
Dennis Morgan and Jack Carson) to make blonde waitress Doris
Day a movie star. At one point, they pass Day off as a brunette
French star at a studio press party, introducing her down a mile-
long staircase on which Errol Flynn had just fenced in Adventures
of Don Juan. Whereupon a facetious Eleanor Parker, one of the
many quickly glimpsed guest stars, comments to Patricia Neal, "They'll
probably make her a blonde." In only her second film, Doris Day
continues to show a rare camera naturalness and comedic flair. And
It's a Great Feeling, in its own free-wheeling way, says more
about the vagaries of movie-making in its day than many epic productions.

22. CHAIN LIGHTNING. Warner Bros. 1950. 94 Mins.

Producer, Anthony Veiller; director, Stuart Heisler; screenplay,
Liam O'Brien, Vincent Evans; suggested by a story by J. Redmond
Prior; camera, Ernest Haller; art director, Leo E. Kuter; editor,
Thomas Reilly; sound, Francis J. Scheid; make-up, Perc Westmore;
special effects, William McGann, Harry Barndollar, H. F. Koenekamp,

Edwin DuPar; set decorator, William Wallace; music, David Buttolph;
orchestrations, Maurice de Packh; wardrobe, Leah Rhodes; assistant
director, Don Page.

Cast: HUMPHREY BOGART (Matt Brennan); ELEANOR PARKER
(Jo Holloway); Raymond Massey (Leland Willis); Richard Whorf
(Carl Trexall); James Brown (Maj. Hinkle); Roy Roberts (Gen.
Hewitt); Morris Ankrum (Bostwick); Fay Baker (Mrs. Willis); Fred
Sherman (Jeb Farley).

   Chain Lightning lands carrying a full cargo of airplane movie
clichés, but with two salient entities in inventory: co-stars Humphrey
Bogart and Eleanor Parker (in a part first mentioned for "Mrs.
Bogart," Lauren Bacall). Both, assuredly, have been seen in more
exciting, exacting roles, despite the lurid (and misleading) advertising which blurbed "When there's a redhead to get close to, he
moves faster than ... CHAIN LIGHTNING!" and "He's a sucker for
speed ... and redheads are his speed!" Yet the leads' personal
chemistry, together and singly, gives fresh impetus to the one about
the self-centered air ace and the worried girl he leaves below. It
may take a couple of scenes for the viewer to suspend credibility
and accept the 51-year-old Bogart as a test pilot in, as his character
calls it, a "Buck Rogers monkey suit," but the actor's legendary
powers of persuasion along with Parker's luminous sincerity maintain
interest in a plotline then long dispatched, even by "B" movies, to
that big hangar in the sky. This was not lost on Louella Parsons,
who consequently gave the film a Best Drama of the Month citation
in Cosmopolitan magazine.
   The story has overtones (but only overtones) of Bogart's
Casablanca (1942). Like that great success, it deals with a pair of
café lovebirds parted during wartime who meet again years later.
Post-credits, Bogart is shown testing a new plane, then the action
goes to flashback for the majority of the running time and we see
Americans Bogart and Parker, as a flyer and a Red Cross worker,
romancing in 1943 London. They are separated when Bogart, a
combat veteran of 25 missions, is sent home where, after the war,
he "stunts" for an air circus, later losing his own small flying school.
Seven years pass. He and Parker meet again at a party given by
aircraft manufacturer Raymond Massey, for whom she now works as
executive secretary. Although still in love with the increasingly
mercenary Bogart, she is dating Massey's idealistic plane designer
Richard Whorf. Bogart joins Massey's company to test jet planes.
Watching him spin and soar, Parker remarks, "He's home, isn't he?"
Whorf, looking at her wistfully, replies, "Is he?" Bogart proposes
to Parker while Whorf invents a new escape-cockpit. When Whorf
dies trying out his safety "pod," to be ejected with parachute from
a malfunctioning plane, Bogart goes up and tests it--successfully.
Back on the ground, Parker asks, "Why did you take a chance,
Matt? Why did you do it?" And in a closing line delivered to recall
his classic "Here's looking at you, kid" from Casablanca, Bogart
explains, "Well, there I was, up 60,000 feet. It was the quickest
way to get down to you."

Bogart is his usual audience-pleasing, mordantly surface me-
first self redeemed by a climactic act of heroism; while Parker. in
her low-hemline "New Look" fashions by Leah Rhodes and a gallery
of soulfully charming close-ups by cinematographer Ernest Haller,
is totally believable and sympathetic, even though something more
than casual dating with Whorf is insinuated.   (In 1950, such things
were still "insinuated.") After they meet again at Massey's home,
she invites Bogart to her smartly appointed apartment, on which,
looking around, he compliments her--an implication being that perhaps Whorf has set her up in it.

The film was one of the first to deal with supersonic air travel.
The scenes of then still new jets in action remain interesting, even
rousing on occasion, in spite of being done mostly with models and
process photography well cut into close shots of the helmeted Bogart
twisting and grimacing in cockpits meant to be climbing the clouds.
Richard Gehman may have been a bit harsh when he wrote in his
1965 book Bogart that Chain Lightning was "brightened only by the
appearance of Eleanor Parker"; but the truth is that it does take
all the considerable attributes of Parker and Bogart to keep the film
airborne.   Even they were not always enough, though, as G.M.
Bennett, an exhibitor from Dunedin, Florida, wrote Boxoffice magazine
after playing it: "We opened fair and dropped off badly the last
two days.   However, our area is made up of older, retired people
and anything that suggests a heart attack they stay away from!"

23.   CAGED.   Warner Bros.   1950.   96 Mins.

Producer, Jerry Wald; director, John Cromwell; screenplay, Virginia
Kellogg, Bernard C. Schoenfeld; camera, Carl Guthrie; art director,
Charles H. Clarke; editor. Owen Marks; sound. Stanley Jones; set
decorator, G. W. Berntsen; technical advisor, Doris Whitney; make-
up, Perc Westmore; music, Max Steiner; orchestrations. Murray
Cutter; assistant director, Frank Mattison; wardrobe. Leah Rhodes.

Cast: ELEANOR PARKER (Marie Allen); Agnes Moorehead (Ruth
Benton); Ellen Corby (Emma); Hope Emerson (Evelyn Harper);
Betty Garde (Kitty); Jan Sterling (Smoochie); Lee Patrick (Elvira
Powell); Olive Deering (June); Jane Darwell (Isolation Matron);
Gertrude Michael (Georgia); Sheila Stevens/MacRae (Helen); Joan
Miller (Claire); Marjorie Crossland (Cassie); Taylor Holmes (Sen.
Donnolly); Frances Morris (Mrs. Roley); Lynn Sherman (Ann);
Queenie Smith (Mrs. Warren); Gertrude Hoffman (Millie); Naomi
Robison (Hattie); Esther Howard (Grace); Marlo Dwyer (Julie);
Wanda Tynan (Meta); Peggy Wynne (Lottie); Edith Evanson (Miss
Barker); Yvonne Rob (Elaine); Ann Tyrell (Edna); Eileen Stevens
(Infirmary Nurse); June Whipple (Ada); Sandra Gould (Skip); Grace
Hayes (Mugging Matron); Don Beddoe (Commissioner Walker); Charles
Meredith (Chairman); George Baxter (Jeffries); Guy Beach (Mr.
Cooper); Harlan Warde (Dr. Ashton); Bill Hunter (Guard); Barbara
Esback (Matron); Gail Bonney, Doris Kemper, Lovyss Bradley, Eva

Nelson, Rosemary O'Neill, Jean Calhoun, Nita Talbot, Tina Menard,
Gladys Roach, Virginia Engels, Claudia Cauldwell, Helen Eby-Rock,
Joyce Newhard, Pauline Creasman, Marie Melish (Inmates); Davison
Clark (Doctor); Pauline Drake (Doctor's Wife); Bill Wayne (Ada's
Father); Doris Whitney (Visitor); Ruth Warren (Miss Lyons).

    Until she made Interrupted Melody five years later, Eleanor
Parker usually said that Caged was her favorite film. Sometimes
even after--it hasn't always been easy for the actress to decide
between the two. A viewer is faced with the same dilemma because
Caged is a dynamic, important work with one of the screen's great
performances by Parker. In its surging, bitter, even harrowing
style leavened by some tough laughs a comedy film might envy, the
production evokes the earlier The Snake Pit (1948), an exposé of
mental hospitals.
    Caged attacks women's prisons to a knockout. The prologue
establishes the graphic, unsparing mood: from inside a moving, dark
van we see a patch of daylight and blurring landmarks through a
small back window as the credits, accompanied only by a wailing
siren, flash on--"Starring Eleanor Parker," etc. At the Women's
State Prison, the vehicle stops, the doors are opened to reveal,
among others, a terrified young Eleanor Parker, a voice instructing,
"Pile out, you tramps. The end of the line." Parker tells her
story to the receiving room worker (Edith Evanson): only 19, she
had been her jobless husband's unwilling accomplice when he was
killed stealing $40 from a gas station. "Five bucks less and it
wouldn't be a felony," yawns her interrogator. Her sentence: ten
to fifteen years for "armed robbery," with a parole hearing in ten
months. She is sent to Isolation, where a ravaged consumptive
(Ann Tyrell) croaks, "Welcome ... to Lysol Lane." Next, the infirmary. "Hope your batch is cleaner than the last lot. We had
to scrub them with brooms," a burly nurse informs Parker. She
learns she is pregnant (which the actress, expecting daughter Sharon,
was in real life). It is becoming clear what the caring, progressive
but constantly thwarted prison superintendent (Agnes Moorehead)
means when she advises Parker, "You weren't sent here to be punished.
Just being here is the punishment." She also informs her that she
cannot go home to have her baby and that she will be working in
the laundry. As the evil matron of Parker's 60-woman "bull pen,"
the mountainous Hope Emerson is introduced munching caramels
and reading a romance magazine, the wall of her room adorned by
a framed, embroidered doily that reads "For Our Dear Matron."
When she learns Parker has no money for "favors," she puts the
new inmate to work scrubbing the floor of her bull pen--"Just like
the cage in the zoo, only you clean it up instead of the keeper."
Parker's barrack mates include husband-killer Betty Garde, a shop-
lifting ring recruiter who tries unsuccessfully for Parker; Jan Sterling,
a "C.P." (common prostitute); Gertrude Michael, a disturbed former
socialite; Olive Deering, who befriends Parker, then, failing her
parole hearing, hangs herself; and the bird-like, simple-minded
Ellen Corby, who has one of the film's funniest (yet valid) monologues:

It's all the judge's fault I'm here. When Joe first beats me
up, I grab his gun and just wing him in the shoulder. Do
they arrest me? No. Then a year later I fires at Joe again
and missed. Do they give me a rap for attempted assault?
No! Then last year I defends myself again with a gun and
the police still treats me like I was poison ivy. And then
finally I finished Joe off for good. Well, it's that judge.
If he'd-a nabbed me the first three times while I was just
practicing, I wouldn't be here now for murder. It's all the
judge's fault.

And Corby again: "It's funny. You get a baby from a guy and 20
years later you finish him off." When another prisoner reveals
that she's been married five times and is asked what's wrong with
that, she replies, "Nothin', if you're not married to 'em all at the
same time, like I was." In the yard, an inmate explains that she
killed her boyfriend when he took her rowing on the lake. "He
slaps me, so I slapped him back," she relates. "You just slapped
him?" asks a companion. "Well, I did have an oar in my hand.
He kept on hittin' me so I kept on slappin' him." Her friend:
"Still with the oar in your hand?" "Uh-huh," answers the narrator.
"What'd you keep on slappin' him for?" wonders one inmate. "Well,
he kept on comin' up."
        Parker's first night in prison is anything but humorous: atop
her bunk in the darkened bull pen, where bar shadows fall across
her pillow, she cowers as a mournful voice sings "Bird in a Cage"
and others cough, sneeze, and cry. Finally, Gertrude Michael
goes berserk and smashes a window with her hands, severing an
artery--"I don't belong in here! I'm Georgia Harrison!" Betty Garde
tells Parker, "You see, kid, in this cage you get tough or you get
killed." Each time the train passes near the compound, the nostalgic
prisoners stop everything and stand still until the sounds of travel
trail off in the distance. Before leaving on a night off, Emerson,
her massive torso incongruous in frilly street dress and hat, saunters
over to her charges. Sterling wisecracks, "I got news for ya. If
that's what dames are wearing now, I'm glad I'm in here." Emerson
proceeds to torment the rapt, frustrated women by suggestively de-
tailing how much she likes her boyfriend to kiss her, adding that
he "just bought himself a brand new car." Snaps Garde, "It must
be a truck." Parker's baby is imminent, keying a small but signifi-
cantly cynical scene: desperately calling outside for a doctor, superintendent Moorehead is connected with a smoke-filled room in which
several men are playing cards. The young woman who answers the
phone lies, "He's not here. He went out on a case," as the camera
pans to the medico in question passed out on a couch. Parker's
mother (Queenie Smith) refuses to take her baby; it is put up for
adoption. In one of the most shattering scenes, Parker, hysterical
at being denied parole, runs into the yard and tries to climb over
the barbed wire fence, ripping open her hand. Soon, well-connected
"vice queen" Lee Patrick enters the prison ("So help me, I never
saw such an old-looking bunch of bags") and also tries to recruit

"cute trick" Parker for when she "flops out of stir," but she resists
her, too. Coming upon old enemy Garde, Patrick says, "Read about
you and Ed. Divorcing him would have been easier." Subsequently,
Emerson beats Garde until she twitches and is "stir-bugs," and in
a particularly horrifying scene she shaves Parker's head--the close-
ups of the stark terror in the actress' expressive eyes as each strand
tumbles past them almost searing the screen. (Actually, wigs were
used to portray Parker's various stages of "baldness.") Another
stunning moment among many: when the grimly impassive Parker,
a little peach fuzz growing in after time in solitary confinement and
the hospital, returns to the bull pen, climbs to her bunk, and
stares straight ahead, her cellmates bang on the furniture in protest.
Then one day in mess hall, Garde uses her fork to stab Emerson
fatally as Parker cries "Kill her! Kill her! Kill her! Kill her!"
Later, after Parker has looked through the bars of the bull pen at
a well-dressed, pitying young woman visitor, she decides to join
Patrick and quickly gets her parole. On the way out, she tells
Moorehead, "For that 40 bucks Tom and I heisted, I certainly got
myself an education." With a "Thanks for the haircut," she throws
her wedding ring in the waste basket. When Moorehead's secretary
(Sheila Stevens) asks what she should do with Parker's file, Moorehead sighs, "Keep it active. She'll be back."

     The seasoned Virginia Kellogg, who co-authored with Bernard
C. Schoenfeld the scathing, Oscar-nominated story and screenplay
of Caged, voluntarily served time in prison to research the riveting
tale. And, although the humor--while welcome and always funny--
sometimes teeters toward vaudeville, Kellogg and collaborator have
written a smashing, generally unairbrushed plea for prison reform.
Along with her dramaturgical know-how, Kellogg also has a spongy
ear for prison jargon: the scenario is filled with atmospheric collo-
quialisms such as "freeside" (outside prison), "behind the iron" (in
prison), "booster" (shoplifter), "pogey" (the infirmary). Caged,
called Locked In during production, was powerful and applicable
then, and it is still powerful and applicable today, just the kind of
film the socially conscious Warner Bros. Studio was always drawn
to in the "golden age." (One of the ads promised "The Most Daring
Revelations Since Prisoner from a Chain Gang!", the company's early
landmark social-protest drama.) Credit goes to John Cromwell,
too, the underrated director of such exceptional films as Of Human
Bondage (1934), The Prisoner of Zenda (1937), Since You Went Away
(1944), The Enchanted Cottage (1945) and Anna and the King of Siam
(1946). Unfalteringly, he has helped to string together an unusually
potent series of scenes, dramatic gems that add up to a brilliant,
devastating whole.

     The contribution of star Eleanor Parker to the success of
Caged cannot be overestimated. Her range is prodigious as she
goes in subtle stages from naive, gaping, teen-aged inmate, wanting
to do what is right, to--horrific months later--cigarette-flicking,
embittered doxy who looks a full ten years older and at last drives
away from her "alma mater" with a car full of hoodlums. They seem
to be two different women, and of course they are, thanks to

Parker's awesome artistry whereby even her vocal timbre undergoes
a metamorphosis from timid, melting tones to, gradually, the brusque,
sandpaper delivery of the later episodes. Near the end, when the
now almost mannishly hardened parolee is ready to leave and Moorehead looks at Parker's early "mug shot" as a frightened, dull-eyed,
pregnant young widow, the effect is startling, to say the least.
Joan Crawford originally brought the part to her attention. As she
somehow usually managed to do, Crawford had got hold of the script,
but felt she was too old for it and told Parker it was perfect for
her. Actually, Cromwell and producer Jerry Wald first had wanted
petite Wanda Hendrix, but Parker fought to be tested and finally
won the role. And the role won her the Volpi Cup as world's best
actress at the Venice Film Festival that year, as well as her first
best actress Academy Award nomination (she lost to Judy Holliday
recreating her stage role of the dumb blonde Billie Dawn in Born
Yesterday).

Parker is supported by a marvelous troupe--Hope Emerson's
sadistic, chiseling, mastodon matron with political connections literally towering above the others. She, too, received a well deserved
Oscar nomination for best supporting actress. Betty Garde is also
sensational, running the gamut from swaggering cell boss to maimed
beating victim to, finally, "hot seat" candidate. Agnes Moorehead
is exemplary as the prison superintendent who is constantly thwarted
by politicians in her attempts at institutional reform. Lee Patrick
is authoritative as the somewhat "butch" vice queen; Gertrude
Michael pitiable as a deranged, aristocratic forger; Ellen Corby funny
as a light-hearted and -headed husband killer; Jan Sterling both
droll and pathetic as an incarcerated Billie Dawn; the excellent,
neglected actress Olive Deering touching as a suicide; Edith Evanson
memorable as a jaded arrivals clerk; and Queenie Smith briefly vivid
as Parker's torn little mother. Noteworthy, too, is the small but
shining contribution of an actress named Lynn Sherman, who plays
a prison trusty with a soft-spoken, trance-like gravity that is
chilling. When Parker asks what she's in for, Sherman's several-beats
pause before answering "Murder" not only drops the blood temperature
but makes a viewer wonder what her story is. The whole film is
flawlessly cast, right down to the frowsiest assortment of bit players
and extras ever assembled on one sound stage. In an article she
by-lined in Screenland magazine in 1950, Eleanor Parker wrote:

> When the picture went into production and the word was
> circulated that 60 women were working together in the
> cramped space of a prison set, that they were not allowed
> to wear any make-up, that their hairdressing was nil, and
> that these conditions were going to prevail for 10 weeks,
> there was a good deal of masculine wagering about how long
> it would be before the scratching and biting began.... The
> announcement may come as a bombshell, but the stark truth
> is that there was not one unpleasant moment during the
> entire shooting schedule. There was no strain, no irritation,
> no boredom. We 60 women worked as a team and enjoyed

it. Between "takes," we would gather around the piano,
while Hope Emerson played. We had quite a respectable
glee club.

Caged, then, contains ensemble acting heights rarely attained
in films. History did not repeat itself when the story was remade
by Warners in 1962 as House of Women, with Shirley Knight, or in
any of the numerous uncredited stage, screen, and TV rip-offs
since the 1950 original. Parker was even asked to appear in one
of the retreads, a 1972 TV movie entitled Women in Chains, but this
time as the cruel matron. Relates her son, Paul Clemens, "Mother's
feeling was, she had played the lead in the best of the women's
prison dramas, and she saw no reason now to play Hope Emerson."
Her old Warner colleague Ida Lupino got the role. Caged does
indeed remain the definitive dramatic portrait of women behind bars
and was directly responsible for the installation of reform programs
at many women's penal institutions.

24.   THREE SECRETS.   Warner Bros./United States Pictures Pro-
      duction. 1950. 98 Mins.

Producer, Milton Sperling; director, Robert Wise; screenplay, Martin
Rackin, Gina Kaus; camera, Sid Hickox; art director, Charles H.
Clarke; editor, Thomas Reilly; sound, Charles Lang; assistant
director, Russell Saunders; dialogue director, Anthony Jowitt;
music, David Buttolph; orchestrations, Maurice de Packh; set decorator, Fred M. MacLean; special effects, William McGann, Edwin
DuPar; wardrobe, Leah Rhodes; make-up, Perc Westmore.

Cast: ELEANOR PARKER (Susan Chase); PATRICIA NEAL (Phyllis
Horn); RUTH ROMAN (Ann Lawrence); Frank Lovejoy (Bob Duffy);
Leif Erickson (Bill Chase); Ted de Corsia (Del Prince); Edmon
Ryan (Hardin); Larry Keating (Mark Harrison); Katherine Warren
(Mrs. Connors); Arthur Franz (Paul Radin); Duncan Richardson
(Johnnie); Nana Bryant (Mrs. Gilbert); Kenneth Tobey (Marine
Officer); Ross Elliott, Rory Mallinson (Reporters).

Today when moviegoers sigh, "They don't make 'em like that
anymore," they mean films like Three Secrets. It's a real "movie"
movie, with well-drawn, well-cast characters and a plot that is not
only clever but suspenseful, keeping the viewer guessing right up
to the end. It begins when a small plane carrying a boy (Duncan
Richardson) and his parents crashes into the Sierra mountains.
Only the child, celebrating his fifth birthday, survives, though he
is trapped on a remote ledge of a mountain. It is then revealed
that he was one of three boys adopted from a Los Angeles foundling
home on the same day five years before.
    As climbers, reporters, and spectators converge at the lodge
near the base of the mountain, Eleanor Parker, happily married to
lawyer Leif Erickson, hears the news and thinks the child could be

hers. She drives to the lodge while a flashback explains her story.
Five years earlier, after being jilted by Marine Arthur Franz, she
finds she is pregnant. She fails in a suicide attempt, after which
her mother (Katherine Warren) convinces her to give up the baby
for adoption. As she takes pen in hand to sign the agreement, she
hesitates, prompting agency head Nana Bryant to ask, "Is it empty?"
Throat-catchingly, Parker replies, "No. It's me," and signs. Back
in the present, she arrives at the lodge and meets tough, ambitious
reporter Patricia Neal, who also had a boy given out for adoption--
same day, same place. "I'm just a reporter covering a story.
Wouldn't it be ironic if it turned out to be my own?" she quips. Neal
then thinks back five years to her marriage to Frank Lovejoy, a
male chauvinist sportswriter who resents her globe-trotting. When
she accepts another overseas assignment, he divorces her and re-
marries, leaving Neal pregnant. She gives up the baby. Next,
Ruth Roman, a notorious ex-convict, shows up at the lodge, drunk
and disorderly. "Three little maids who lost their way," she observes, "waiting together. It's very funny." She tells Parker and
Neal her story. Five years before, she was a pregnant dancer with
a soon tiring producer boyfriend who tried to pay her off. She
bludgeoned him to death. During imprisonment for manslaughter,
her child was born (recalling the preceding Caged), and she gives
him to the same home as Parker and Neal; the boy is adopted on
the same day as theirs. As the rescuers approach the mountain
ledge, Parker sends for her husband, telling him of her wartime
indiscretion. He is understanding. It is then learned that the boy
on the mountain is Roman's son. When he is safely brought down,
Parker and her husband plan to adopt him.

  Patricia Neal once said that Parker "loathed playing that part
(in Three Secrets)," possibly because she may have felt it less
colorful than the other two leads. But it doesn't show. Neither
does the fact that in real life the actress was pregnant with her
second child, daughter Sharon, though cinematographer Sid Hickox
"had a heck of a time trying not to shoot her in profile," to believe
Photoplay at the time. With her beautifully modulated voice, Parker
earns her top billing with a sensitive, touching, knowing execution
of the woman among the three with the strongest maternal instinct.
"She scores decisively," said "Brog." in Variety. The lanky Neal,
however, does come close to taking top honors as the dedicated
journalist who--to the strains of "I Get a Kick Out of You"--loves
her husband but not quite as much as her job. Despite the sexist
charges of the era that she isn't a woman because she prefers to
work, she makes her wise-cracking but compassionate scribe not
only likable but moving. One flavorful bit: when she returns after
a long European assignment to her news desk, rummages nostalgically
through it, lights up a cigarette and grimaces, realizing it is from
a pack she put in the drawer a year ago. Ruth Roman is convincing and is likewise affecting when she gives up her child to
Parker at the finish. Registering strongly, too, are Ted de Corsia,
in a particularly interesting turn as the dead producer's glibly insidious, peripatetic factotum; and Katherine Warren, as Parker's

self-contained mother who finally breaks down in a hospital corridor
when she holds her soon-to-be-adopted infant grandson. Fresh from
his first big success with the prizefighting drama The Set-Up (1949),
versatile director Robert Wise pulls all the drama possible from the
taut Martin Rackin-Gina Kaus screenplay, helping to make Three
Secrets an all-around solid, edge-of-the-seat entertainment.

25. VALENTINO. Columbia. 1951. Technicolor. 103 Mins.

Producer, Edward Small; associate of producer, Jan Grippo; director,
Lewis Allen; screenplay, George Bruce; camera, Harry Stradling;
music, Heinz Roemheld; music supervisor, David Chudnow; editor,
Daniel Mandell; art director, William Flannery; set decorator, Howard
Bristol; special effects, John Fulton; costumes, Gwen Wakeling,
Travis Banton; dance director, Larry Ceballos; make-up, Ern West-
more; hair, Marie Clark; Technicolor color consultant, Robert Brower.

Cast: ELEANOR PARKER (Joan Carlyle); ANTHONY DEXTER (Rudolph
Valentino); Richard Carlson (William King); Patricia Medina (Lila
Reyes); Joseph Calleia (Luigi Verducci); Dona Drake (Maria Torres);
Lloyd Gough (Eddie Morgan); Otto Kruger (Mark Towers); Marietta
Canty (Tillie); Paul Bruar (Photographer); Eric Wilton, Charles
Coleman (Butlers); Robin Raymond (Chef's Girl); Almira Sessions
(Mail Clerk).

     Valentino was an Italian immigrant, a gigolo, the "great lover"
among movie stars and died young. That is pretty much where
fact ends in the "biographical" film Valentino. The complexities
of this silent screen phenomenon, as well as his marriages to two emascu-
lating women (Jean Acker and Natacha Rambova), are omitted from
the trite screenplay credited to George Bruce but on which a long
line of writers had toiled. So is any overt mention of the rumored
homosexuality that caused newsmen then to dub him "The Pink Powder
Puff," though at one early point his major-domo (Joseph Calleia)
does tell a rival gigolo, "For $50 Rudy would teach even you to
tango."
     Following a "10-year search" by producer Edward Small,
Anthony Dexter, né Walter Fleischmann of Nebraska and a schoolteacher turned stage actor, is "introduced" as Valentino. It was
said that the theater's Katharine Cornell recommended him for the
role. But despite a superficial resemblance to the star, bolstered
by make-up and lighting, he is strictly an animated, somewhat
jowly eight-by-ten glossy. In fact, Dexter's slit-eyed posing and
stiff, pigeon-like strut suggest a characterization wholly derived
from scrutiny of Valentino stills. On the other hand, Eleanor
Parker, with top billing in her first film since leaving Warner Bros.,
does bring some feeling and professionalism to the story as the
"mystery blonde" Valentino meets on the boat to America. They fall
in love, and he learns that she is actually "one of the biggest stars
in Hollywood," a "Joan Carlyle" also referred to as "America's Dream

Girl." According to publicity for <u>Valentino</u>, Carlyle is a "composite" of the women in Rudy's life, but this gracious blonde lady really is like none of the manipulators, barracudas, and "vampires" closely associated with poor Rudy. (Alice Terry, however, a co-star of Valentino's, thought otherwise. Claiming that Parker was portraying her, she sued Columbia for suggesting that she had an affair with Valentino. She settled out of court in 1953 for a sum described as "substantial.") In Hollywood, Valentino quickly wins the star-making role of Julio (here pronounced "Jew-lio" by everyone) in <u>The Four Horsemen of the Apocalypse</u>, going on to ignite the screen with Carlyle in <u>The Sheik</u>. Near the end, disregarding "appendicitis," Valentino leaves his sickbed and, enlisting the aid of a bogus fiancée (Patricia Medina) to avoid embroiling the married Carlyle in a scandal, entrains for New York where he dies.

Except for the train and his demise (in 1926 at 31), none of this has a basis in fact, either. And the cause of his death was actually peritonitis resulting from a perforated ulcer. Still, a juggling--even omission--of facts would be excusable if the end product proved entertaining. Unfortunately, this is only sporadically so in <u>Valentino</u>. Among the items on the plus side, Dexter does a lusty whip tango with Medina (as the most sympathetic "other woman" ever), the "Valentino Tango" theme is infectious and there is some color in the Hollywood setting. But all are at the mercy of the script, which shows none. Eleanor Parker is given such lines as "Oh, Rudolph Valentino you are impossible!" and "Oh, Rudolph Valentino you're hopeless!" <u>Time</u> magazine said, "Its dialogue sounds as hackneyed as silent subtitles read aloud." Nevertheless, in sumptuous outfits by Gwen Wakeling and Travis Banton that must have accounted for half the production's budget, Parker is the one thing consistently worth watching in <u>Valentino</u>. As photographed in soft Technicolor aureoles by Harry Stradling, her warm beauty fairly glows. "Eleanor Parker brings to her star role a quiet warmth and quality," wrote "Brog." in <u>Variety</u>, "that helps to make Dexter look better than he actually is." Fleischmann/Dexter, trying to live down the fiasco of <u>Valentino</u> and a few subsequent films, eventually gave himself yet another name, Walter Craig, and when last heard from was teaching drama at a public school in Eagle Rock, California.

26. A MILLIONAIRE FOR CHRISTY.   20th Century-Fox. 1951. 91 Mins.

Producer, Bert E. Friedlob; director, George Marshall; screenplay, Ken Englund; story, Robert Harari; art director, Boris Leven; music, Victor Young; camera, Harry Stradling; editor, Daniel Mandell; sound, Frank Webster.

Cast: FRED MacMURRAY (Prof. Peter Ulysses Lockwood); ELEANOR PARKER (Christy Sloane); Richard Carlson (Dr. Roland Cook); Una Merkel (Patsy); Kay Buckley (June Chandler); Douglas Dumbrille (A. K. Thompson); Raymond Greenleaf (Benjamin Chandler); Nestor

Paiva (Mr. Rapello); Chris-Pin Martin (Fat Mexican); Walter Baldwin
(Mr. Sloane); Ralph Hodges (Bud); Byron Foulger (Sam); Ralph
Peters (Collector); Gene Gericko (Office Joker); Jo-Carroll Dennison
(Nurse Jackson); John Indrisano (Mechanic); Billy Snyder (Photo-
grapher); Charles Williams (Reporter); Al Hill (Cab Driver); Emmett
Lynn (Hermit); Julian Rivero (Thin Mexican); Lane Chandler (Tall
Reporter); Almira Sessions (Myrtle); Everett Glass (Dr. Whipple);
Emmett Vogan (Fat Reporter); Robert Bice (Reporter with Tape
Recorder); Sam Flint (Mayor).

    A Millionaire for Christy is, if not the last stand for the
screwball comedy, certainly one of the final innings in the major
league for that romantically wacky genre popularized in the 1930s
by such directors as Frank Capra (It Happened One Night), Gregory
LaCava (My Man Godfrey), Leo McCarey (The Awful Truth) and Howard
Hawks (Bringing Up Baby). At the helm is old hand George Marshall, who directed the hilarious but unheralded slapstick farce
Murder, He Says (1945), starring Fred MacMurray, with whom he
worked often. He is teamed again with MacMurray, one of the earliest
and most adept citizens of daffydom, the feminine lead in Christy
going to Eleanor Parker in a rare but expert light moment. Unfortunately, the film, produced by Parker's husband, Bert Friedlob,
arrived after the madcap vogue had given way to more sophisticated
comedies such as All About Eve (1950). It did reasonably well,
but probably would have done far better if it had been dropped down
in the Depression-hit thirties when movie audiences flocked to "escapist" entertainments that lifted them as far away from troubled
reality as possible.
    Perhaps influenced by Carole Lombard, the late, preeminent
platinum blonde screwball of Hollywood's thirties who had played a
particularly similar role in Hands Across the Table (1935) opposite
MacMurray, Parker turned bright blonde to personify ditsy "Christy."
A poor San Francisco legal secretary, she is entrusted with revealing
to syrupy radio philosopher Fred MacMurray that he has just in-
herited $2,000,000. Her friend (Una Merkel) convinces her to try
and trap the newly rich broadcaster while she's at it: "For one day
be a scarlet woman. The rest of your life you can be virtuous."
Arriving at his Los Angeles apartment as he is dressing to leave
for his wedding to socialite Kay Buckley, Parker pretends to swoon
in his arms. Unable to go through with her plot, however, she
rambles on about his uncle dying ... his $2,000,000 inheritance ...
signing the papers. But he has already rushed off to his wedding.
Cleaning woman Almira Sessions enters, sees Parker talking to herself and remarks, "Gee, you're nuttier than the rest!" Parker
follows him to his betrothed's estate, the marriage site, where, sobbing
from something in her eye, she is mistaken by everyone including
the bride-to-be for a cast-off girlfriend of the groom. The nuptials
are canceled as MacMurray drags the protesting Parker off to La
Jolla, California, where his old friend Richard Carlson runs a psychiatric clinic. Driving in his honeymoon car along the foggy coast
highway, they suddenly detour into the surf, getting drenched.

Seeking shelter, they come upon a group of rambunctious Mexican
section hands living in a boxcar. In the film's zaniest, most evocative
sequence, MacMurray and Parker (now clad in a Mexican blanket)
spend the night with the men drinking tequila and dancing. Later,
the two engage in a smooching session on the fog-shrouded beach
that, as underscored by the sweet old Bing Crosby/Ned Washington/
Victor Young song, "I Don't Stand a Ghost of a Chance with You,"
is surprisingly lyrical as well as laughable--murmurs Parker, "I feel
like such a heel. I mean, spending your honeymoon with you."
Arriving at La Jolla, psychiatrist Carlson, coveting MacMurray's
fiancée, convinces his buddy to court Parker, whom he claims is
1) mentally ill, 2) loves MacMurray (true) and 3) might otherwise
commit suicide. "Oh, this is insane!" scoffs Parker, told of the
plot. "That's my racket," reassures Carlson. Eventually, Carlson
and Parker trick MacMurray--who doesn't believe the story of his
inheritance--into giving away his $2,000,000 to several charities.
Soon after he realizes what he has done, for some reason he also
realizes he loves Parker in a boisterous, Capra-esque ending replete
with clamorous media people, grateful orphans, a Salvation Army
band, and the police. As the couple runs to escape the bedlam, they
are hoisted aboard a departing train by their Mexican friends.
Parker handles this fast-paced folderol as if she had spent all her
professional life taking pratfalls, being dragged through rooms,
clambering down fire escapes, and getting soaked. As Louella
Parsons wrote:

> The big surprise is the customarily romantic and dramatic
> Eleanor Parker doing out-and-out slapstick and at the same
> time being entirely winsome and charming. Miss Parker,
> it turns out, is a delightful comedienne with an almost un-
> canny sense of timing. She fully deserves the Cosmopolitan
> Citation I am awarding her for the Best Performance of the
> Month.

Parker pairs smoothly with MacMurray. Particularly amusing
is the early scene in which, having feigned a faint in the new
millionaire's arms, she keeps "coming to" and batting her eyes at
him, while he nonchalantly keeps tossing a cold cloth over her whole
face. By 1951, MacMurray could play this kind of role in his sleep,
but he never dogs it, proving again that he has always been one
of Hollywood's most underrated leading men. As the sticky airwaves
philosopher sponsored by, as he must put it, "The prune juice
that's a shot in the arm!", Fred MacMurray joins Eleanor Parker in
making A Millionaire for Christy, as New York Times critic A. H.
Weiler put it, "an infectious trifle, as harmless and palatable as a
bon bon."

27. DETECTIVE STORY. Paramount. 1951. 103 Mins.

Producer-director, William Wyler; associate producers, Robert Wyler,

Lester Koenig; based on the play by Sidney Kingsley; screenplay,
Philip Yordan, Robert Wyler; art directors, Hal Pereira, Earl Hedrick;
sets, Emile Kuri; camera, Lee Garmes; editor, Robert Swink; costumes, Edith Head; process work, Farciot Edouart; make-up, Wally
Westmore.

Cast: KIRK DOUGLAS (Jim McLeod); ELEANOR PARKER (Mary
McLeod); WILLIAM BENDIX (Lou Brody); Cathy O'Donnell (Susan);
George Macready (Karl Schneider); Horace McMahon (Lieut.
Monahan); Gladys George (Miss Hatch); Joseph Wiseman (Burgler);
Lee Grant (Shoplifter); Gerald Mohr (Tami Giacoppetti); Frank Faylen (Galla-
gher); Craig Hill (Arthur); Michael Strong (Lewis Abbott); Luis
Van Rooten (Joe Feinson); Bert Freed (Dakis); Warner Anderson
(Sims); Grandon Rhodes (O'Brien); William "Bill" Phillips (Callahan);
Russell Evans (Barnes); Edmund Cobb (Ed); Burt Mustin (Willie);
James Maloney (Mr. Pritchett); Catherine Doucet (Mrs. Farragut);
Ann Codee (Frenchwoman).

Under the aegis of William Wyler, one of Hollywood's most
honored, prestigious directors, Detective Story is a hard-hitting,
effective transferal to film of Sidney Kingsley's 1949 Broadway success
covering one dramatic day in a New York City police station. The
precinct remains the main set on screen as well. Most conspicuous
among those arrested are young embezzler Craig Hill, man-crazy
shoplifter Lee Grant, cat burglar Joseph Wiseman, and sleazy abortion-
ist George Macready. The latter gets beaten up by intolerant,
brutal sergeant Kirk Douglas. "Every time I look at one of those
babies," explains Douglas, "I see my old man's face." His father,
whom Douglas claims was criminally inclined, had driven his mother
insane. Douglas and wife Eleanor Parker love each other, but are
unhappily childless. When he discovers that, pregnant and unwed
before they met, she had availed herself of Macready's services he
cannot forgive her. "You're everything you always said you hated
in your own father," Parker retorts. He tells her he'll take her
home. "What for? So you can drive me to an insane asylum?" She
leaves him.
Grant and Wiseman, repeating their stage characterizations, have
not scaled down their work to accommodate the propinquity of the
cameras, overplaying grossly. But in the lead roles created on the
boards by Ralph Bellamy and Meg Mundy, Douglas and especially
the deglamourized Parker (wearing only the minimum street make-up)
achieve, in their scorching, anguished scenes together behind cramped
precinct doors, emotional crises and climaxes of a rarely intimate
intensity in films. Said Sam Lesner in The Chicago Daily News:

> Eleanor Parker, as the wife, who hears herself called "tramp"
> by her once worshipping husband, and Kirk Douglas, as
> the hate-corroded spouse who turns detective on his own
> heart, are superb.

Said "Herb." in Variety:

William Wyler, with a dream cast of truly pro thesps and a
powerful, human story, again hits full stride in Detective
Story. The producer-director has polished the legit hit by
Pulitzer prize-winner Sidney Kingsley into a cinematic gem
that can't be less than surefire at the b.o. [boxoffice]....
Miss Parker plays the wife with a dignity and emotional depth
that makes a dramatic highlight of the scene in which she
is forced to reveal her past and another in which she and
Douglas think they have come to a reconciliation only to
realize a moment later that Douglas' perverted mind again
can't compromise.

Wyler once said that Parker's role, giving her less screen
footage than she was used to at the time, was longer in the original
scenario which contained a scene that "opened up" the play to show
the detective and his wife at home. Wyler then felt that this interlude diminished the tension of the story and cut it from the shooting
script. Also cut from play-to-screen were comparisons made between
Douglas' tactics and a police state, deemed too controversial at a
time when Communist infiltration of the film industry was being charged.
Despite the abbreviation of her part from the script first submitted
to her, as well as the fact that she was still filming some of the
comedy A Millionaire for Christy, Eleanor Parker went on to win her
second best-actress Academy Award nomination in a row. Curiously,
the top-billed, focal Kirk Douglas, who had prepared by playing
the role on stage in Phoenix, Arizona, was not nominated. Parker
lost to Vivien Leigh in A Streetcar Named Desire. William Wyler was
nominated as best director, but George Stevens won for A Place in
the Sun, and Lee Grant was nominated as best supporting actress,
losing to Kim Hunter for A Streetcar Named Desire.

28. SCARAMOUCHE. M-G-M. 1952. Technicolor. 118 Mins.

Producer, Carey Wilson; director, George Sidney; based on the novel
by Rafael Sabatini; screenplay, Ronald Millar, George Froeschel;
art directors, Cedric Gibbons, Hans Peters; set decorators, Edwin
P. Willis, Richard Pefferie; costumes, Gile Steele; make-up, William
Tuttle; Technicolor consultants, Henri Jaffa, James Gooch, montages,
Peter Ballbusch; music, Victor Young; sound, Douglas Shearer;
special effects, A. Arnold Gillespie, Warren Newcombe, Irving G.
Ries; camera, Charles Rosher; editor, James E. Newcom.

Cast: STEWART GRANGER (André Moreau); ELEANOR PARKER
(Lenore); JANET LEIGH (Aline de Gavrillac); MEL FERRER (Noel,
Marquis de Maynes); Henry Wilcoxon (Chevalier de Chabrillaine);
Nina Foch (Marie Antoinette); Richard Anderson (Philippe de Val-
morin); Robert Coote (Gaston Binet); Lewis Stone (Georges de Val-
morin); Elizabeth Risdon (Isabelle de Valmorin); Howard Freeman
(Michael Vanneau); Curtis Cooksey (Fabian); John Dehner (Doutreval);
John Litel (Dr. Dubuque); Jonathan Cott (Sergeant); Dan Foster

(Pierrot); Owen McGiveney (Punchinello); Hope Landin (Mme. Frying
Pan); Frank Mitchell (Harlequin); Carol Hughes (Pierrette); Richard
Hale (Perigore); Henry Corden (Scaramouche, the Drinker); John
Eldredge (Clerk); Mitchell Lewis (Major-Domo); Ottola Nesmith (Lady
in Waiting); Dorothy Patrick (Dorie); John Sheffield (Flunkey);
Douglass Dumbrille (President); Frank Wilcox (DeCrillon); Anthony
Marsh (Capelier); John Crawford (Vignon); Bert LeBaron (Fencing
Opponent); Barbara Ruick (Actress).

Originally intended as a musical for Gene Kelly (fresh from
The Three Musketeers), everything about Scaramouche is on target,
making it one of the cinema's greatest swashbuckling adventures.
Set during the days preceding the French Revolution, the film
brought Stewart Granger his finest part as André Moreau, the playboy
born on "the wrong side of the blanket" now sworn to vengeance
against the callous marquis (Mel Ferrer) who has killed his dissident
friend (Richard Anderson). Meanwhile, he masquerades as the
masked clown Scaramouche with a troupe of traveling players among
whom is his occasional girlfriend, the tempestuous Lenore (Eleanor
Parker). After besting the nobleman in a climactic duel, only to
discover they are actually brothers, he marries his adversary's ward
(Janet Leigh), while in one of the most sophisticated gag endings
in an action epic the resilient Lenore walks off with a new swain
--Napoleon!
Granger not only fakes the fencing with aplomb, but plays
with enormous humor and style, his often grand manner musical readings
rendering to his dialogue the resonance of poetry. Audiences--and
Granger--may have the wife of director George Sidney, M-G-M drama
coach Lillian Burns, to thank for some of his effectiveness. According
to leaks from the set, after the shooting was completed Burns, dissatis-
fied with the quality of the sound recording, took it upon herself to re-
assemble almost the entire cast and personally direct them in the un-
detectable looping, or dubbing, of about 90 percent of the film. Clearly,
however, Granger had the ability and panache for a far more important
career than was to be his lot. Photoplay magazine, tabulating readers'
votes, gave him one of their venerable Gold Medal awards for giving
one of the year's most popular performances in Scaramouche.
Enacting her first role under her new M-G-M contract, Parker
has never been more dazzling, wearing long red wigs and, as the
feisty Columbine, the elaborate (and, in the prosaic 1950s, daring)
facial make-up of her stylized commedia dell'arte trouping chores with
stunning effect. Truly, as critics discerned, "a revelation," she
endows both plot and playlet with knockabout gusto and classical
stature. Ava Gardner had turned down the role; the reason becomes
obvious: the beauteous but limited Gardner must have known she
could never have approximated the skills required of the part and
which are Parker's in abundance. In his rave review in The New
York Times, Bosley Crowther wrote:

It is really Eleanor Parker who wins the female prize as the
red-headed fire-brand of the theatre who keeps our hero on

the go. We are very happy to inform you that she goes
off with Napoleon at the end. No less would be worthy of
the lady.

Parker and Granger, furthermore, sported the most impressive
romantic profiles since Garbo and John Barrymore in the same studio's
Grand Hotel 20 years before. Off-camera, they were less compatible.
For one of their several stormy scenes together, Parker had to slap
him but through several takes kept pulling her punches, not wanting
to hurt her co-star. Finally, director George Sidney insisted that,
for the sake of credibility, she really had to hit him. Which she
did, and a furious Granger refused to speak to her for the duration
of the shooting, unless it was dialogue for the film. In 1981 Granger
wrote his autobiography, Sparks Fly Upward, spending several
pages on Scaramouche but completely omitting the name anywhere
of probably his most felicitous leading lady, Eleanor Parker.
    The rest of the cast is also optimum, Janet Leigh (replacing
Elizabeth Taylor) being especially charming in her powdered wigs,
with Nina Foch offering a piquant cameo as Marie Antoinette. The
Ronald Millar-George Froeschel screenplay has rare wit for a film
of its genre: when a middle-aged suitor (Howard Freeman) gives
Parker a diamond bracelet, saying he thought of her eyes and went
out and bought it, she purrs, "Just my eyes? How sweet. I must
see that you start thinking about all of me." The direction of George
Sidney--unsung overseer of some of Hollywood's most colorful entertainments, including Anchors Aweigh, The Three Musketeers, Annie
Get Your Gun, Show Boat and Kiss Me. Kate--brings wonderful
dash to the richly mounted proceedings. For instance, the modest
scene in which Granger agrees to take the desirous Parker to Paris
so he can study fencing--proclaiming for her the instructor's name:
"Perigore of Paris!"--takes on an almost euphoric bravura as the
striking pair, in a rickety horse-drawn cart, speeds out of sight
down an old country road. Immensely helpful, too, is Victor Young's
superb musical score highlighted by a rousing action theme and lush
romantic underscoring. Deserving landmark status is the brilliant
Technicolor photography of pioneer cinematographer Charles Rosher,
with its misty lakeside mornings, sunlit rose arbors, plushly appointed playhouses and night-blue village streets dotted by golden
windows. And still talked and written about is the film's climax, the
duel (sans music) between Granger and Ferrer in a Parisian theater--
in the boxes, on their ledges, down the hall and Grand Stairway,
through the audience, up on the stage and into a soon gutted prop
room. At six-and-a-half minutes, it was called the longest duel ever
filmed. It is almost surely the most spectacular, even though the
triumphant, slightly beefy Granger, according to more studio scuttle-
butt, in real life was not as skilled at fencing as the slim Mel Ferrer
and necessitated several retakes because he kept dropping his sword.
This happened one afternoon when Granger's wife, actress Jean
Simmons, was visiting the set, whereupon the short-tempered actor
picked up the weapon and threw it, just missing Simmons' head.
    For the record, M-G-M previously had made Scaramouche

as a 1923 silent, with Ramon Novarro in the lead and, as the marquis, Lewis Stone, who here plays Granger's elderly adoptive father. There is no question, however, which version left the more lasting impression. Director Sidney recently said that wherever he goes on his frequent travels around the world, "cab drivers, doormen, when they learn who I am, cry 'Scaramouche! Scaramouche!'"

29. ABOVE AND BEYOND. M-G-M. 1953. 122 Mins.

Producers-directors, Melvin Frank, Norman Panama; screenplay, Frank, Panama, Beirne Lay, Jr.; story, Lay, Jr.; camera, Ray June; music, Hugo Friedhofer; conductor, André Previn; art directors, Cedric Gibbons, Malcolm Brown; sound, Douglas Shearer; set decoration, Edwin B. Willis, Ralph Hurst; editor, Cotton Warburton; montages, Peter Ballbusch; special effects, A. Arnold Gillespie, Warren Newcombe; women's costumes, Helen Rose; hair, Sydney Guilaroff.

Cast: ROBERT TAYLOR (Col. Paul W. Tibbets); ELEANOR PARKER (Lucey Tibbets); James Whitmore (Maj. Uanna); Larry Keating (Maj. Gen. Vernon C. Brent); Marilyn Erskine (Marge Bratton); Larry Gates (Capt. Parsons); Stephen Dunne (Maj. Henry Bratton); Robert Burton (Gen. Samuel E. Roberts); Hayden Rorke (Dr. Ramsey); Larry Dobkin (Dr. Van Dyke); Jack Raine (Dr. Fiske); Jonathan Cott (Dutch Van Kirk); Jeff Richards (Tom); Dick Simmons (Bob); John McKee (Wyatt Duzenberry); Patrick Conway (Radio Operator); Christie Olsen (Paul Tibbets, Jr.); William Lester (Driver); Barbara Ruick (Mary Malone); Jim Backus (Gen. Curtis E. LeMay); G. Pat Collins (Maj. Gen. Creston); Harlan Warde (Chaplain Downey); Crane Whitty (Gen. Corlone); Don Gibson (Dexter); John W. Baer (Captain); John Close (Co-pilot); Lee MacGregor (Gen. Roberts' Aide); Ewing Mitchell (Gen. Wolfe); Mack Williams (Gen. Irvine); Sam McKim (Captain); Robert Forrest (M. P. Officer); Dabbs Greer (Haddock); Dorothy Kennedy (Nurse); John Hedloe (Lt. Malone); Frank Gerstle (Sgt. Wilson); John Pickard (Miller); Gregory Walcott (Burns); Roger McGee (Johnson); Robert Fuller (Extra).

Above and Beyond, starring Robert Taylor and Eleanor Parker, is a powerful, true drama as well as one of its leading lady's most controversial films. The story, which gives new meaning to the expression "dead serious," tells of Paul W. Tibbets, the United States Army Air Force pilot who dropped the first atomic bomb on Hiroshima, much of the time concentrating, for maximum audience empathy, on the tremendous pressure this top secret operation put on his marriage. While most reviewers of the day lauded the tense, documentary-like preparations for the bombing which was calculated to save many American lives and end World War II, and embraced the love story as candid and involving, there were notable dissenters who felt that dwelling to such an extent on the Colonel's "domestic squabbles" trivialized one of humankind's most frightening, devastating

events. Much later, when consciousnesses had been raised and anti-
war stances became fashionable, there was additional retrospective
criticism for a "hero" who had precipitated the deaths of 80,000
Japanese. At the time of release, though, the majority of critics
saw much to praise in this grim but scrupulously reconstructed,
meritoriously acted tale, with Kate Cameron and the New York Daily
News bestowing their highest rating, four stars ("... Packs Terrific
Punch," read the headline); Louella Parsons giving it the "Best
Drama" of the month citation in Cosmopolitan ("Eleanor Parker ...
in a moving performance") and the elite National Board of Review
voting it one of the ten best films of the year. Most audiences
sided with proponents of Above and Beyond, finding the personal
story of the man in charge of the first atomic bombing not only
tenderly presented but a relevant, revealing footnote to history.

In Robert Taylor and Eleanor Parker, M-G-M has the perfect
players to drum dramatic life into Paul Tibbets--laconic, dedicated
leader of this horrific secret mission--and his wife, Lucey, loving
but baffled and, for a while, alienated by her husband's furtiveness.
Their story, for which Col. Tibbets himself was a technical advisor,
is narrated to excellent effect by the limpid-voiced Parker. It
starts in 1943, when the couple has been married five years, though
they have only been able to live together about seven weeks. After
flying many missions overseas, Taylor is sent home to whip into shape
the new B-29 bomber, hitherto "a death trap." Taylor and Parker,
with one small son, are soon expecting another child, though he is
constantly being called away on Air Force business. "Some day I'm
going to have a baby and you're going to be there when he's born,"
Parker grumbles. The atomic bomb is being developed, and he is
given the job of commanding the B-29 that will loose the first one
over a Japanese target to be determined by weather conditions then.
As plans for the attack are set into motion under Taylor, Maj. Gen.
Larry Keating warns him, "This must be the best-kept secret of the
war." Operation Silverplate, as the project is called, begins at the
Wendover, Utah, desert air base to which, for security reasons, the
wives soon also are moved. Security officer James Whitmore tries
to talk Taylor out of sending for Parker. "You're the one man who
shouldn't bring his wife out here," he advises. "I think you're
going to be too tough to live with." Back home, Parker is about
to give birth. Leaving her other child with her mother-in-law, who
is named Enola Gay Tibbets, she drives herself to the hospital,
ruminating, "Enola. Backwards, it spells alone." After the arrival
of their second son, Taylor relents and moves her to the base with
the children. Parker, struggling with the primitive conditions of
their cramped accommodations and her husband's sudden, cryptic
departures, turns edgy, imploring the tight-lipped Taylor, "For
Heaven's sake, stop taking yourself so seriously!" In one welcome ,
fact-based comic interlude, Parker gives a "plumber" (Larry Dobkin)
she has seen in white coveralls around the base $2 to fix her kitchen
sink; in actuality, he is a nuclear physicist. The pressure mounts
when President Truman authorizes dropping the bomb on Japan.
Parker, frustrated by Taylor's silence, becomes increasingly rebellious

and is put under surveillance as a security risk. Taylor sends his
hurt young wife away. In August 1945, the B-29 named Enola Gay
(after Taylor/Tibbets' mother, only shown in a photograph) takes
off for Japan, where Hiroshima's good weather makes that city the
target. Despite the known outcome, there is considerable suspense
as well as horror generated in this passage. Taylor informs his men
they'll be seeing "the biggest explosion in history." When the bomb
detonates, the inside of the plane goes white for a few seconds as
the huge mushroom cloud billows upward. "God!" exclaims Taylor.
Hiroshima is in flames. Later, he is reunited with Parker who at
last understands the reasons for her husband's secrecy.

Again, Robert Taylor--his celebrated widow's peak grown
slightly craggy after almost 20 years in films--admirably meets one
of his greatest challenges as the miserable but totally committed
real-life colonel, his natural reserve working well as a man described
as not easily showing emotion. It is entirely in keeping with such
an individual that he should ponder only briefly the morality of
being responsible for the deaths of enemy thousands, then get on
with the job of ending the war. Parker, as a woman who has spent
years meeting her husband in airports between planes and who must
now try to deal with his oppressive taciturnity, is immensely human
and attractive in her confusion. On behalf of Parker, quick bows
to hair stylist Syndey Guilaroff for her painstakingly casual, medium-
length coiffure of cascading blonde waves; and to Ray June, a prolific cinematographer from silent days who also photographed Metro's
1947 feature about the development of the atomic bomb, The Beginning
or the End, and who has given the feminine lead in Above and Beyond
several shimmeringly intense close-ups. They had faces then, for
sure, to borrow a line from Gloria Swanson in 1950's Sunset Blvd.,
and they knew how to prepare, light, and photograph them. Today,
this often seems a lost art. Of course few today have the basic
material to work with of an Eleanor Parker. Elsewhere, facsimiles
of assorted officers and their wives come and go, but Above and
Beyond belongs to Taylor and Parker in the first of three teamings
for the extremely compatible actors soon rumored to be a romantic
twosome off-screen as well. Under the producing-directing colors
of, astonishingly, comedy specialists Melvin Frank and Norman Panama
(who also wrote the telling screenplay with ex-B-29 pilot Beirne
Lay, Jr.), this magnetic pair gives an object lesson in movie star
acting of the special sort that put the "golden" into Hollywood's
Golden Age.

In 1980, Patrick Duffy and Kim Darby appeared as Paul and
Lucey Tibbets in a three-hour NBC-TV movie called Enola Gay.
There was, as they so often say of remakes, no comparison.

30. ESCAPE FROM FORT BRAVO. M-G-M. 1954. Ansco Color.
       98 Mins.

Producer, Nicholas Nayfack; director, John Sturges; screenplay,
Frank Fenton; story, Philip Rock, Michael Pate; music, Jeff Alexander;

camera, Robert Surtees; color consultant, Alvard Eiseman; art
directors, Cedric Gibbons, Malcolm Brown; set decorators, Edwin
B. Willis, Ralph Hurst; women's costumes, Helen Rose; special
effects, Warren Newcombe; hair, Sydney Guilaroff; make-up, William
Tuttle; editor, George Boemler.

Cast: WILLIAM HOLDEN (Capt. Roper); ELEANOR PARKER (Carla
Forester); JOHN FORSYTHE (Capt. John Marsh); William Demarest
(Campbell); William Campbell (Cabot Young); John Lupton (Bailey);
Richard Anderson (Lt. Beecher); Polly Bergen (Alice Owens); Carl
Benton Reid (Col. Owens); Howard McNear (Watson); Alex Montoya
(Chavez); Forrest Lewis (Dr. Miller); Fred Graham (Jones); William
Newell (Symore); Frank Matts (Kiowa Indian); Charles Stevens
(Eilota); Michael Dugan (Sims); Valerie Vernon (Girl in Bar); Phil
Rich (Barman); Glenn Strange (Sgt. Compton); Harry Cheshire
(Chaplain); Eloise Hardt (Girl); Richard P. Beedle (Confederate
Lieutenant).

Not the most original Western ever, and sans the Indian rights
consciousness then seeping into Hollywood output, the old-fashioned
Escape from Fort Bravo is still endowed with enough plusses to place
it among the fifties' best horse operas. It has William Holden and
Eleanor Parker heading a fine cast; John Sturges' panoramic direction;
magnificent scenery filmed at New Mexico and Death Valley, California;
and unusually snappy repartee for the genre by veteran screenwriter
Frank Fenton. To top it all off, there is a 25-minute Indian battle
climax that ranks with the most exciting ever staged. While the
species was not always taken seriously by critics, the reviews for
this one were very good, with Time magazine one of the most extrava-
gant:

> Escape from Fort Bravo, riding hard on the hoofbeats of
> Shane and High Noon, should prove to the movie public that
> the old mare is what she used to be--and maybe more. Direct-
> or John Sturges' Bravo is in some ways the best Western
> since 1943's memorable Ox-Bow Incident.... The four leading
> actors do excellent work. Actress Parker is spirited and
> warm as the heroine....

The time, the Civil War; the place, Fort Bravo, Arizona Terri-
tory, where unsmiling, by-the-book Union Captain Holden treats the
Confederate prisoners harshly. "When I see you work at soldier-
ing," comments his colonel (Carl Benton Reid), "I'm glad we're in
the same army." Reid's daughter (Polly Bergen) is about to marry
a lieutenant (Richard Anderson), which brings her Texas school-
friend (Parker) to the fort for the ceremony. The first glimpse
of this beautiful visitor clues viewers that here is no mere maid of
honor: as her stagecoach is attacked by "the deadly Mescalero
Indians," she defends herself with a small but effective revolver.
Actually, Parker is the girlfriend of one of the rebel captives (John
Forsythe), coming to the fort to effect his escape with three others

(William Demarest, William Campbell, John Lupton). Immediately
recognizing that the tough, smart Holden will be their main obstacle,
she moves to divert his attention. She invites him to the fort
dance, coquettishly warning, "I should tell you, Captain. I can
be a little trouble." To which he replies, "I believe that." She
adds, "But then, you look big enough to handle a little trouble."
Parker quickly discovers another side of the outwardly stern, increasingly attracted captain when he shows her the flowers he takes
pains to grow in his desert backyard. "A green thumb and an
iron hand," she observes, intrigued. After the wedding, Parker
muses, "Women always look beautiful when they're married and the
men always look scared." Retorts Holden, "They both get over it."
She arranges for the Confederates to escape in a merchant's covered
wagon, and after Holden proposes she impetuously goes with them,
realizing that she, too, has fallen in love with the enemy. When
Holden catches up with them in the desert, they are under siege
from a band of Indians. All are trapped overnight in a large sand-
hole as the Indians continually rain arrows and bullets on them.
Massacre seems certain until cowardly poet Lupton redeems himself
by escaping and sending back the Cavalry. Forsythe has been
killed (as have Demarest and Campbell), leaving Holden and Parker
to ride off together.
    Upon reflection, however, their way hardly seems clear:
one can't help wondering how the rulebook Union captain will manage
marriage to, and the implied happy ending with, a Confederate spy
whose machinations have resulted in several deaths. This curious
inconclusiveness leaves enough drama for a sequel (which never
came). Such loose ends are easily overlooked, though, when ex-
pertise is so prevalent elsewhere. Near the peak of a popularity
which would shortly see him win the best actor Oscar for Stalag 17
(1953), Holden convincingly embodies the two sides of the dedicated
soldier and cuts a dashing figure in uniform, too. Parker is incisive
in her emoting and, her red-blonde, meticulously styled hair sparkling
by both moon- and sunlight, resplendent in her luxuriant Helen Rose
costumes (though it would have taken a train, not a stagecoach, to
haul their bulk). As John McCarten wrote in The New Yorker,
"Eleanor Parker demonstrates that the desert air does just as much
for a girl's complexion as a couple of weeks at Helena Rubinstein's."
The dependable Demarest is outstanding as the tobacco-spitting old
"reb" whose running banter with young rebel Campbell provides
most of the humor ("Why don't you just take a nice nap," Demarest
advises as the Indians threaten, "and I'll wake you when you're
dead"). And in the end it also provides pathos, as they die together
from Indian bullets, the old man straining to pat the younger's
now limp hand. Talented Polly Bergen is wasted. At first she
appeared set for the feminine lead, but the studio finally decided
to go with a bigger name, giving Bergen the nothing role of the fort
bride. Whereupon she left Hollywood and established herself as a
television personality in New York.
    Director John Sturges (whose next film was the even more

widely acclaimed <u>Bad Day at Black Rock</u>) evokes John Ford in his
sensitivity to the grandeur of nature and the scope of his material,
adroitly capturing every facet of the tale; and he is aided greatly
by Robert Surtees' breathtaking cinematography of red mountains,
white sand, and blue skies. Jeff Alexander's versatile score of
stirring marches, romantic folk ballads, and lyrical pastoral themes
is a help as well.

M-G-M originally shot the story in the new 3-D, evident from the
fists, tomahawks, arrows, spears, and even snakes tossed at the
audience. By the time of general showings, however, the dimensional
projection gimmick was acquiring an aura of low-budget exploitation
undesirable for a major M-G-M release with a leading man soon to
win the Academy Award. The 3-D, which was to prove short-lived
anyway, was discarded, though <u>Fort Bravo</u> was subsequently said
to be the first M-G-M picture to be lensed specifically for the
growingly popular wide screen in an aspect ratio of 1.66 to 1. Still,
the production proves once again that it isn't the size, shape or
depth of the screen that really matters. It's the content that counts,
and in its classic, straightforward approach to Western adventure,
<u>Escape from Fort Bravo</u> delivers on most counts.

31. THE NAKED JUNGLE. Paramount. 1954. Technicolor. 95
Mins.

Producer, George Pal; associate producer, Frank Freeman, Jr.;
director, Byron Haskin; assistant director, Herbert Coleman; screen-
play, Philip Yordan, Ranald MacDougall; based on the short story
<u>Leiningen Versus the Ants</u> by Carl Stephenson; camera, Ernest
Laszlo; music, Daniele Amfitheatrof; costumes, Edith Head; make-up,
Wally Westmore; second unit director, Arthur Rosson; second unit
cameraman, Loyal Griggs; special photographic effects, John P.
Fulton; process photography, Farciot Edouart; art direction, Hal
Pereira, Franz Bachelin; set decoration, Sam Comer, Grace Gregory;
Technicolor color consultant, Richard Mueller.

Cast: ELEANOR PARKER (Joanna Leiningen); CHARLTON HESTON
(Christopher Leiningen); Abraham Sofaer (Incacha); William Conrad
(Commissioner); Romo Vincent (Boat Captain); Douglas Fowley
(Medicine Man); John Dierkes (Gruber); Leonard Strong (Kutina);
Norma Calderon (Zala); John Mansfield (Foreman); Ronald Alan
Numkena (Indian Boy); Bernie Gozier, Jack Reitzen, Rodd Redwing,
Pilar Del Rey, John E. Wood, Jerry Groves, Leon Lontoc, Carlos
Rivero (Bits).

The Naked Jungle has, among other virtues, something unique
in the science-fiction genre: a truly adult love story that is every
bit as absorbing as the melodrama created by the special effects
department. Some of the Philip Yordan/Ranald MacDougall screenplay
is even racy by 1954 standards. While often condescending, if not

downright hostile to films of its category, even the critics registered
approval: "Literate as well as dramatic"--Bosley Crowther, The
New York Times; "Masterfully utilizes an offbeat subject"--Milton
Luban, The Hollywood Reporter; "One of the truest, most literate,
most adult love stories the screen has seen in a very long time"--
Ruth Waterbury, Los Angeles Examiner.

The year is 1901 and top-billed Eleanor Parker, as "Leiningen's
woman," has journeyed from New Orleans to the South American
cacao plantation of American Charlton Heston, the proxy husband
she has never seen. Heston, who brags that he has built his impressive universe out of the jungle with his bare hands and is in
fact a virgin, having had "no time" for women, is startled by the
sexually aggressive, lush Parker in her sleekly lovely (if impractical)
period Edith Head outfits. "Leave something on me. I'm getting
chilly," entreats Parker, observing his initial gaze at her décolletage.
The dialogue grows increasingly sophisticated for a film of its species.
"Frankly, you're not what I expected," the groom explains. "Am I
worse or better?" she asks. "Just ... more," replies Heston. Their
exchanges peak after Parker tells him she had a previous husband
who died. Disturbed, he shows her his piano, noting it was brought
up the river 2,000 miles. As she sits down and plays, he adds
that the only condition for the things he has purchased for his home
has been that they not be used. "The piano you're sitting at,"
he sneers, "was never played before you came here." Her rejoinder:
"If you knew more about music, you'd know that a piano is better
when it's played. This is not a very good piano!" Later, she tells
him that she became his bride because she was looking for "the
strength and purpose" missing in her first husband. As he is
preparing to send her back to the United States, the Marabunta--
mile after mile of man-eating "soldier ants"--begin their decimating
march toward the plantation. South American commissioner William
Conrad reveals that the ants had come 27 years before but that "a
hundred years would be too soon." Heston hopes the moat around
his property will safeguard them, but the billions of intelligent ants
cross the water on leaves. We see vistas devoured, human skulls
picked clean. Ultimately, Heston blows up a dam, flooding his property and killing the ants. He and Parker, whose courage has helped
bring them together, embrace.

The imposing Heston is in top form, from his first appearance,
stooped and dirty from the fields, to his closing stance, wet but
triumphant. The ants are goose-pimply, as is the Daniele Amfitheatrof
music score, which becomes creepily discordant whenever the Marabunta are mentioned. And the settings--largely Paramount sound
stage and backlot--are skillfully interwoven with some Florida second
unit work. Towering above all like the studio's alpine logo, however,
is Eleanor Parker. As "Brog." in Variety noted, "For Miss Parker
it is a particularly good characterization, warm and human." Ironically, the character of Joanna Leiningen was not even in the famous
1938 Esquire short story that inspired the film, but was created
out of whole cloth for the film. In the book Byron Haskin, by Joe
Adamson, director Haskin said that the screenplay for The Naked

Jungle was originally written for "a gamine, someone like Leslie
Caron," a less attractive leading lady who, he felt, would have been
more believable traveling so far to be with a husband she's never
met. This changed when the elegant Parker became available--"There
is some difference between Eleanor Parker and Leslie Caron!" ex-
claimed Haskin. With all due respect to Haskin, who with producer
George Pal has done a first-rate job (as they did on the previous
year's still highly regarded The War of the Worlds), it would be hard
to imagine anyone equalling Parker in the role. She compels total
conviction as this exquisite, witty, emancipated but pained young
woman, her expressive voice squeezing the last ounce of meaning
and drama from every line, her porcelain, red-haired beauty in
Technicolor upstaging, even, mountains of soldier ants.
       In 1970, she told Ft. Lauderdale News Amusement Editor Bob
Freund, "The Naked Jungle was great fun and it made more money
for Paramount than any other picture they released that year....
It was very popular in Europe and South America. I still get letters
addressed to the 'Marabunta Lady'." When Parker's character in
the film elects to stay behind with her husband and help him fight
the marauding Marabunta (a name, incidentally, director Haskin
claims to have coined), he remarks, "You're quite a woman." Replies Eleanor Parker, "You're right." Quite a woman indeed.

32. VALLEY OF THE KINGS. M-G-M. 1954. Eastman Color. 85
     Mins.

Director, Robert Pirosh; screenplay, Pirosh, Karl Tunberg; suggested
by historical data in Gods, Graves and Scholars by C. W. Ceram;
camera, Robert Surtees; editor, Harold F. Kress; music, Miklos
Rozsa; costumes, Walter Plunkett.

Cast: ROBERT TAYLOR (Mark Brandon); ELEANOR PARKER (Ann
Mercedes); Carlos Thompson (Philip Mercedes); Kurt Kasznar
(Hamed Bachkour); Victor Jory (Taureg Chief); Leon Askin (Valentine
Arko); Aldo Silvani (Father Anthimos); Samia Gamal (Dancer).

       With Valley of the Kings, M-G-M obviously hoped to duplicate
the boxoffice bonanza a few years earlier of its King Solomon's Mines.
Again, Robert Surtees is cinematographer and Walter Plunkett costume designer. And again, two men and a woman (Robert Taylor,
Carlos Thompson, Eleanor Parker) set off on a quest through exotic
and sometimes dangerous terrain, circa 1900, this time Egypt instead
of Africa. There are times, in fact, when Valley of the Kings,
promoted as "the first Hollywood-produced picture made on location
in Egypt," actually looks like a remake of King Solomon's Mines.
       Wrapped in her Plunkett outfits that sometimes appear mys-
teriously like a mirage in the middle of the desert, a radiant Parker
portrays the determined English daughter of a famed archaeologist.
She has returned to the land of the Nile to continue her late father's
search for the pharaoh's tomb that would confirm the Old Testament

account of Joseph in Egypt. Says one character of her, "When
children were learning the alphabet, she was out on digs." She
enlists the aid of idealistic American archaeologist Taylor and is
also accompanied on the journey by her husband (Thompson, a handsome Latin inexplicably neglected by Hollywood), who eventually
resorts to murder in his scheme to loot the pharaoh's treasure.
Other perils of Parker and Taylor include the inevitable sandstorm.

Shot at most of the actual locales, the film puts the actors in
front of some impressive scenery, but little imagination is used in
the presentation of it. The characters are one-dimensional, allowing
the performers no opportunity to create living, or simply entertaining,
characters, and the direction is clumsy. Nevertheless, reporting
that the timeless beauty of Egypt and Eleanor Parker are the only
distinctions of Valley of the Kings brings to mind Bette Davis'
abiding final lines to married lover Paul Henreid in Now, Voyager:
"Oh, Jerry, don't let's ask for the moon. We have the stars."

33. MANY RIVERS TO CROSS. M-G-M. 1955. Eastman Color. 94
     Mins.

Producer, Jack Cummings; director, Roy Rowland; screenplay, Harry
Brown, Guy Trosper; story, Steve Frazee; camera, John Seitz;
music, Cyril J. Mockridge; editor, Ben Lewis; assistant director,
Ridgeway Callow; costumes, Walter Plunkett; hair, Sydney Guilaroff;
make-up, William Tuttle.

Cast: ROBERT TAYLOR (Bushrod Gentry); ELEANOR PARKER (Mary
Stuart Cherne); Victor McLaglen (Cadmus Cherne); Jeff Richards
(Fremont); Russ Tamblyn (Shields); James Arness (Esau Hamilton);
Alan Hale, Jr. (Luke Radford); John Hudson (Hugh); Rhys Williams
(Lige Blake); Josephine Hutchinson (Mrs. Cherne); Sig Ruman
(Spectacle Man); Rosemary DeCamp (Lucy Hamilton); Russell Johnson
(Banks); Ralph Moody (Sandak); Abel Fernandez (Slangoh); Darryl
Hickman (Miles); Betty Lynn (Cissie); Dorothy Adams (Mrs. Crawford);
Louis Jean Heydt (Mr. Crawford); Richard Garrick (Preacher Ellis).

In the divertingly rowdy backwoods farce called Many Rivers to
Cross, Eleanor Parker not only has the most physical role of her
career, but probably the most physical role of any leading lady of
the 1950s. She appears as the pretty but "most impatient maiden
in the virgin West" whom her old Indian bodyguard (Ralph Moody)
has nicknamed "Steppin' Woman--move fast, track good, shoot
straight." She also wields a wicked whip and knife. After she
rescues the wounded wanderer named Bushrod Gentry (Robert Taylor)
from Shawnee Indians, she takes him to the old Kentucky home she
shares with her parents (Victor McLaglen, Josephine Hutchinson)
and four brothers (Jeff Richards, Russ Tamblyn, John Hudson,
Russell Johnson). "I found this'un and it's mine," declares Parker's
bellicose Mary Stuart Cherne, who has set her bonnet--helmet?--for
him. Although Gentry seems to have spent equal amounts of time

trapping furs and avoiding being trapped himself by amorous females, he has clearly met his match in this single-minded, blazing redhead. "He'll take a lot of gettin'," warns her mother. "Well," drawls Mary Stuart, suddenly stabbing the kitchen table with a knife, "I got a lot of get!" When her quarry tries to bolt, she brings him back at gunpoint, instigates a fistfight between him and her local boyfriend (Alan Hale, Jr.) and pretends to be pregnant, forcing a shotgun wedding with Gentry. The beleaguered trapper finally makes it to the woods; she pursues and they bed down in a clearing for the night. As the unresponsive groom accidentally falls down a bank, his alarmed, still chaste bride cries out, "Did you break anything, Bushrod?" Eventually they part and Mary Stuart heads for home, but is chased by Indians. The backtracking Gentry saves her, asking, "What did you do to get those Indians so mad at you?" Her boast: "I outran 'em, that's what!" Finally, trapped in a cave where she inadvertently, hilariously thwarts Gentry's every effort to rout the last attacker, she once again reverses the tradition of male-to-the-rescue and furiously dispatches the Shawnee with a cracking whip. Running to the groggy Gentry, she exclaims, "Bushrod, I can't fight you off any longer. You won me!"

   The woodsy gusto of Many Rivers to Cross recalls the same studio and producer's Seven Brides for Seven Brothers, the surprise success of which the previous year probably prompted the usually lush M-G-M to make such an uncharacteristic film with two equally off-beat, slapstick roles for the generally more decorous co-stars, Robert Taylor and Eleanor Parker. (Russ Tamblyn and Jeff Richards, Parker brothers in Rivers, also appeared in Seven Brides.) The newer film doesn't hit the target quite as often as Parker's "sure shot" Steppin' Woman, a first cousin to Annie Oakley, and the male brawling, while used for comic effect, seems excessive; but for the most part Rivers flows smoothly. It is a send-up of the Indians-versus-the pioneers staple always filmed by Hollywood from such a serious and one-sided viewpoint. The slant is still one-sided as far as the ever-bloodthirsty Indians are concerned, but everything else is amusingly spoofed. And at least Parker's old Indian companion is given some of the brighter lines, which actor Ralph Moody, in long grey wig, delivers with sardonic drollery. While marching through the forests on the scent of her runaway groom, Parker swears to the trailing elderly retainer that she'll kill Bushrod Gentry when she catches him, and he groans, "You kill this old Indian first."

   The normally stolid Taylor, though no one's idea of a farceur, seems to be enjoying his unaccustomed role as Bushrod Gentry-- one of the great character names in film comedy that, perhaps intentionally, sounds like one of Hollywood's male starlets of the time (Rock Hudson, Tab Hunter, Race Gentry). "Eleanor Parker Kicks Robert Taylor Awake," read the headline for the Chicago Daily News review of Many Rivers to Cross, the last of the actress' three pictures with Taylor. In her 1987 book Gable's Women, Jane Ellen Wayne (who also had authored one on Robert Taylor) wrote, "Parker was Taylor's favorite leading lady, and she complemented him on the screen more than any other actress."

In a part first planned for Janet Leigh, Parker's zeal and facility with knockdown comedy amazed those who remembered her more ladylike characterizations. It is a performance to leave one breathless and gratified, and if one happened to be Eleanor Parker, black and blue as well, because the actress did all her own stunts and was particularly bruised and achy after the climactic donnybrook in the cave. Her frequent drawling bursts of "Booshroddd!" are consigned to memory with Marlon Brando's "Stellahhh!"

The screenplay of Harry Brown and Guy Trosper shows a keen (and often comically fractured) understanding of frontier language and lore, and it has been done to a turn by director Roy Rowland. Though originally from New York City, M-G-M's little-publicized Rowland also displayed a sure (if more restrained) hand with two earlier bucolic films, the charming Our Vines Have Tender Grapes (1945) and The Romance of Rosy Ridge (1947). A final kudo for music director Cyril J. Mockridge's sharp usage of Saul Chaplin's bouncy, folky theme song, "The Berry Tree" ("The higher up the berry tree, the sweeter grow the berries/The more you hug and kiss a gal, the more she wants to marry"). It is sung briefly early in the action by the coonskin-capped Taylor, traipsing light-heartedly through the woods, and later reprised by the stalking, like-outfitted Parker, establishing just the right jaunty tone for the wild and wacky adventure. The temptation is to call the show a backwoods Taming of the Shrew, except that Parker's "gumptious little feist" remains, thankfully, delightfully untamed--for 1955, maybe even outrageously so.

34. INTERRUPTED MELODY. M-G-M. 1955. Eastman Color. 106 Mins.

Producer, Jack Cummings; director, Curtis Bernhardt; screenplay, William Ludwig, Sonya Levien; based on her life story by Marjorie Lawrence; art directors, Cedric Gibbons, Daniel B. Cathcart; operatic recordings supervised and conducted by Walter Du Cloux; musical supervision, Saul Chaplin; operatic sequences staged by Vladimir Rosing; dramatic music score adapted and conducted by Adolph Deutsch; camera, Joseph Ruttenberg, Paul C. Vogel; editor, John Dunning; make-up, William Tuttle; costumes, Helen Rose; hair, Sydney Guilaroff; set decoration, Edwin B. Willis, Jack D. Moore; special effects, Warren B. Newcombe; recording supervisor, Wesley C. Miller; music advisor, Howard Gelman; assistant director, Ridgeway Callow; color consultant, Alvord Eiseman.

Cast: GLENN FORD (Dr. Thomas King); ELEANOR PARKER (Marjorie Lawrence); Roger Moore (Cyril Lawrence); Cecil Kellaway (Bill Lawrence); Peter Leeds (Dr. Ed Ryson); Evelyn Ellis (Clara); Walter Baldwin (Jim Owens); Ann Codee (Mme. Gilly); Leopold Sachse (Himself); Stephen Bekassy (Comte Claude des Vigneux); Charles R. Keane (Ted Lawrence); Fiona Hale (Eileen Lawrence); Rudolf Petrak, William Olvis (Tenors); Stapleton Kent (Station Man);

Ann Howard, Donna Jo Gribble, Janet Comerford (Contestants);
Phyllis Coghlan, Ivis Goulding, Jean Fenwick (Mothers); Doris Lloyd
(Volunteer Worker); Alex Fraser (Adjudicator); Penny Santon (Gilly's
Secretary); George Davis (Elderly Diner); Eugene Borden (French
Headwaiter); Jerry Martin (Taxi Driver); Gabor Curtiz (Tenor's
Manager); Claude Stroud (George); Doris Merrick (Nurse); André
Charlot (Bertrand); Sandra Descher (Suzie); Charles Evans (Director
of Metropolitan); Martin Garralaga (Dr. Ortega); William Forrest
(Dr. Richards); Stuart Whitman, Robert Dix (Men on Beach); Paul
Bryar (Florida Conductor); Eileen Farrell (Louise); Bess Flowers,
Maj. Sam Harris (Bits).

   Eleanor Parker has said that the inspiring Interrupted Melody
is her favorite among her films, and it's easy to see why. Cast
as the real-life Marjorie Lawrence, blonde opera star crippled by
polio in her prime, Parker has one of the most spectacular women's
roles of the sound period. She was not, however, first choice.
In 1952, M-G-M purchased Lawrence's autobiography as a vehicle
for Lana Turner; subsequent visions of the "sweater girl" swathed
in kimono as Madame Butterfly ended those plans. Next up, Greer
Garson, who by the time the studio got around to filming the story
had left M-G-M. Enter Eleanor. During preproduction, Lawrence
herself had been tapped to do the actual singing on the soundtrack,
but time and illness having taken their toll, she was not up to the
strenuous vocal demands of the part. The sturdier young Eileen
Farrell was hired, her flexible, honey-textured soprano exercised
on a wide musical repertoire helping to put the film's soundtrack
among the most exquisite ever recorded. It was a production that
made opera accessible to the masses as perhaps no other big studio
motion picture before or since. The selections are among the most
familiar, melodious, and dramatic of the popular operas, staged with
great color and dash as well as pantomimed with tremendous flair
and vivacity by Parker in a stunning succession of multihued wigs
and costumes. Her dubbing in several languages to Farrell's musical
soundtrack is letter-perfect, too. (In earlier show business film
biographies, Larry Parks in The Jolson Story and Susan Hayward
in the similar With a Song in My Heart had done equally extensive,
notable dubbing to another star's singing, but to popular music and
in English.) Although she was no opera-goer, actress Parker catches
with uncanny accuracy the bravura style of the era's "grand opera"
prima donna (though few have been as traffic-stoppingly beautiful).
So wholeheartedly does Parker throw herself into the performing of
the arias, in fact, that when she throws back her head and opens
wide her mouth it is not only almost impossible to believe she is not
doing the actual singing but there is also a certain suspense as one
wonders just how long her tonsils will be able to keep from popping
out for a CinemaScope "first." One critic, expressing wonderment
at her fervor, wished he had been on the M-G-M stage to hear the
sounds Parker actually had emitted.
   Parker's whole performance is unforgettable. She begins as
an Australian farm girl riding horseback to a vocal competition. She

wins first prize, a scholarship to study voice in Paris. There, she
is refused admittance to teacher Ann Codee, busy giving a lesson
to an ample diva who is unable to hit her high notes. In the court-
yard, Parker hears this and belts out the troublesome aria with a
flourish. Impressed, Codee beckons her from a window, and a year
of intense study commences. (The unique thing about this scene
is that the singer who cannot quite hit her notes is played, for this
one brief episode, by none other than Eileen Farrell, Parker's singing
voice on the soundtrack.) Parker soon makes her debut in Monte
Carlo singing "Musetta's Waltz" from Puccini's La Bohème, and is an
immediate success. On the night of her triumph, she meets American
doctor Glenn Ford, having a last fling before returning to the states
after a year of research at the Sorbonne. They are attracted to
each other, go dancing, drink too much and part. She does the
Finale to Act I from Verdi's Il Trovatore, "One Fine Day" from
Puccini's Madama Butterfly, and the "Habanera" and "Seguidilla"
from Bizet's Carmen. Invited to sing in Paris, she renders "My
Heart at Thy Sweet Voice" from Saint-Saëns' Samson and Delilah,
perhaps the operatic highlight of the film. Wearing a long, strawberry
blonde wig and diaphanous gown draped with beads, she is a visual
and (thanks to Farrell) vocal knockout as she slinks about the stage
seducing Samson. Her Delilah easily upstages the libretto's electrical
storm, not to mention a hapless Samson. At the Metropolitan Opera
House in New York, she is signed to sing Brunnhilde in Wagner's
Götterdämmerüng, but argues with her director (Leopold Sachse).
He insists she follow tradition and walk her horse into Siegfried's
funeral pyre; but as a country girl familiar with horses she insists
she should ride the animal across the stage and into the flames
because only at a gallop would a horse enter an inferno. On opening
night she does it her way, creating a sensation. She meets Ford
again, they fall in love and marry.

While rehearsing Wagner's Tristan and Isolde in South America,
she is stricken with polio and crippled. She stops singing. Parker
and Ford move to Florida where he devotes himself to her therapy.
But she grows more and more despondent at the slow progress and
one day angrily refuses his help. To get her to move, Ford puts
her old recording of "My Heart at Thy Sweet Voice" on the record
player. "Turn it off!" she screams from the couch as her singing
envelops the room. "I'll never forgive you!... Please, Tom, turn
it off! Damn you, turn it off!" She rolls onto the floor with a thud
and slowly crawls to the table holding the record player, knocking
it over. "You've moved!" he cries. She begins to sing again--
"Annie Laurie"--and is booked to guest with the Florida Philharmonic,
backing out at the last minute. In one of the most moving scenes,
she tries to kill herself but is stopped by Ford. Hysterical, she
falls out of her wheelchair, and Ford cradles her in his arms, sobbing
for help. Seing how distraught he has become, his wife's own
tears subside as the patient now tries to calm the doctor.

It is World War II, and she agrees to sing for wounded servicemen in the local hospital. Accompanied only by a piano as she
weaves about the ward in her wheelchair, she does "Over the

Rainbow." Judy Garland may have sung the definitive version of
this song in a barnyard, but the crystal-pure Farrell vocal combined
with the Parker performance and the heart-rending setting and
direction make this interpretation a close second. Encouraged by
the reaction, Parker now goes overseas to entertain servicemen--
aboard ship, on rainy, muddy back roads, in jungles where she
sings "Don't Sit Under the Apple Tree." Finally, Australia, where,
in yet another memorable scene, she tears into the rousing Aussie
anthem "Waltzing Matilda" from her wheelchair on a train platform as
her country's soldiers depart. She is ready for her comeback
at the Met as Isolde clad in flowing blonde wig and robes and wearing
leg braces. Seated for most of her scenes, near the end of the opera
she stands and, aided by the braces while holding onto prop rocks,
walks a few difficult steps and finishes the aria. The audience
cheers; the camera pulls back as the prima donna bows. The End.

Parker's scope was never more impressive as she goes from
unsophisticated farm girl, giddy at her first success, to glamorous,
strong-minded international star, loving, playful wife, and then
despairing paraplegic who eventually fights her way back into the
spotlight and life--truly the role of a lifetime. This was not lost
on the critics who gave her the reviews of her career: "Electrifying"
(Bosley Crowther, The New York Times), "Socko" ("Brog.", Variety),
"Outstanding" (England's Picturegoer magazine), "Academy Award
caliber" (columnist Ed Sullivan). In Redbook, Florence Somers
selected Interrupted Melody "Picture of the Month," writing, "Eleanor
Parker gives her finest performance [in] a distinguished film."
Parker was nominated for her third best-actress Oscar, but M-G-M
chose to put its promotional clout behind four-time nominee Susan
Hayward in their bigger boxoffice I'll Cry Tomorrow, another biography
of a musical star (Lillian Roth). Both lost to Anna Magnani for
Paramount's The Rose Tattoo.

Although top-billed in a role first planned for James Stewart,
Glenn Ford has a far less showy assignment yet manages to give
one of his most skillful, deeply felt enactments. He makes this
husband's love and dedication immensely touching and real. Roger
Moore, almost two decades before he became James Bond, has a major
supporting role as Parker's ambitious manager brother and is almost
indecently young and handsome in it. Curtis Bernhardt, who had
directed Bette Davis as jealous twins (A Stolen Life), Joan Crawford
as lovelorn schizophrenic (Possessed), and Jane Wyman as sacrificing
nursemaid (The Blue Veil), had served his basic training for the
pyrotechnics of Eleanor Parker as crippled diva. He rises mightily
to the demands of the dramatic material which is consistently engrossing, even candid for 1955 autobiography: there is the then unusual
use of a four-letter expletive, while Marjorie Lawrence's ulterior
character is not glossed over for likability as she for a time sullenly
resists her husband's loving ministrations and gives in to depression.
Special mention must be made of the sensitive screenplay by William
Ludwig and Sonya Levien, which won the best story and screenplay
Academy Award that year; the dazzling, Oscar-nominated costumes
by Helen Rose; the vivid staging of the operatic sequences by Vladimir

Rosing--indeed the outstanding work of the entire music department.
Interrupted Melody is not only the probable peak of Eleanor Parker's
career, but a film whose many riches make it one of the most adult
and involving musicals ever.

35. THE MAN WITH THE GOLDEN ARM.   United Artists/Carlyle
     Production. 1955. 119 Mins.

Producer-director, Otto Preminger; based on the novel by Nelson
Algren; screenplay, Walter Newman, Lewis Meltzer; music, Elmer
Bernstein; orchestrations, Frederick Steiner; camera, Sam Leavitt;
editor, Louis R. Loeffler; art director, Joseph Wright; set decorator,
Darrell Silvera; costume supervisor, Mary Ann Nyberg; men's ward-
robe, Joe King; women's wardrobe, Adele Parmenter; make-up,
Jack Stone, Bernard Ponedel, Ben Lane; hair, Helene Parrish, Hazel
Keats; sound, Jack Solomon; music editor, Leon Birnbaum; assistant
directors, Horace Hough, James Engle; production manager, Jack
McEdward; producer's assistant, Maximilian Slater.

Cast: FRANK SINATRA (Frankie Machine); ELEANOR PARKER (Zosh);
KIM NOVAK (Molly); Arnold Stang (Sparrow); Darren McGavin (Louie);
Robert Strauss (Schwiefka); John Conte (Drunky); Doro Merande
(Vi); George E. Stone (Markette); George Mathews (Williams); Leonid
Kinskey (Dominowski); Emile Meyer (Bednar); Shorty Rogers, Shelly
Manne (Themselves); Frank Richards (Piggy); Will Wright (Lane);
Tommy Hart (Kvorka); Frank Marlowe (Antek); Joe McTurk (Meter
Reader); Ralph Neff (Chester); Ernest Raboff (Bird Dog); Martha
Wentworth (Vangie); Jerry Barclay (Junkie); Lennie Bremen (Taxi
Driver); Paul E. Burns (Suspenders); Charles Seel (Landlord).

    Irrespective of its theatricality and melodrama, The Man with
the Golden Arm is a grimly arresting experience. In 1955 it was a
shocking, controversial one: the most graphic examination of drug
addiction yet seen on the American screen, with a particularly harrowing "cold turkey" scene well played by Frank Sinatra in the title
role. The film was responsible for changing the Motion Picture
Production Code. Although it was denied a seal of approval by
the censoring code because of the hitherto taboo drug addiction
theme, United Artists released it anyway, causing a furor because,
as a member of the Motion Picture Association of America, the company had sworn not to distribute a film without a seal of approval.
United Artists quit the Association. Producer-director Otto Preminger
and United Artists then carried the battle a step further when they
successfully demanded that the code be restructured to permit films
about narcotics abuse.
    Sinatra is junkie Frankie Machine, a card-game dealer who re-
turns to his Chicago slum after six months in a federal narcotics
hospital determined to live a straight life as a big band drummer.
In a claustrophobic, Street Scene-ish set of front stoops and flashing
neon, overrun by dimwits, finks, harridans, hustlers, floozies and

pushers, he soon succumbs to old ways and loses his chance with
the band. Parker portrays Zosh, his ignorant, beer-swigging wife,
"crippled" three years before in a car accident caused by her husband's drunkenness. Neurotic and clinging, totally unsympathetic,
she is actually able to walk but pretends to be wheelchair-bound to
keep Frankie guilt-ridden and attendant. Eventually, her deception
is discovered by drug peddler Darren McGavin, whom she then
pushes to his death over a high railing. When the police come, she
throws herself from the back porch of her tenement and dies, freeing
Frankie to go off with Molly, played by Kim Novak as a rather too
lushly upholstered local strip-joint B-girl who has been helping him
overcome his habit.

Parker is the only player who seems to be attempting a seamy
Chicago accent, which is especially noticeable in her innumerable
pronunciations of "Frankie" as a very nasal "Frinkie." Although
excessively jittery in early scenes, in later moments of cold terror
when found out, first by McGavin and then the police, she expresses
the unstable wife's glassy-eyed, cornered horror with chilling power.
According to some, though, she was not ideally cast. Screenwriter
Walter Newman, for one, felt she was too patrician-looking, that
Shelley Winters would have been more believable as "a lowlife slob."
And, in truth, Parker does not concern herself as much with the
character's vulgar externals as she had in Of Human Bondage.
Preminger, with a casting ingenuity not exactly unheard of in Holly-
wood, reportedly thought of her for the wheelchair-confined malingerer
because he had just seen her as a cripple in Interrupted Melody.
Nevertheless, Parker's Zosh created an impression and is curiously
a performance often mentioned first when her name comes up today.
And in Hollywood it has always been important for an actor to be
seen in a successful movie, which The Man with the Golden Arm was.
It marks a high point in the career of erstwhile band singer Frank
Sinatra, who was nominated by the film Academy as best actor
(Ernest Borgnine won for Marty).

36. THE KING AND FOUR QUEENS. United Artists/Russ-Field-
     Gabco Production. 1956. De Luxe Color. 83 Mins.

Executive producer, Robert Waterfield; producer, David Hempstead;
director, Raoul Walsh; screenplay, Margaret Fitts, Richard Alan
Simmons; story, Fitts; camera, Lucien Ballard; music, Alex North;
editor, David Bretherton; editorial supervision, Louis R. Loeffker;
assistant director, Tom Connors, Jr.; costumes, Renie, Oscar Rod-
riguez, Marjorie Henderson.

Cast: CLARK GABLE (Dan Kehoe); ELEANOR PARKER (Sabina);
Jo Van Fleet (Ma McDade); Jean Willes (Ruby); Barbara Nichols
(Birdie); Sara Shane (Oralie); Roy Roberts (Sheriff Larrabee);
Arthur Shields (Padre); Jay C. Flippen (Bartender); John Compton
(Boone McDade--cut from film); Dayton Lummis (Dr. Amos Whitmore--
cut from film); Bill Tom (Indian Boy).

If The King and Four Queens has any distinction besides the
teaming of Clark Gable, "The King of the Movies," and Eleanor
Parker, it is that it suffered the most drastic altering from script
to released film of any Parker feature. This is puzzling because as
Gable's first producing venture (partnered with Jane Russell and
her husband, Robert Waterfield) he could have been expected to
exert a more stabilizing influence over matters. What might have
been a delightful, original, even exciting Western spoof was reduced,
therefore, to the mildest of entertainments by the injudicious, unex-
plainable cutting of many important scenes. The reasons do not
appear to have been budgetary because much of the missing material
was shot--scene stills remain attesting to that.

Gable is perfectly cast in a story that could have exploited
his romantic image to a fare-thee-well. An Old West desperado, he
rides into the ghost town of Wagon Mound inhabited only by a rifle-
toting crone (Jo Van Fleet) and her four comely young daughters-in-
law (Parker, Jean Willes, Barbara Nichols, Sara Shane). It seems
that two years before, Van Fleet's four outlaw sons stole $100,000
worth of gold and during a fire in the barn where they were trapped,
only one escaped alive. The problem is, nobody knows which one--
he never came back. So the women wait. So does the gold, its
hiding place in Wagon Mound known only to Van Fleet. Gable in-
gratiates himself into the household, planning to uncover the gold
and make off with it. Meanwhile, he dallies a bit with Willes, a sultry,
knife-brandishing Mexican; Nichols, a buxom blonde dancer "who
is dumb but could hardly be called a case of arrested development"
(William K. Zinsser in his New York Herald Tribune review); Shane,
a prim young woman in mourning black; and, most seriously, with
Parker, the "flaming redhead" whom Gable describes as "tougher than
wang leather, smarter than spit and colder than January." The
women raise chickens and trade them for supplies. But, sighs Parker,
"The hens aren't laying." "Maybe you need a new rooster," suggests
Gable. With Parker, he also ventures, "You wouldn't wait two years
for any man. Money, a pile of it--that would be worth waiting for."
Towards the end, she reveals to Gable that she was not really married
to one of Van Fleet's boys. The escaped son had told her about
the gold the night before he was killed, whereupon she had decided
to go after it. Spying on Van Fleet, Gable and Parker discover the
location of the loot, steal it and bolt. As the sheriff (Roy Roberts)
and his men approach, Gable tosses Parker a bag of gold with in-
structions to meet him at a rendezvous. He then returns the booty
to the sheriff, explaining that he has kept only the reward money.
Just as it begins to look like Parker has absconded, he suddenly
finds her carriage waiting for him on the side of a road. Warily,
they drive into the sunset.

The ending seems abrupt, tacked-on, unconvincing, as if
something else first had been planned to close the proceedings. And
indeed it had. The whole second half of the film, in fact, is almost
totally different from the script Parker signed to do; much of the
interesting seeming material had been filmed. In the 83-minute released version, we never see the escaped outlaw son, but in the early

draft of the film he had appeared to confront the escaping Gable and
Parker, then was killed in a buckboard crash. He was played by
one John Compton, whose whole role wound up on the cutting room
floor. So did character actor Dayton Lummis' part as a doctor.
There was a much-publicized outdoor scene of Parker, clad only in
a large striped blanket, necking with Gable that did not materialize
in the film. There was a rain-drenched sequence in which Gable and
Parker retrieve the stolen gold from a river that did not make it
to the final picture. There was even a scene of Parker, tended by
Van Fleet and Gable, giving birth to Gable's son at the end that
never showed up. Under these circumstances, it is a miracle that
the film makes any sense at all. It is impossible to discern how much
credit (or discredit) is due prolific director Raoul Walsh, nevertheless
once again embroiled in the critical cutting of Eleanor Parker scenes:
she had faced cameras for the first time in his They Died with Their
Boots On (1942), but when the film ran long was cut out entirely.
     The actors, however, are right there, up front in their respon-
sibilities, and trouping nicely with the tattered goods left them in
The King and Four Queens. Gable is ideal, 55 years old now but
still twinkling at the sight of women and gold as no one else ever
could; his rascally humor, as always, takes the onus off the most
preposterous situations. And Parker is a worthy match: beautiful,
strong, shrewd, with a larcenous streak as long as the Santa Fe
Trail. In roles not picked clean, the pair could have struck sparks
to equal the screen's most electric male-female combinations. Van
Fleet, playing her specialty (a woman years older than herself), is
a tough old buzzard who can also be unexpectedly moving when
talking about her four dead sons ("They were bad--bad clear through.
I had to take their part, though"). Nichols, the least devious of the
four brides for four brothers, is a quintessential fifties peroxide
dimwit (though the story is set many decades earlier), while Shane
seems right as the wife in whom still waters apparently run deep. An
overlooked "pro," Willes makes her strutting, posing Latin Mae West
work.
     Ominously, much of the action was staged in and around St.
George, Utah, where the Howard Hughes production The Conqueror
also had just been shot and near where there had been 87 recent
atomic bomb test explosions. Years later, after most of the principals
of The Conqueror, including stars John Wayne and Susan Hayward,
director Dick Powell and supporting actress Agnes Moorehead, had died
from cancer, and many children from Southern Utah were dying from
leukemia in accelerated number, hundreds of St. George residents
filed suit against the federal government, claiming exposure without
warning to large doses of radiation. The King and Four Queens is
scarcely worth the hazards, travail, and frustrations involved. Called
The Last Man in Wagon Mound during pre-production, the film is
far from the last word in Westerns. A cutting room orgy saw to
that. But an able cast toiling amid perhaps deceptively scenic Utah
locations makes a passable diversion of what remains.

92   Eleanor Parker

37. LIZZIE. M-G-M/Bryna Production. 1957. 81 Mins.

Producer, Jerry Bresler; director, Hugo Haas; screenplay, Mel
Dinelli; based on the novel The Bird's Nest by Shirley Jackson;
camera, Paul Ivano; editor, Leon Barsha; music, Leith Stevens;
associate producer, Edward Lewis; art director, Rudi Feld; set
decorator, Darrell Silvera; make-up, Frank McCoy; hair, Helene
Parrish; men's wardrobe, Norman Martien; women's wardrobe, Sabine
Manela; sound, Jack Solomon; in charge of production, Barney Briskin.

Cast: ELEANOR PARKER (Elizabeth Richmond); Richard Boone (Dr.
Neal Wright); Joan Blondell (Aunt Morgan); Hugo Haas (Walter Bren-
ner); Ric Roman (Johnny Valenzo); Dorothy Arnold (Elizabeth's
Mother); John Reach (Robin); Marion Ross (Ruth Seaton); Johnny
Mathis (Nightclub Singer); Jan Englund (Helen Jameson); Carol Wells
(Elizabeth, age 13); Karen Green (Elizabeth, age 9); Gene Walker
(Guard); Pat Golden (Man in Bar); Dick Paxton (Waiter); Michael
Marks (Bartender).

   The Three Faces of Eve, starring Joanne Woodward, and Eleanor
Parker's Lizzie, released first, have so much in common it's surprising there weren't repercussions (read: litigation). Both films
opened in 1957, both deal with young women afflicted with triple-split,
or multiple, personality who were traumatized in childhood by events
involving their mothers, and both are finally brought to healthy one-
ness through hypnosis conducted by an understanding psychiatrist.
Eve was based on a recent much-discussed actual case and book,
while Lizzie was adapted by Mel Dinelli from an obscure Shirley Jackson
novel, The Bird's Nest (in which the affliction had been five personalities). Unsurprisingly, there was only room at the party for one
girl with three personalities, and Eve proved to be the more popular
miss. Although Lizzie came out about six months before Eve, it was
inadequately promoted. The latter, meanwhile, starred a relative
newcomer, Woodward, and the film industry and audiences tend to be
taken by a new face in a colorful role, especially when said role
arrives pre-publicized. Consequently, Eve became the seen and
talked-about production, Woodward going on to win that year's best-
actress Oscar. Lizzie, however, is a dramatization with much more
vitality, mainly due to Parker's mesmerizing chameleon with three
different, completely separate personalities who are sometimes not
even aware of each other. Eve, on the other hand, unwinds in flat,
slow fashion with a Woodward who viewed today appears drab in all
three hats. If Joanne Woodward deserved an Academy Award for her
characterization, Eleanor Parker deserved three--one for each sharply
defined character (though her bad-girl Lizzie is limned, and received,
with the most relish: "I must confess," wrote Arthur Spaeth of the
Cleveland News, "her wanton Lizzie mostly proved to be my kind of
woman"). The headline for Frank Quinn's review in the New York
Daily Mirror read: "Eleanor Parker is A-1 in 3-in-1 Role," with
Quinn remarking:

It is a wide range of characters the capable actress enacts as a disturbed girl suffering from multiple personality. She plays three separate and distinct persons with haunting dramatic effect.

In a 1973 issue of TV Guide, Judith Crist looked back in admiration:

[Lizzie is] a neglected but fascinating 1957 film, which boasts a stunning performance by Eleanor Parker.... By freaky (or literary) coincidence, the case-based Three Faces of Eve was a best-seller when this movie was released and the film version thereof came out later that year, with Joanne Woodward winning a best actress Oscar for her portrait of the triple-personalitied heroine. But for my money Miss Parker does as well with the role.

Her director, Hugo Haas, agreed, and then some. In Films in Review, he told writer James K. Loutzenhiser:

Lizzie was badly exploited. Because Joanne Woodward was a surprise newcomer, The Three Faces of Eve beat Lizzie. But I still believe that Eleanor Parker was better and more logical.

Admittedly, Lizzie, made by Kirk Douglas' independent Bryna Productions, was completed in three weeks on a very limited budget, and may be the chilliest-looking movie ever shot around the usually oppressively sunny Los Angeles. (At least one location, the area's Blessed Sacrament Church, was used for a scene described by Parker in the release print, but the actual episode was cut prior to opening although still mentioned in publicity for the film as well.) The story's few settings are seemingly photographed through a grey scrim, perhaps to reflect the neurotic heroine's headachy, sleepless, foggy state.

When prim, nervous Elizabeth Richmond (Parker) arrives at her museum job, a fellow worker comments, "I've learned one thing. Never ask her how she feels." As played by Parker in baggy cardigan sweater, hair pulled back tightly, her every move an effort, it is immediately apparent that this is a girl with problems. Quickly established, for one thing, is that she has been getting poison-pen letters, the latest reading, "Watch out for me. I know all.... One of these days I may even kill you. Lizzie." She is, of course, unknowingly sending them to herself. Elizabeth lives with her alcoholic, horse-playing Aunt Morgan (Joan Blondell), enduring with quiet resignation the older woman's endless prattle. Until one evening, after wearily asking her aunt if she ever thought she was losing her mind, she abruptly stops in the shadows on the stairway to her room and lashes out in an unfamiliar, strident voice, "You drunken old slut!" Inside, she faces the mirror, pencils her eyebrows, smears on dark lipstick, piles her hair on top of her head, ties Elizabeth's

plain blouse across her midriff, and sneaks off to the local tavern
--in full regalia as Lizzie, the wicked, lustful personality. Swaggering
past the men at the bar, she growls, "Hope you get your eyes full,
boys." She picks up the museum maintenance man (Ric Roman).
In the morning, when Aunt Morgan finds liquor bottles in Elizabeth's
room, she wisecracks, "With both of us drinking, I'll have to order
by the case!" Elizabeth remembers nothing of her wild night, as
usual. After Lizzie ferociously throws a bottle at her aunt, Walter
Brenner (Hugo Haas), a writer neighbor, arranges for Elizabeth
to see his psychiatrist friend, Dr. Neal Wright (Richard Boone).
Many weeks of treatment ensue. Under hypnosis, the coarse, evil
Lizzie reveals herself to Dr. Wright, boasting, "I'm getting stronger
and stronger and someday soon I'm taking over." Before long, a
third personality, the pleasant, normal Beth, emerges--"It seems I've
just awakened from a long sleep." Dr. Wright concentrates on devel-
oping Beth who, it is explained via flashbacks, was traumatized by
two events when she was a youngster: shoving her drunken, floozie
mother (Dorothy Arnold) into a chair, soon after which the already
ailing woman died; and being raped by her mother's boyfriend (John
Reach). Following a striking scene in Elizabeth's room where the
warring alter egos confront each other in a three-way mirror, Beth
at last rises the sweetly smiling victor.

   Actress Parker, her black-eyebrowed, white-faced, lipstick-
daubed, teeth-gnashing Lizzie far more sinister than Joanne Woodward's
pale Eve evil, suggests a contemporary, female Dr. Jekyll and Mr.
Hyde. Shivers erupt, for instance, after the mousy Elizabeth pads
to a window, suddenly to turn around as the smirking, licentious,
potentially dangerous Lizzie. And Parker has a particularly un-
erasable moment when a hysterical Lizzie is jolted back to reality
by Dr. Wright clapping his hands in her face; at this instant, the
young woman's darkly outlined, feral eyes resemble two stark Hallo-
ween moons. Hers is a powerfully unfettered study, made all the
more extraordinary by the skimpy, hurried look elsewhere of the
81-minute production.

   Hugo Haas, whose unique fifties specialty was producing,
directing, writing, and starring in low-budget films about older men
and young chippies, functions only as director-actor here, yet still
seems to have spread himself a bit thin. Wisely, he stood back to
allow his star free rein. Ditto Joan Blondell, who reciprocates with
an amusingly broad turn as the bathrobe-wearing, bourbon-loving
aunt with a distrust of psychiatrists ("Wonder if he's gonna send me
three bills?"), though a bit more slips through of new singer Johnny
Mathis' saloon wailing than is absolutely necessary to the plot. A
facetious Time magazine cautioned that the film would "probably be
pretty confusing to the old-fashioned moviegoer who thinks that when
a girl isn't single it's because she's married"; but on the whole Lizzie
is an engrossing update of Robert Louis Stevenson's Jekyll-Hyde
classic, thanks largely to the continuing splendid artistry of Eleanor
Parker.

38. THE SEVENTH SIN. M-G-M. 1957. 92 Mins.

Producer, David Lewis; uncredited producer, Sidney Franklin; direct-
or, Ronald Neame; uncredited director, Vincente Minnelli; screenplay,
Karl Tunberg; based on the novel The Painted Veil by W. Somerset
Maugham; music, Miklos Rozsa; camera, Ray June; art directors,
William A. Horning, Daniel B. Cathcart; set decoration, Edwin B.
Willis, Fred MacLean; special effects, A. Arnold Gillespie, Lee LeBlanc;
assistant director, William McGarry; make-up, William Tuttle; wardrobe
for Eleanor Parker, Helen Rose; editor, Gene Ruggiero; hair, Sydney
Guilaroff.

Cast: ELEANOR PARKER (Carol Carwin); BILL TRAVERS (Dr. Walter
Carwin); GEORGE SANDERS (Tim Waddington); JEAN PIERRE AUMONT
(Paul Duvelle); Francoise Rosay (Mother Superior); Ellen Corby
(Sister St. Joseph); Judy Dan (Mrs. Waddington); Frank Tang (Dr.
Ling); Kam Tong (Col. Yu); Eddie Luke (House Boy); Leslie Denison
(Gov. Neville); Jennifer Raine (Other Woman); Phyllis Stanley (Dorothy
Duvelle); Bruce Lester (Allan); William Yip (Chinese Owner); Gai
Lee (Chinese Waiter); Georges Saurel (First Gentleman); George
Chan (Town Elder); Henry S. Quan (House Boy); James Hong (Chi-
nese Officer); Owen McGiveney (Butler); Esther Ying Lee (Secretary);
David Chow (Chinese Businessman).

     In 1957, an increasingly unrestrained motion picture medium
was beginning to take on new, previously taboo subjects while old
themes were coming in for more candid treatment. The Seventh Sin,
with its unspiked sin-and-reformation theme, seemed to many then,
as Howard Thompson in his New York Times critique commented,
"slightly unreal, long ago and far away," a return to W. Somerset
Maugham country of stuffy Englishmen, fallen wives, obedient natives,
"tiffin," and bridge before dinner. Based on Maugham's 1925 novel
The Painted Veil, it had been filmed previously by M-G-M in 1934
under that title with Greta Garbo, Herbert Marshall, and George
Brent. Updated only to 1949, the obviously apprehensive makers
shying away from any attempts to pass it off as totally contemporary
drama, this time the stars are Eleanor Parker, Bill Travers, and Jean
Pierre Aumont, under the direction of England's Ronald Neame, in
his American debut.
     Despite the somewhat dated "white man's burden" colonialism
inherent in its story, the production deserved a wider audience
than it received, if only for the top-billed Parker's emotion-charged,
uncompromising characterization of an errant American wife who has
come to Hong Kong with her British bacteriologist husband (Travers).
And then there is her ravishing appearance: alluringly photographed
by Ray June, she is dressed by Helen Rose in a number of soignée
Oriental-type ensembles probably inspired by Charles LeMaire's recent
similar, Oscar-winning outfits on Jennifer Jones in 20th Century-
Fox's Love Is a Many Splendored Thing (1955)--the much-appreciated
Hong Kong ambience of which, in fact, may have given M-G-M the
idea to remake the Maugham story. Sin also benefits from Karl

Tunberg's cultivated, even occasionally epigrammatic screenplay.
As Dorothy Masters wrote in the New York Daily News:

> The soundtrack of The Seventh Sin is in itself almost worth
> the price of a ticket. The lively banter will be envied by
> all of us people whose brilliant repartée is inevitably framed
> several hours too late.

When Travers discovers the shallow, selfish Parker's affair with
diplomat Jean Pierre Aumont, he whisks her off to a remote Chinese
village where he has volunteered to fight a cholera epidemic. There,
befriended only by cynical, n'er-do-well settler George Sanders, who
tries to heal the breach, she turns out of boredom to helping the
overworked nuns in a local orphanage. Gradually, engaged in the
first selfless, meaningful activity of her life, she grows into a more
sensitive individual who at last comes to love her husband. He,
however, dies from cholera.

The filming, mostly done on the M-G-M lot in Culver City,
California (with some second unit background photography in Hong
Kong), was troubled. As it neared completion, Dore Schary was
ousted as studio head, and the new order had no interest in a project
begun by the previous regime. Director Neame and producer David
Lewis, resenting this, left the film, the final scenes of which were
directed, without credit, by Vincente Minnelli. (Sidney Franklin
stepped in to replace Lewis, also sans credit.) According to Minnelli
in his autobiography, I Remember It Well, the actors didn't get along
with each other, either. The result, while no world-beater and
generally considered misbegotten by most of those involved, nevertheless contains much of interest and garnered a circlet of decent reviews: "The movie is well worth seeing"--Paul V. Beckley, New York
Herald Tribune; "A fascinating and absorbing picture"--Hank Grant,
The Hollywood Reporter. The latter also praised the leading lady
as "simply great. [Miss Parker] leaves no doubt as to every emotion
she feels, yet never spilling over into maudlin pathos." Paul M.
Bruun, in his Miami Beach Sun review column entitled "Bruun over
Miami," concurred: "Eleanor Parker possesses a most expressive
face and voice and first-caliber acting abilities." The New York Times
likewise commended her:

> Exquisitely gowned and looking as cool as a cucumber, cholera
> or no cholera, Miss Parker makes a sincere, even moving
> heroine, in spite of (at least to this viewer) her almost
> blinding beauty. It's a tough part; Miss Parker tackles it
> like a professional.

Sanders, too, brightens the sometimes static dramaturgy with
his patented world-weary, dry delivery of the wittier lines. When
someone remarks that Parker, assisting the nuns, has "a willing
spirit," Sanders replies, "I like willing women." France's Francoise
Rosay has presence as a wise Mother Superior, while Aumont is well
cast in his early, brief chore. Unfortunately, the stolidity of Travers'

role stymies the actor's attempts to bring it to life, leaving <u>Picturegoer</u>
critic Margaret Hinxman to wonder "why Miss Parker didn't go off
the rails long before." One of the least-known and rarely seen of
Eleanor Parker's starring films, <u>The Seventh Sin</u> warrants reappraisal.

39. A HOLE IN THE HEAD. United Artists/SinCap Production. 1959.
     De Luxe Color. 120 Mins.

Producer-director, Frank Capra; screenplay, Arnold Shulman; based
on the play by Shulman; music, Nelson Riddle; camera, William H.
Danierls; art director, Eddie Imazu; editor, William Hornbeck; sound,
Fred Lau; costumes, Edith Head; hair, Helene Parrish; make-up,
Bernard Ponedel.

Cast: FRANK SINATRA (Tony Manetta); EDWARD G. ROBINSON
(Mario Manetta); ELEANOR PARKER (Eloise Rogers); Carolyn Jones
(Shirl); Thelma Ritter (Sophie Manetta); Keenan Wynn (Jerry Marks);
Eddie Hodges (Allie Manetta); Joi Lansing (Dorine); George DeWitt
(Mendy); Jimmy Komack (Julius Manetta); Dub Taylor (Fred); Connie
Sawyer (Miss Wexler); Benny Rubin (Mr. Diamond); Ruby Dandridge
(Sally); B. S. Pully (Hood No. 1); Joyce Nizzari (Alice); Pupi
Campo (Master of Ceremonies); Dave Willock (Waiter--cut from film).

   Frank Capra's <u>A Hole in the Head</u> is very entertaining, by
turns warm and funny, although something a bit more high-voltage
might have been expected from a hook-up with some of the screen's
most electric talents. After a lay-off from feature directing for eight
years, Capra, lionized for his socially oriented (if occasionally
preachy) comedies of the thirties and forties, returned to direct a
message-free story which screenwriter Arnold Shulman had first done
on television and then in 1957 for the New York stage. One of the
top casts of the day helped to make Capra's comeback an event:
Frank Sinatra, Edward G. Robinson, Eleanor Parker, Carolyn Jones,
Thelma Ritter, Keenan Wynn, and young Eddie Hodges, recently of
Broadway's <u>The Music Man</u>. Originally, the plot dealt with Jews in
Miami Beach, but Capra (no doubt because he and his male lead are
of Italian origin) changed them to Italians over the protests of author
Shulman. Actually, only the names were made Italianate; the dialogue
retains the Yiddish rhythms and humor, and the two main characters
(Sinatra and Robinson) continue as Miami Beach hotel proprietor and
Bronx department store owner. While this seems incongruous at
first, the especially deft (and Jewish) Robinson's handling of the
Semitic-slanted yocks ("Bum!" he repeatedly calls his penniless brother)
soon makes the viewer forget the none-too-credible alteration.
   Sinatra plays a n'er-do-well, girl-chasing, would-be promoter
who is also a widower with an adoring small son (Hodges). "You
must have been behind a pole or something the afternoon they handed
out daddies," he tells the unconvinced lad. About to be evicted for
non-payment of rent from the tacky beachfront hotel he runs, he
asks his visiting merchant brother (Robinson) for $5300. Replies

the baleful, conservative Robinson, who has come to his younger
brother's financial rescue many times, "You know how many garter
belts I gotta sell to make $5300?" He promises Sinatra he will set
him up in his own business, a five-and-ten, if he will settle down and
marry a nice local widow he and his wife (Ritter) know. She turns
out to be the attractive Parker, who a couple of years before had
seen her husband and child drown before her eyes. Now living alone
and lonely, she seems interested in Sinatra, is immediately charmed
by his son, but is embarrassed by the obvious matchmaking. Alone
with Sinatra after a while she says, "You know what the worst part
of my day is? Having to walk into a grocery store and order one
lamb chop." Although Sinatra at first feigns interest in her to get
money from his brother, by the end he, Parker, and Hodges are
romping by the surf, clearly headed for a future that will make up
in togetherness what it may lack in financial security.

Actor Sinatra's task is not easy, requiring him as it does to
be likable while being an irresponsible chiseler, a man whose impossible
dream is to con wealthy old friend Keenan Wynn into bankrolling a
Disneyland in Miami's low-rent South Beach area. But he carries it
off with sympathy and personality, enjoying a particularly disarming
scene one evening on the beach when he and his son duet Sammy
Cahn and Jimmy Van Heusen's Oscar-winning song, "High Hopes."
(Paul Douglas had starred in the part of Broadway.) As noted,
Robinson is most accomplished in the humor department; while it is
no "Mario Manetta" who says things like "Now I'm first worried," the
veteran actor shrewdly refrains from playing against the Jewish
material and gets the loudest laughs and applause with his expertly
timed gibes.

Parker has too little to do as the widow created on stage by
Lee Grant. If, as photographed by Garbo's favorite cameraman,
William H. Daniels, Parker's statuesque, red-haired looker doesn't
quite live down to Robinson's description of her as "a nice little
woman," she brings a lovely, quiet dignity to the proceedings.
"Eleanor Parker is touchingly responsive," wrote Bosley Crowther
in The New York Times (while calling the film "a perfect entertainment"). Her role was somewhat larger in the original concept: she
had a restaurant scene with Sinatra that was cut from the release
print, probably because the running time then was more than two
hours, quite long for a comedy. We see the pair walking Miami
streets to the place "for a cup of coffee," but the scene inside--while
pictured in publicity for the film--never appears.

As Sinatra's bongo-playing, free-spirited tenant girlfriend,
Carolyn Jones has a more colorful assignment (literally), although her
bright garb, jet-black braids and Man-Tan glow suggest the story's
South Beach might make a better reservation than Disneyland.
Eschewing her usual tart-tongued specialty, Ritter is fine as Sinatra's
caring sister-in-law, as are young Hodges as his son and Wynn as
the promoter friend who ultimately turns on him. Connie Sawyer,
the only player retained from the stage cast, has a hilarious cameo
as a spinster living quietly by day with her mother, but at night
becoming a boozy party girl who staggers up the hotel staircase

yelling, "Geronimo!"   Director Capra makes acute use of Miami's
flashy neon locations and overall keeps his tasty brew bubbling.

40. HOME FROM THE HILL. M-G-M/Sol. C. Siegel Production.
     1960. Metrocolor. 150 Mins.

Producer, Edmund Grainger; director, Vincente Minnelli; screenplay,
Harriet Frank, Jr., Irving Ravetch; from the novel by William Hum-
phrey; camera, Milton Krasner; editor, Harold F. Kress; music,
Bronislau Kaper; conductor, Charles Wolcott; art directors, George
W. Davis, Preston Ames; set decorators, Henry Grace, Robert
Priestley; color consultant, Charles K. Hagedon; assistant director,
William McGarry; costumes, Walter Plunkett; make-up, William Tuttle;
hair, Sydney Guilaroff; sound, Franklin Milton; special effects, Robert
R. Hoag.

Cast: ROBERT MITCHUM (Capt. Wade Hunnicutt); ELEANOR PARKER
(Hannah Hunnicutt); George Peppard (Rafe Copley); George Hamilton
(Theron Hunnicutt); Everett Sloane (Albert Halstead); Luana Patten
(Libby Halstead); Anne Seymour (Sarah Halstead); Constance Ford
(Opal Bixby); Ken Renard (Chauncey); Ray Teal (Dr. Reuben Car-
son); Guinn "Big Boy" Williams (Hugh Macauley); Charlie Briggs
(Dick Gibbons); Hilda Haynes (Melba); Denver Pyle (Marshal Bradley);
Dan Sheridan (Peyton Stiles); Orville Sherman (Ed Dinwoodie); Dub
Taylor (Bob Skaggs); Stuart Randall (John Ramsey); Tom Gilson
(John Ellis); Rev. Duncan Grey, Jr. (Minister); Joe Ed Russell
(Foreman); Burt Mustin (Gas Station Attendant).

     Home from the Hill is two-and-a-half hours long, but there is
not a dull minute in it. Adapted from William Humphrey's engrossing,
elegiac first novel, screenwriters Harriet Frank, Jr. and Irving
Ravetch are brilliantly faithful to the spirit if not the letter of the
original--Eleanor Parker's character, for instance, was a withered
crone in the book but is a still tantalizingly beautiful redhead in the
film. It is, furthermore, one of Vincente Minnelli's most macho
directorial efforts, a sweeping contemporary melodrama of tangled
relationships that takes on the proportions of Greek tragedy.
     Robert Mitchum is the pivotal figure, and it's an impressive
one that casts its wide-brimmed shadow over the proceedings, including the stretches when he isn't even on view. He portrays
"Captain" Wade Hunnicutt, a wealthy northeast Texas land baron who
hunts wild boar and (it is impossible to resist saying) wild whore
with equal verve. As the film opens, he is shot in the shoulder by
an angry young husband. "I'll tell you somethin'. I can't even
remember which one she was," Wade admits later to George Peppard,
as Rafe, the devoted young hired hand who lives in a cabin on his
land. "Well, he's only got one woman, so he's got no trouble keepin'
straight," replies Rafe in the tangy, indigenous language with which
the writers vivify their script. When his doctor (Ray Teal) advises
that "This sportin' life's gonna do you in yet," Wade defines his

creed: "It's my right to cross any man's fence when I'm hunting."
His embittered wife, Hannah (Parker), knows of his infidelities, and
while they have remained under the same rich roof, they have not
slept together for years. She has raised their 17-year-old son,
Theron (George Hamilton), keeping him innocent of the masculine
excesses of "the Captain's" world. When Theron passes some men
whittling in town, one asks, "Ain't that the Captain's boy?" Another
answers, "Captain's boy, nothin'. That's Hannah's boy." Wade decides to take over the naive lad's education. "You said he was mine
if I stayed," protests Hannah. "Well ... I stayed." To which Wade
responds, "Behind a locked door. From here on out, that boy is
mine." He puts Theron in the care of the slightly older, woodsy
Rafe, who teaches him to shoot.

One of the film's most exciting segments is the hunting sequence
in which Theron, to win paternal approbation, sets out to track the
wild boar that has been poaching on Wade's land. Racing through
blurry brush, past darting animals and sulphur pits of yellow smoke
and quicksand, he corners the beast in a thicket only to see his
dogs tossed high in the air. Resting for the night, he continues
in the morning when he encounters the charging boar. A direct
shot through the snout kills him; Theron, exhausted, falls to the
ground where his proud father soon finds him. At the party for
him that night, the porker is roasted on a spit while Wade tries to
patch things up with Hannah, who tells him, "You're too late, Wade,
with too little." Then, "Shall I tell you why you still find me attractive after all these years? Because you can't have me. Because you
never will." Meanwhile, Theron is having his own problems with the
opposite sex: arriving to pick up his party date, Libby Halstead
(Luana Patten), he is turned away at the door by her angry father,
Albert (Everett Sloane). In Parker's best scene, which she plays
with almost palpable emotion, Hannah tells her son that Albert Halstead's behavior had nothing to do with him--"Your name was all
he saw.... Everyone knows about your father.... He's been notorious since he was your age." She goes on to reveal that she hasn't
lived with the Captain since before Theron was born because, upon
returning from their honeymoon, she found a girl in their house
with her husband's illegitimate child--who grew up to be Rafe. (The
mother soon died.) Theron is furious with his father for not acknow-
ledging Rafe: "As far as I'm concerned there's only one bastard in
this family, and I don't mean it's Rafe." Theron gets Libby pregnant,
but Rafe marries her. For the depressed Theron's sake, Wade and
Hannah decide to try again with their marriage. Their plans end
abruptly when Libby's father hears gossip that Wade is actually the
father of his daughter's newborn child. Albert's mind snaps, and he
fatally shoots Wade. Theron chases him to the sulphur pits, kills
him, and runs away. At the end, Hannah and Rafe stand by Wade's
grave stone on which she has given the young man his long-sought
recognition. He reads: "Wade Hunnicutt ... Beloved Father of
Raphael and Theron."

With its pungent, idiomatic dialogue, charged confrontations
and rueful aura that permeates nearly every scene, Home from the

<u>Hill</u> resembles classical theater. Certainly Robert Mitchum's larger-than-life "hero" has the stature of high-powered drama, with the star turning in one of his most skillful jobs in a role first mentioned for Clark Gable. His drawling but forceful, almost poetically rhythmic readings of the wryly accurate regional lines are faultless, and he manages to create sympathy for this hulking feudal lord who, beneath the swagger, dissolution and violence, does love his wife and sons-- at least as Mitchum wisely delineates him. His warped machismo is best verbalized by the local doctor, the wisest (if quickly dispatched) character in the story, while dressing the wound inflicted by a cuckolded husband:

> It's gettin' to where a man isn't a man around here anymore unless he uses up a car a year, goes down a road at a hundred miles an hour, owns six or seven fancy shotguns, knows six or seven fancy ladies....

Parker, in a part coveted by Bette Davis that is also her first as the mother of a grown individual, likewise is superb, conveying every nuance of this once life-loving young woman who, after being hurt, shuts out everything and everyone except her son. Eventually, this suppression makes her physically ill, and the sight of the actress clutching her stomach in agonized, frozen horror before her murdered husband is one not easily forgotten. Since the focus is so often on the younger people in the plot, Parker is off the screen for considerable periods, and at least one of her major moments was cut before release: a dramatic sick room scene in which she is comforted by Hamilton. Nevertheless, like Mitchum, Parker makes every word--sentence--speech--spill over with uncontainable passion. It is one of her most underrated performances. Because they were youthful newcomers in meaty, sympathetic roles, Peppard and Hamilton drew most of the media attention at the time; it is probable that neither has ever acted quite so well again. On the other hand, the seasoned Everett Sloane, in his difficult smaller assignment, overdoes the hysterics.

Aside from the already lauded robust yet stylish direction and knowledgeable screenplay ("One of the few film scripts in which I didn't change a word," director Minnelli said later--Harriet Frank, Jr., and Irving Ravetch went on to write another trenchant modern Western about an ignoble character, 1963's <u>Hud</u>), accolades go to Milton Krasner's fluid camera work on location in Texas and Mississippi, as well as in Hollywood; and Bronislau Kaper's complementary music score with its hauntingly mournful main theme. The art department deserves a laurel, too. The set for Mitchum's den, for instance-- with its huge stone fireplace, sleeping hounds, deep leather chairs, weapons, and animal trophies--brings to mind an only thinly civilized cave of some primeval force. It tells the viewer as much about the owner as ten pages of dialogue could. Voted one of the year's ten best films by, among others, the National Board of Review (also naming Robert Mitchum best actor for this picture and <u>The Sundowners</u>), the New York <u>Daily News</u>, and the New York <u>Daily Mirror</u>, <u>Home from the Hill</u> is a top credit for almost everybody concerned.

41. RETURN TO PEYTON PLACE. 20th Century-Fox. 1961. De
     Luxe Color. 122 Mins.

Producer, Jerry Wald; director, José Ferrer; screenplay, Ronald
Alexander; based on the novel by Grace Metalious; music, Franz
Waxman; associate producer, Curtis Harrington; camera, Charles G.
Clarke; art directors, Jack Martin Smith, Hans Peters; set decorators,
Walter M. Scott, Fred MacLean; assistant director, David Hall; cos-
tumes, Don Feld; editor, David Bretherton; make-up, Ben Nye;
hair, Helen Turpin; sound, Bernard Freericks, Warren B. Delaplain;
orchestrations, Leonid Raab; vocal, Rosemary Clooney.

Cast: CAROL LYNLEY (Allison MacKenzie); JEFF CHANDLER (Lewis
Jackman); ELEANOR PARKER (Connie); Mary Astor (Roberta Carter);
Robert Sterling (Mike Rossi); Luciana Paluzzi (Raffaella); Brett
Halsey (Ted); Gunnar Hellstrom (Lars); Tuesday Weld (Selena Cross);
Kenneth MacDonald (Dexter); Joan Banks (Mrs. Humphries); Emerson
Treacy (Bud Humphries); Wilton Graff (Dr. Fowlkes); Jennifer Howard
(Mrs. Jackman); Laura McCann (Miss Wentworth); Bob Crane (Peter
White); Bill Bradley (Mark Steele); Tim Durant (John Smith); Casey
Adams (Nick Parker); Pitt Herbert (Mr. Wadley); Warren Parker
(Lupus Wolf); Arthur Peterson (Selectman); Hari Rhodes (Arthur);
Leonard Stone (Steve Swanson); Collette Lyons (Mrs. Bingham);
Charles Seel (Counterman); Carol Veazie, Helen Bennett (Interviewers);
José Ferrer (Reporter).

Peyton Place (1957), adapted from Grace Metalious' best-selling
novel about raunchy doings in a small New England town, was beautifully photographed in Maine, the rare case when a film outclassed
the book. At the request of the producer, Jerry Wald (who also
had been in charge of Eleanor Parker's The Very Thought of You,
Pride of the Marines, and Caged), author Metalious then wrote a
strained, even trashier but less successful sequel, Return to Peyton
Place. This time, unfortunately, Wald's film version was on a par
with the book. Maybe the actors from the first picture read the
script, because none returned to Peyton Place, now created on 20th-
Fox sets.
     Carol Lynley takes on the central role of Allison MacKenzie
(evidently the Metalious prototype), who scandalizes her conventional
hamlet with a first novel depicting lurid recent events there. Tuesday
Weld is the traumatized Selena Cross, acquitted stepfather killer
courted by ski instructor Gunnar Hellstrom, whom she incessantly
"meets cute"--bumping into him, literally, on highways, in restaurants,
on ski slopes. As Constance MacKenzie, Eleanor Parker plays the
part originated by Lana Turner, the dress shop owner married to
school principal Mike Rossi (Robert Sterling); but the character here
is reduced merely to sideline worrying that illegitimate daughter
Lynley is getting into trouble in New York as she herself had done
years before. Parker, slim and lovely, has perhaps the most peri-
pheral, least substantial role of the half dozen or more principals.
In a part rejected by Bette Davis, Joan Crawford, and Margaret

Leighton, Mary Astor fares best as the bitchy, possessive, possibly
incestuous Roberta Carter, who tries to wreck the marriage of son
Ted (Brett Halsey) and his Italian bride, Raffaella (Luciana Paluzzi).
Return to Peyton Place, made right after Parker's Madison
Avenue but released first, is directed in astonishingly sloppy fashion
by José Ferrer. Following the book and the shooting script, he
builds his story toward a climactic fire to be set by Astor and blamed
on Paluzzi, who is assiduously established as careless with cigarettes
("How many times do I have to tell you to put your cigarettes in the
ashtray?")--then drops the conflagration completely from the action!
To give Ferrer the benefit of some doubt, it is possible that control
was taken away from him by the studio. Oddly, too, only 20th
Century-Fox's young contract players are shown and identified in
curtain call footage. Maybe the old pros had seen the picture.

42. MADISON AVENUE. 20th Century-Fox. 1962. 94 Mins.

Producer-director, Bruce Humberstone; screenplay, Norman Corwin;
based on the novel The Build Up Boys by Jeremy Kirk; music, Harry
Sukman; orchestrators, Leo Shuken, Jack Hayes; art directors,
Duncan Cramer, Leland Fuller; set decorators, Walter M. Scott, John
Sturtevant; make-up, Ben Nye; sound, Donald McKay, Walter B.
Delaplain; camera, Charles G. Clarke; editor, Betty Steinberg; hair,
Helen Turpin.

Cast: DANA ANDREWS (Clint Lorimer); ELEANOR PARKER (Anne
Tremaine); JEANNE CRAIN (Peggy Shannon); EDDIE ALBERT (Harvey
Ames); Howard St. John (T. C. Jocelyn); Henry Daniell (Stipe);
Kathleen Freeman (Miss Haley); David White (Brock); Betti Andrews
(Miss Katie Olsen); Jack Orrison (Mayor of Bellefield); Yvonne Peattie
(Miss Mulloy); Arlene Hunter (Miss Horn); Doris Fesette (Blonde);
Grady Sutton (Dilbock); Leon Alton (Maitre d'); the Sylte Sisters
(Vocal Trio); Ronnie Brown (Piano Accompaniment).

Although one of the screen's most determinedly intricate looks
at the "cut-throat" world of big-time public relations, the modest-
budgeted Madison Avenue is primarily notable for co-starring (with
Dana Andrews) two of the profession's most august beauties and
mothers: Eleanor Parker and Jeanne Crain. At the time of its
release, Crain had six children (eventually to be seven) and Parker
was the mother of four; both look as trim and fresh as ingenues.
They have no dialogue together, but are the visions a viewer recalls with greatest pleasure after seeing the film. Originally, Parker's
role was meant for model-turned-actress Suzy Parker (no relation)
and Crain's for Joan Collins. Each took a studio suspension rather
than play the parts.
Andrews portrays Clint Lorimer, a New York public relations
"sharpshooter" fired by T. C. Jocelyn (Howard St. John) when he
fears the younger man is planning to steal his company's multimillion-
dollar Associated Dairies account. Lorimer then sets out to do just

that. When he learns that Cloverleaf Milk, a minor subsidiary of
Associated, is handled by a small, failing Washington ad agency
owned by dowdy Anne Tremaine (Parker), he convinces her to take
him on as partner. He rejuvenates the agency and Tremaine, whom
he teaches to dress and make up more alluringly. Meantime, except
when she's a useful "contact," he neglects his long-time journalist
girlfriend, Peggy Shannon (Crain). Tremaine falls in love with him,
and while he finds it expedient to encourage her, the feeling is not
mutual. Lorimer and Tremaine build up Cloverleaf sales and company
President Harvey Ames (Eddie Albert) until he becomes head of
Associated Dairies, "one of the major corporations in America." In
frustration over her dead-end relationship with Lorimer, Tremaine
grows ruthless--a secretary (Kathleen Freeman) observes, "I think
it's kind of exciting around here today. Miss Tremaine fired six
people." Ames and the now treacherous Tremaine become engaged,
whereas Lorimer, after squelching the inflated, incompetent Ames'
political plans, returns to Shannon and former boss Jocelyn.

Parker has an interesting "Eliza Doolittle" sort of role which
she plays to perfection. For her first scene in the then tomb-like
ad agency, she is the wan personification of failure in a prison issue
dress and twisted braid on the back of her head. As Lorimer remarks, "You look like a refugee from a nursing school, or a novel
by Louisa May Alcott.... You could moor a tugboat with that braid."
Her "Henry Higgins" tells her how to dress for success, the metamorphosis bringing a stunningly chic but soon hard and spiteful
Parker who turns on her mentor in the end. According to publicity,
her hair was dyed a new "pink champagne" color for the part, and
Howard Thompson in The New York Times opined that "Miss Parker
... never looked more ravishing." Crain's task is more sedentary,
requiring her mainly to sit around bars and apartments waiting for
her ever-scheming "huckster," but the actress is sleekly poised and
attractive. She and Dana Andrews, however, are a long way from
the homespun charm of their 1945 hit State Fair. By dint of natural
affability, Andrews, hardly ever off screen, keeps his character--
whose flashes of same seem purely accidental--from being abhorrent;
and the other players provide satisfactory creations as well, especially
Albert's doltish milk executive, St. John's unctuous PR chief, and
Freeman's veteran secretary.

Norman Corwin's screenplay is basically conversational, though,
as well as a trifle contrived and "inside"--the subject matter is in-
trinsically not of burning interest to the average viewer. Long-time
director Bruce Humberstone, perhaps best known for a number of
color musicals, tries to keep his black-and-white drama moving, whenever possible playing up the personal tumult with which an audience
can identify, and is at least wholly successful in drawing workmanlike
performances from his cast. Completed in less than a month on
November 28, 1960, but not released till March 1962, Madison Avenue
is a not unintelligent try at something more pithy and off the beaten
track than standard populist program fare, but the scenario simply
has not engendered sufficient dramatic sparks to make it crackle.
It remains for the durable beauty and charm of leading ladies Eleanor
Parker and Jeanne Crain to give Madison Avenue its real appeal

43. PANIC BUTTON. Yankee Production/Gorton Associates. 1964.
    90 Mins.

Producer, Ron Gorton; director, George Sherman; screenplay, Hal
Biller; based on a story by Gorton, dramatized by Gorton, Mort
Friedman; camera, Enzo Sarafin; music, Georges Garvarentz.

Cast: MAURICE CHEVALIER (Phillipe Fontaine); ELEANOR PARKER
(Louise Harris); JAYNE MANSFIELD (Angela); MICHAEL CONNORS
(Frank Pagano); Akim Tamiroff (Pandowski); Carlo Croccolo (Guido);
Vincent Barbi (Mario).

    Signed to star in the comedy Panic Button, filming in Italy,
Eleanor Parker took her family to the production's Rome base for
several months, settling in a villa on the Appian Way. She got to
shoot in Venice, too. Parker appears opposite France's legendary
septuagenarian entertainer Maurice Chevalier and on screen looks
at least a decade younger than her own 40 years. Thus concludes
the credit side of the ledger. Produced by a 28-year-old novice named
Ron Gorton, formerly a football-baseball pro, who also dreamed up
the original story on which Hal Biller based the screenplay, Panic
Button was directed by George Sherman, known (if at all) for a
quarter-century of quickie Westerns. Jayne Mansfield, Michael
Connors, and Akim Tamiroff are the other names familiar to Americans
in the compact cast.
    There was trouble immediately, with the stateside press--
courtesy, obviously, of a disgruntled producer--trumpeting the
difficulties in a steady barrage of publicity that recalled, though
did not quite rival, the torrent of bulletins from the Roman set of
the recent Elizabeth Taylor-Richard Burton Cleopatra. Filming took
place during the spring and summer of 1962. Visiting Rome (where
film production was at an all-time high, putting the city very much
in the world movie news), columnist Sheilah Graham promptly wrote,
"Producer Ron Gorton told me Eleanor Parker pulled a Marilyn Monroe
and didn't show up for the first three days of filming. Eleanor is
usually so cooperative that there have to be two sides heard from
in this battle." Variety explained that "Eleanor Parker's illness has
delayed Ron Gorton's Panic Button a few days." A few weeks into
the shooting, Sheilah Graham was at it again: "Producer Ron Gorton
lost 18 pounds making the picture between fights with Eleanor Parker."
Graham another time: "After the first day of work, [Parker and
Gorton] have not spoken to each other; the producer communicates
with his star by letter, even when they are within a few inches of
each other on the set!" Then Dorothy Manners reported, "There's
no love lost between stars Jayne Mansfield and Eleanor Parker,"
adding that Michael Connors had been unable to work on the film
for a while because of a bee sting on the lip. Meanwhile, Chavalier
told the slavering Sheilah Graham:

        This picture has been tough on me physically. I had to spend
        one hot day in Rome at the beach encased in bandages. In

Venice I wore the uniform of a nun and it was a hundred
in the sun. I had to do the Twist with Jayne and that has
injured people half my age. It was rough--especially when,
in the middle of the dance, Jayne lost her bra.

Production finally wrapped, but the worst setbacks were to
come. In September 1963, Warner Bros. and Seven Arts, which had
given Gorton $1,000,000 to make the film, viewed a rough cut and
decided against releasing it. An irate Gorton vowed to release it
himself. Subsequently, Louella Parsons, in one of her last columns,
revealed that "Panic Button has finally come out from under a bushel
of lawsuits and will be released.... Panic Button was mostly plagued
with salary suits." More than two years after completion, the single-
minded producer did indeed bring out the film himself, which, for
the few nimble enough to catch it, was seen to be hardly worth all
the fuss. In the Los Angeles area it was shown on the bottom of
double bills. In New York the film premiered at a 42nd Street grind
house where it was ignored by the daily reviewers. The impulse
is to suggest that if producer Gorton had spent more time steering
the ship and less complaining to columnists, Panic Button might not
have sunk.

The plot: an American business concern must pay heavy income
taxes unless it can lose half a million dollars in a month. To accom-
plish the latter, company representative Connors is sent to Rome to
produce a phony TV pilot film. Chevalier, a washed-up movie actor
who lives in a women's hotel run by Parker, his ex-wife, is hired to
star along with call girl Mansfield, under the direction of seedy
drama coach Tamiroff. A psychological version of Romeo and Juliet,
the film flops as serious drama but, owing to Chevalier's machinations,
goes on to win the award for most original new comedy at the Venice
TV Film Festival. None of the players, pros all, are seen to parti-
cular advantage in Panic Button--though, as noted, Eleanor Parker
still looks like a million. The picture is a harmless, fitfully amusing
if bluntly directed lampoon of film-making in Italy, so much the fashion
in that early period of "runaway production."

44. THE SOUND OF MUSIC. 20th Century-Fox/Argyle Enterprises.
    1965. De Luxe Color. 171 Mins.

Producer-director, Robert Wise; associate producer, Saul Chaplin;
screenplay, Ernest Lehman; from the stage musical with music and
lyrics by Richard Rodgers, Oscar Hammerstein II, book by Howard
Lindsay, Russel Crouse, suggested by Maria von Trapp's story;
music, Rodgers, Hammerstein; additional words and music, Rodgers;
music supervised, arranged, conducted by Irwin Kostal; production
design, Boris Leven; camera, Ted McCord; choreography, Marc
Breaux, Dee Dee Wood; costumes, Dorothy Jeakins; puppeteers, Bil,
Cora Baird; second unit supervision, Maurice Zuberano; vocal supervision, Robert Tucker; editor, William Reynolds; additional photography, Paul Beeson; sound, Murray Spivack, Bernard Freericks;

assistant director, Ridgeway Callow; dialogue coach, Pamela Danova;
music editor, Robert Mayer; set decorations, Walter M. Scott, Ruby
Levitt; special effects, L. B. Abbott, Emil Kosa, Jr.; make-up, Ben
Nye; hair, Margaret Donovan.

Cast: JULIE ANDREWS (Maria); CHRISTOPHER PLUMMER (Capt.
von Trapp); ELEANOR PARKER (Baroness Elsa Schraeder); Richard
Haydn (Max Detweiler); Peggy Wood (Mother Abbess); Charmian Carr
(Liesl); Heather Menzies (Louisa); Nicholas Hammond (Friedrich);
Duane Chase (Kurt); Angela Cartwright (Brigitta); Debbie Turner
(Marta); Kym Karath (Gretl); Anna Lee (Sister Margaretta); Portia
Nelson (Sister Berthe); Ben Wright (Herr Zeller); Daniel Truhitte
(Rolf); Norma Varden (Frau Schmidt); Gil Stuart (Franz); Marni
Nixon (Sister Sophia); Evadne Baker (Sister Bernice); Doris Lloyd
(Baroness Ebberfeld); Maria von Trapp and daughter (Extras).

Right from the start, The Sound of Music acquired a reputation
as a film whose sweet story and sunny, melodic Rodgers and Hammerstein songs were enough to give the unwary diabetes. It seemed a
bum rap when the film came out, and still seems so. Producer-
director Robert Wise had the last laugh, of course, when Music went
on to become an all-time boxoffice champion, grossing $200,000,000
and winning five Academy Awards, including best picture and best
director. Based on the 1959 Broadway musical play that had starred
Mary Martin as Maria von Trapp and which ran for four years, the
film was splendidly shot by cinematographer Ted McCord in and around
Salzburg, Austria--incredibly photogenic and apparently unchanged
from the late-thirties setting of the fact-based plot.
The film stars Julie Andrews, fresh from her best-actress Oscar
for Mary Poppins (1964), as the equally positive and indomitable
convent postulant who prefers the Alps to the Abbey, the valleys
to the vespers. There is one of the great openings: as cameras
pan down through wisps of clouds at snow-capped mountains, quaint
villages, Rhine castles, and glassy lakes and rivers, the hoydenish
Andrews suddenly appears in the sun-drenched foothills of the Tyrol
to sing the title song, the credits following. The Mother Abbess
(Peggy Wood) then dispatches the young non-conformist to a nearby
estate where stern Christopher Plummer, a retired Navy captain and
widower, needs a governess for his seven frisky children. Huddling
together during thunderstorms and singing "My Favorite Things,"
gamboling about the countryside to the strains of "Do Re Mi," Andrews
wins over the youngsters. She also soon wins the Captain away from
his glamorous fiancée (Eleanor Parker). They marry and, when the
Nazis invade Austria, become the Trapp Family Singers, warbling
their way across the border to Switzerland.
Andrews and Plummer are charming and an elocution teacher's
dream, though the aged Peggy Wood lacks the authority of the stage's
Patricia Neway as the Mother Abbess. And her dubbed vocal of the
rousing "Climb Ev'ry Mountain" is further muted by the odd decision
to photograph it mostly in shadows--a rare time when director Wise
does not live up to his name. As the free-loading impresario who

introduces the musical von Trapps to their new career, the distinguished character actor-director Richard Haydn strikes a pleasing wry
note among the several English-accented Austrians. Parker, crowned
by a none-too-flattering, irrelevant blonde wig (Marion Marlowe, who
created her part on Broadway, employed her own brunette tresses),
receives "And Eleanor Parker as the Baroness" billing in the concilia-
tory fashion of the day for veteran stars. The role, furthermore,
is neither large nor wholly worthy, especially since the character's
songs were cut before filming began. Grievously absent is the score's
most sophisticated tune, "How Can Love Survive?", sung on stage
by the baroness and the impresario. In it, they wonder how wealthy
lovers, who don't have to starve together in a garret, manage to
stay in love, going on to sing:

> You're fond of bonds and you own a lot.
> I have a plane and a diesel yacht.
> Plenty of nothing you haven't got.
> How can love survive?

Although both Parker and the film could have used this taste
of tangy satire, the songless actress still manages to introduce a
welcome worldliness as Plummer's visiting girlfriend who, as he
describes her, is "lovely--charming, witty, graceful--the perfect
hostess." Playing up to him, she remarks, "Oh, I am amusing, I
suppose, and I do have the finest couturier in Vienna and the most
glittering circle of friends and I do give some rather gay parties....
But take all that away and you have just wealthy, unattached little
me, searching just like you." She is at her brittle, bitchy best when
Plummer sists down with his children to strum and sing "Edelweiss"
and she asides to Haydn, "Why didn't you tell me to bring along my
harmonica?" While her character is not very sympathetic--she sends
Andrews packing for the Abbey at one point and secretly plans, after
snaring their father, to dispose of the children at boarding school--
Parker makes her final balcony renunciation of Plummer touching, even
slyly amusing. Looking towards the night, where an idling, lovelorn
Andrews is lost in dreams and the dark, a moist-eyed Parker exits
cracking, "Somewhere out there is a young lady who I think ... will
never be a nun." She has accomplished the far from easy feat of
making the Baroness both hissable and likable, and her departure
regrettable.

Long and cheerful, an unswerving family entertainment whose
Nazis don't even seem very threatening ("Ruritanian Reich," head-
lined the patronizing Newsweek critic), The Sound of Music is among
the most tuneful, visually beautiful, and skillfully assembled musicals
ever. Director Wise's early training as an editor on Citizen Kane
(1941) and other films is evident throughout, particularly in the
numbers wherein, for almost every new line of the song, he cuts
sharply, putting those performing in one breathtaking locale after
another. The result was fantastically successful, the kind of movie,
as they say, only the public loved.

II. Professional Credits

109

45. THE OSCAR. Embassy. 1966. Pathécolor. 119 Mins.

Executive producer, Joseph E. Levine; producer, Clarence Greene; director, Russell Rouse; screenplay, Harlan Ellison, Rouse, Greene; based on the novel by Richard Sale; music, Percy Faith; music supervisor, Irving Friedman; orchestrators, Leo Shuken, Jack Hayes; art directors, Hal Pereira, Arthur Lonergan; set decorators, Robert Benton, James Payne; gowns, Edith Head; women's wardrobe, Glenita Dinneen; Stephen Boyd's wardrobe, Robert Magahay; assistant director, Dick Moder; dialogue coach, Leon Charles; choreography, Steven Peck; sound, Harry Lindgren, John Wilkinson; camera, Joseph Ruttenberg; editor, Chester W. Schaeffer.

Cast: STEPHEN BOYD (Frank Fane); ELKE SOMMER (Kay Bergdahl); MILTON BERLE (Kappy Kapstetter); ELEANOR PARKER (Sophie Cantaro); JOSEPH COTTEN (Kenneth H. Regan); Jill St. John (Laurel Scott); Tony Bennett (Hymie Kelly); Edie Adams (Trina Yale); Ernest Borgnine (Barney Yale); Ed Begley (Grobard); Walter Brennan (Orrin C. Quentin); Broderick Crawford (Sheriff); James Dunn (Network Executive); Peter Lawford (Steve Marks); Jack Soo (Sam); Jean Hale (Cheryl Barker); Peter Leeds (Bert); Karen Norris (Secretary); Army Archerd (Reporter); Edith Head, Bob Hope, Hedda Hopper, Merle Oberon, Hal Pereira, Frank Sinatra, Nancy Sinatra (Themselves).

The Oscar is no The Bad and the Beautiful (1952), which also dealt with the rise and fall of a Hollywood heel. While that film was beautifully written, directed, and played, the production of moment is overwritten, loosely directed and unevenly played. Eleanor Parker, in the half-dozen or so scenes allotted her, easily wins top plaudits in a role mentioned early for Rita Hayworth, Jennifer Jones, and Merle Oberon (who winds up playing a cameo as herself). Nevertheless, the garish tabloid plot keeps you looking, and its tarnished Tinsel Town--with a number of the incidents and characters thinly veiled from real life--provides some color and intrigue.
   The Oscar fades in during Academy Award festivities as nominated louse Stephen Boyd anxiously waits to see if his name is called as best actor. The story then flashes back to his beginning as "spieler" at smokers for his stripper girlfriend (Jill St. John). He leaves her, she dies bearing his stillborn child, and he heads for New York, where he comes under the tutelage of older Hollywood talent scout Eleanor Parker. She also falls in love with him, taking to heart agent Milton Berle's cheerful observation to her, "You're 42. There are many good minutes for you." But as Boyd's long-time buddy Tony Bennett reveals, "No woman's any better than his mother. She didn't care who she slept with." Seems the youthful Boyd was traumatized when, after taking his father to the place where his mother was engaged in an assignation, his dad killed himself. As soon as Parker gets him a film contract, he throws her over, too. In her big scene, played from her large bed following their last night of love-making, she tells the dressing, indifferent Boyd, "Don't break a leg getting out of here." They argue and he retorts, "I'm

going, old lady." A hot property now, he marries Elke Sommer, an
intellectual (!) who dresses like the lead in Debbie Does Hollywood
but, we are asked to believe, is a sketch artist at the studio for no
less than the noted couturière Edith Head. He gets a glimpse of what
he fears might be his fate when he spots Peter Lawford working as
a maître d' in a restaurant. "What happened?" asks a stunned Boyd.
"He was a good actor--made more movies than I have." He is soon
cheating on Sommer and alienating everyone in sight, including his
agent (Berle), studio boss Joseph Cotten and, finally, Bennett and
Sommer.

Several stars appear as themselves at the simulated Academy
Award ceremonies; when the best actor's name is read at the end,
Frank Sinatra steps on stage for the statuette. Boyd, who has
staked everything on winning, crumbles into his seat. Actor Boyd
hams it and is snarlingly unpleasant throughout, leaving one to wonder
how he was able to charm so many people. In addition, his suppressed
natural Irish accent occasionally sounds more Jamaican than American.
The German Sommer seems to have learned her lines phonetically.
Singer Bennett has surprising power, though, in the dramatic role
of Boyd's incredibly constant shadow, and Milton Berle is sincere
as the most sympathetic, soft-spoken agent on record. Jill St. John
is a believable bimbo, less so as an actress, but then she has some
of the film's ripest dialogue. Following a set-to with Boyd, she
squeals, "This is one stupid, round-heels broad who's finished, done,
D-O-N-E, done!" One Jean Hale appears as a bitchy blonde star
who has the public mannerisms of Marilyn Monroe but, in a typical
lapse of taste, is made up and named (Cheryl Barker) to resemble
Oscar executive producer Joseph E. Levine's recent "blonde bomb
sell" Carroll Baker. A showy small part that in the screen's halcyon
years might have made a star of someone capable like Lana Turner,
it is wasted by Hale whose delivery of the caustic dialogue is limp.
To say that Eleanor Parker shines in such company is hardly to hand
her an Oscar, but she is the most credible and involving person in
sight, even when she vengefully bad-mouths Boyd to Cotten, causing
him to be dropped by the studio.

As this writer reported in his Record World magazine review
at the time, "Miss Parker's professionalism (three times a best actress
nominee herself) and classic face make the numerous other femmes
look--in the classic Hollywood vernacular for which this screenplay
has such an affinity--like so many pieces of meat." In spite of everything, The Oscar: The Film is still a better show than, most years.
The Oscar: The Telecast, and at just under two hours, shorter, too.

46. AN AMERICAN DREAM. Warner Bros. 1966. Technicolor. 103
    Mins.

Executive producer, William Conrad; director, Robert Gist; screen-
play, Mann Rubin; based on the novel by Norman Mailer; camera,
Sam Leavitt; art director, LeRoy Deane; editor, Geroge Rohrs; sound,
M. A. Merrick; set decorator, Ralph S. Hurst; assistant director,

Sherry Shourds; music, Johnny Mandell; costumes, Howard Shoup;
make-up, Gordon Bau; hair, Jean Burt Reilly.

Cast: STUART WHITMAN (Stephen Rojack); JANET LEIGH (Cherry
McMahon); ELEANOR PARKER (Deborah Kelly Rojack); Barry Sullivan
(Roberts); Lloyd Nolan (Barney Kelly); Murray Hamilton (Arthur
Kabot); J. D. Cannon (Lt. Leznicki); Susan Denberg (Ruta); Les
Crane (Nicky); Warren Stevens (Johnny Dell); Joe DeSantis (Eddie
Ganucci); Stacy Harris (Det. O'Brien); Paul Mantee (Shago Martin);
Harold Gould (Ganucci's Lawyer); George Takei (Ord Long); Kelly
Jean Peters (Freya).

Despite the portentous title An American Dream, this torpid
adaptation of Norman Mailer's novel is banal melodrama. Eleanor
Parker, who has said that her role as Deborah Kelly Rojack might
have put her in contention for a supporting Oscar if a couple of her
significant scenes hadn't been cut, appears as the decadent daughter
of "the eighth richest man in the United States" (Lloyd Nolan) and
wife of born-poor TV personality Stuart Whitman. Left only brief
footage at the beginning, it is still enough for her to make off with
the film's acting honors: the sting of her virtuoso virulence is felt
throughout. One of the advertising lines was "This is Mrs. Rojack.
Be glad you're not Mr. Rojack." Another: "She's the stuff that
dreams are made of. Or is it nightmares...." Utilizing an incredible
variety of vocal speeds and octaves, she attacks the all-out theatrics
of her segment with operatic gusto.
    Parker's whole part consists mainly of a verbal and physical
battle with Whitman in the penthouse apartment of the building her
father built and named for her. Wearing only a thin robe and a
long strand of whirling pearls, also drunk, profane, and smoking a
small cigar, she boasts to her husband of ten years that one of her
many lovers has just left and that she has thought of having Whitman
killed. They tumble about the apartment, Whitman proclaiming his
disgust for her "sick parties, perverted friends," the alternately
snarling and cooing Parker confessing that she had "bought my own
little private war hero" as she removes her wedding ring and presses
it against his nose. The mêlée winds up on the patio where, during
a struggle, she falls 30 floors to her death. For the London Daily
Mirror review, the headline read, "After Miss Parker, Everyone Dies."
The notice went on to discern:

> An acid, shrewish performance by Eleanor Parker as a rich,
> alcoholic wife gets (the film) away to a tough, crackling
> start.... But from the moment Eleanor Parker regrettably
> exits, the film trails off into a soggy blend of police pro-
> cedure, turgid romance and mild gangsterdom.

Stuart Whitman proves a disagreeable "hero," free with his fists
and evidently none too bright: on the same night that the police
accuse him of murdering his wife, he resumes with stoic girlfriend
Janet Leigh, now consort of the local Mafia which ultimately guns him

down. The "American dream"? According to Lloyd Nolan's character, it's "that everything will come out all right in the end." Unfortunately, this was not prophetic for the veteran actor. In Australia, where (like England) the picture was released as See You in Hell, Darling, Nolan's whole part was cut, as were the entire roles of Murray Hamilton and Kelly Jean Peters.

47. WARNING SHOT. Paramount/Bob Banner Associates Production. 1967. Technicolor. 100 Mins.

Producer-director, Buzz Kulik; screenplay, Mann Rubin; based on the novel 711--Officer Needs Help by Whit Masterson; camera, Joseph Biroc; editor, Archie Marshak; production manager, Bill Davidson; assistant director, Howard Roessel; sound, Joe Edmondson; art director, Roland Anderson; set decorator, Bob Nelson; costumes, Edith Head; make-up, Wally Westmore; hair, Dorothy White; men's wardrobe, John Anderson; music, Jerry Goldsmith; special effects, Paul K. Lerpae.

Cast: DAVID JANSSEN (Sgt. Tom Valens); ED BEGLEY (Capt. Roy Klodin); KEENAN WYNN (Sgt. Ed Musso); SAM WANAMAKER (Frank Sanderman); LILLIAN GISH (Alice Willows); ELEANOR PARKER (Doris Ruston); Stephanie Powers (Liz Thayer); George Grizzard (Walt Cody); George Sanders (Calvin York); Steve Allen (Perry Knowland); Carroll O'Connor (Paul Jerez); Joan Collins (Joanie Valens); Donald Curtis (Dr. James Ruston); Walter Pidgeon (Orville Ames); John Garfield, Jr. (Police Surgeon); Bob Williams (Judge Gerald Lucas); Jerry Dunphy (TV Newscaster); Vito Scotti (Designer); Brian Dunne (Rusty); Romo Vincent (Ira Garvin); Norma Clark (Shari Sherman).

If an outstanding cast and good timing could insure a film's success, the forties-styled whodunnit Warning Shot would have been Academy Award material. Several generations of illustrious motion picture actors are represented--indeed, Lillian Gish, then celebrating 55 years before cameras, goes back almost to the beginning of the medium. The slick, tough, if hardly original basic premise about a Los Angeles police detective accused of being trigger-happy could have been lifted from the headlines of the day, excluding, of course, the increasingly melodramatic plot complications.

David Janssen, fresh from his popular television series The Fugitive, has one of his better roles in a lackluster big-screen career as the cop whose dedication has caused estrangement from his wife (Joan Collins). On a stakeout with his partner (Keenan Wynn) to apprehend a sex murderer, he shoots and kills a man he claims drew a gun first but who turns out to be a respected doctor (Donald Curtis). And Curtis' gun cannot be found. The physician leaves a widow (Eleanor Parker) and son (Brian Dunne). Janssen, reviled for "police brutality," is indicted for manslaughter. With fewer than ten days before his trial, he sets out to track down the missing weapon and the story behind it. He calls on Gish, an elderly spinster

treated by Curtis on the fatal night who is also mourning the death
of her dog. Further investigation reveals that Curtis had been a
losing gambler who suddenly came into a great deal of money. Someone attempts to kill Janssen, then murders Curtis' nurse (Stephanie
Powers). Finally, Janssen and local airline pilot George Grizzard dig
up Gish's dead dog, interred with his playthings. Among them is the
toy wooden pistol Curtis actually had been trying to discard after
being accosted by Janssen; the dog, knowing Curtis' scent, had
picked it up and brought it home. Hidden in the toy, Janssen discovers heroin. The good doctor, on his frequent "mercy trips" to
Baja, had been part of a narcotics syndicate for which Grizzard had
been the middleman, making flights to every big city on the Pacific
coast. Grizzard also is uncovered as Powers' killer.

Other big names in the company, emoting ably in sometime one-
scene cameos, are Ed Begley, as Janssen's superior officer; Sam Wanamaker, the deputy attorney; George Sanders, the late doctor's broker;
Steve Allen, a TV commentator; Carroll O'Connor, the deputy coro-
ner; Walter Pidgeon, a criminal attorney; and, as a police surgeon,
John Garfield, Jr., whose father, in the forties, was one of Eleanor
Parker's most vivid leading men. Parker, representing the merry
widow whose idea of mourning is martinis with black olives, has only
one big scene in which she attempts to seduce Janssen. She seems
to be enjoying herself hugely, though, passing that pleasure along to
the viewer in the film's brightest vignette. For Variety, "Murf."
wrote:

> Eleanor Parker, who electrified as the sodden dame in An
> American Dream, again essays a similar unsympathetic role,
> certainly within her versatile acting range, but, hopefully,
> not to become impartial casting.

The Independent Film Journal commented:

> The supporting cast is a large and recognizable one, but none
> of the players are on screen long enough to make a definite
> impression, with the exception of Parker, who scores in her
> excesses, nostrils flaring and red hair tumbling.

Aspiring to be nothing more than good, escapist entertainment,
Warning Shot hits its mark. Major credit belongs to the straightforward yet mobile storytelling savvy of television director Buzz
Kulik, and to Mann Rubin's smartly formula screenplay with its potent
jabs at California culture (the pet cemetery in the dénouement, for
instance, is filled with fire hydrant-decorated plots).

48. THE TIGER AND THE PUSSYCAT. Embassy/Fairfilm s.p.a.
     Production. 1967. Pathé Color. 105 Mins.

Executive producer, Joseph E. Levine; producer, Mario Cecchi Gori;
director, Dino Risi; screenplay, Agenore Incrocchi, Furio Scarpelli;

camera, Sandro D'Eva; music, Fred Buongusto; art direction, Luciano
Ricceri; editor, Marcello Malvestiti; costumes-set decoration, Ezio
Altieri; sound, Vittorio Massi; English dialogue, John Douglas.

Cast: VITTORIO GASSMAN (Francesco Vincenzini); ANN-MARGRET
(Carolina); ELEANOR PARKER (Esperia); Caterina Boratto (Delia);
Eleanora Brown (Luisella); Antonella Steni (Pinella); Fiorenzo Fioren-
tini (Tazio); Giambattista Salerno (Luca); Jacques Herlen (Monsignor);
Luigi Vanucchi (Company President).

Filmed in Rome, The Tiger and the Pussycat is an improvement
over Eleanor Parker's previous Italian-made film, Panic Button.
Although the story of the older man who makes a fool of himself
over a young girl goes back to the beginning of the movies (and, no
doubt, to the beginning of man), the Italians responsible for this
version have staged the doings with blithe invention, and the stars,
Vittorio Gassman and the cast's only Americans, Ann-Margret and
Eleanor Parker, acquit themselves nobly. Gassman, especially, has
a field day as an active Roman businessman nicknamed "The Tiger,"
who has been married for years to Parker. They have two grown
children (Eleanora Brown, Giambattista Salerno) and, via Brown, at
age 45 Gassman has just become a grandfather. Suddenly, he feels
old age encroaching. When his son attempts suicide over an art
student girlfriend (Ann-Margret), "Tiger" Gassman visits "Pussycat"
Ann-Margret, who flirtatiously tells him she prefers mature men.
They begin an affair. Trying to keep up with his youthful paramour,
he neglects his work, suffers pulled muscles in go-go clubs, pleads
fatigue when Parker wants to make love, and finds that dental appoint-
ments interfere with his attempts to cut a dashing figure. Eventually,
he loses his job and almost has a nervous breakdown, while Ann-
Margret runs off to study in Paris. Sadly, he returns home where,
taking his place at the family table, his young son turns to him,
smiles faintly and murmurs, "It's okay, Dad. We all go through it."
Made for English-speaking audiences, The Tiger and the Pussycat, in the Italian fashion then, was filmed without a soundtrack,
the dialogue dubbed in later. And the disparity is sometimes all
too apparent. Parker has said that working with a director (Dino
(Risi) who spoke only a few words of English, while she spoke only a
few words of Italian, was often "maddening," although it doesn't show
in the sympathetic aplomb with which she carries off an undemanding
role, marred only by distracting, unbecoming black wigs. A number
of critics remarked on "husband" Gassman's myopia, including Ann
Guarino in the New York Daily News:

> Eleanor Parker is outstanding as the devoted, suffering wife.
> Her dignified portrayal of an elegant and attractive woman
> makes it hard to believe that a mature, intelligent man would
> consider leaving her.

For Variety, "Werb." remarked.

Eleanor Parker is standout as the attractive. understanding
wife and mother.... Her top portrayal often adds a note of
implausibility to Gassman's foray.

Perhaps ironically, the film did much better business in Italy
than in America, the market for which it primarily was made, despite
some applause from the stateside reviewing stand. For instance,
Frances Herridge in The New York Post hailed it as "a gem of a
film.... It doesn't sink into soap opera and it knows how to end the
fun. It is a thorough delight." Actually not quite a thorough delight (for one thing, the pace slackens considerably in the second
half), it does have its charms. James Powers in The Hollywood
Reporter:

The script has some bright notes, particularly its use of
black-and-white film flashes as pictorial representations of
thoughts or desires on the part of the characters involved.
They punctuate the film and propel it. Fred Buongusto's
music score is a lively accompaniment to the events, and provides an amusing and memorable theme.

The production was called The Tiger in Italy, where it took
the David di Donatello Award as best picture of 1967, Gassman winning
the best-actor nod. (The "Pussycat" was added to the title for
American showings so that moviegoers wouldn't think it was a jungle
story, as well as to give prominence to the then blooming Ann-
Margret, who was better known in the states than Gassman.) And
Gassman is flamboyantly right in a characterization that has him almost constantly on screen. At M-G-M with Parker in the early fifties
(just long enough to do a few pictures and marry and divorce Shelley
Winters), Gassman nearly played Parker's husband once before: he
was announced for that role in Valley of the Kings (1954), but it
finally went to Carlos Thompson. Here, the Italian actor's work has
a warm Mediterranean kineticism that is just what the plot of The
Tiger and the Pussycat, well into its ninth life, needs to keep purring.

49. EYE OF THE CAT. Universal/Joseph H. Schenck Enterprises,
     Inc., Production. 1969. Technicolor. 102 Mins.

Producers, Bernard Schwartz, Phillip Hazelton; director, David
Lowell Rich; screenplay, Joseph Stefano; camera, Russell Metty, Ells-
worth Fredericks; editor, J. Terry Williams; art directors, Alexander
Golitzen, William D. DeCinces; music. Lalo Schifrin; assistant director,
Joseph Cavalier; sound, Waldon O. Watson, Frank H. Wilkinson.

Cast: MICHAEL SARRAZIN (Wylie); GAYLE HUNNICUTT (Kassia);
ELEANOR PARKER (Aunt Danny); Tim Henry (Luke); Laurence
Naismith (Dr. Mills); Jennifer Leak (Poor Dear); Linden Chiles (Ben-
detto); Mark Herron (Bellemondo); Annabelle Garth (Socialite).

Eye of the Cat, a potentially exciting, still occasionally effective thriller, is marred by a fumbling script, the incongruous sunny prettiness of its San Francisco setting and erratic direction. The opening scene, for instance, in which well heeled emphysema sufferer Eleanor Parker, observed by an amber cat, has a serious attack at the beauty parlor is directed in so muddled a fashion that aleurophobia (fear of cats) is made to seem the cause of her spell. Actually, she keeps "damn near 100 cats" in her hilltop mansion; it is her errant ward (Michael Sarrazin), returned home to murder "Aunt Danny" for her fortune, who has the paralyzing fear of felines.

Parker, in long black wig evidently dictated by unsubstantiated references to her interest in the occult, is repeatedly called an "old lady" but is far from that. Although confined to a wheelchair part of the time, she is still attractive and vital--maybe a shade too much so for the lonely woman said to be mortally ill. It is an unsympathetic role, too, as she inexplicably mistreats the favored Sarrazin's younger brother (Tim Henry), who stayed to care for her. The scene stealer is "Tullia," the well-trained and photographed tabby whose graceful, omnipresent menace is amplified by slow-motion stealth and chilling close-ups of its expressive face.

50. SUNBURN. Paramount/Hemdale Leisure Corp./United Artists Theatre Circuit. 1979. Color. 101 Mins.

Executive producers, Derek J. Dawson, John Quested; producers, John Daly, Gerald Green; director, Richard C. Sarafian; screenplay, Daly, Stephen Oliver, James Booth; based on the novel The Bind by Stanley Ellin; associate producer, David Korda; camera, Alec Phillips, Jr.; first assistant directors, Steve Barnett, Mario Cisneros; set dresser, Dick Purdy; costumes, Moss Mabry; make-up, Leonard Engelman; hair, Barbara Lorenz; stunt coordinator, Carey Loftin; stunt arranger, Paul Baxley; editor, Geoff Foot; music, John Cameron.

Cast: FARRAH FAWCETT-MAJORS (Ellie Morgan); CHARLES GRODIN (Jake Dekker); ART CARNEY (Al Marcus); JOAN COLLINS (Nera Ortega); ELEANOR PARKER (Mrs. Thoren); Robin Clarke (Karl); Joan Goodfellow (Joanna); Jorge Luke (Vasquez); Jack Kruschen (Gela); Alejandro Rey (Fons Ortega); John Hillerman (Webb); Bob Orrison (Milan); Alex Sharpe (Kunz); William Daniels (Crawford); Keenan Wynn (Mark Elmes); Seymour Cassel (Dobbs); Steven Wilensky (Elmer Jones); Joe L. Brown (Milton Beam).

Quitting the TV series Charlie's Angels while her pin-up posters still heated the walls and dreams of young males everywhere, Farrah Fawcett-Majors hoped to have a career in "major motion pictures." The terminally coiffured sex symbol did not find it in Sunburn, a painless but decidedly lightweight caper opus that more closely resembles a movie made for her dreaded television than a theater film. The production also did nothing for Eleanor Parker who, while co-starred prominently in her first big-screen role in ten years, is thrown only a few fleeting appearances.

Although played primarily for chuckles, the story begins with the purported accidental car crash death in Acapulco of an affluent, elderly industrialist.   His insurance company, liable for $5,000,000 payable to his widow (Parker) and suspecting foul play, hires private investigator Charles Grodin to go to Mexico and determine if fraud is the name of the game.   Enter model Fawcett-Majors, a cute but klutzy blonde chatterbox whom Grodin, for cover, hires to pose as his wife at a villa in sunny, beachfront Acapulco.   There they meet the dead man's frightened widow and two children (Robin Clarke, Joan Goodfellow); his lawyer (Alejandro Rey) and his nymphomaniac wife (Joan Collins); and the villa's renting agent (John Hillerman). Lured out of retirement to help the bogus (but increasingly attracted) young marrieds is veteran investigator Art Carney.   Eventually, they discover that the dead man was a Nazi murderer who built a new life in Acapulco, later to be found out and blackmailed by the Mexican Mafia.   After a couple of new murders, hairbreadth escapes, and a car chase through the streets of Acapulco straight out of TV's The Dukes of Hazzard, a letter left by the late Nazi reveals not only that he committed suicide but the name of the blackmailers.   The insurance company saves $5,000,000, and Grodin, Fawcett-Majors, and Carney are handsomely rewarded.

The audience is not so lucky.   The scenery, when the cars slow up long enough for a look, seems picturesque and the writing, directing, and acting are, if rarely inventive, at least breezy.   But the weary plot just isn't strong enough for real impact.   The most vivid memory left by Sunburn is of a solid, name cast valiantly pressing on.   Charles Grodin gets some laughs as the slightly "jerky" but intrepid gumshoe, disregarding a self-conscious improvisational tendency to stammer like a James Stewart mimic; and Farrah Fawcett-Majors, starlet-delectable in (and out of) her Moss Mabry couture even when conking villains with that age-old feminine weapon the frying pan, is hard to dislike--except, perhaps, by women's libbers. Art Carney extracts traces of humor and humanity from a fairly stock "game old-timer" part; while a pre-Dynasty Joan Collins indulges in some surprisingly lively slapstick wherein, on the verge of a drunken blackout, she tries to seduce Grodin ("Be cruel to me, Darling!").   There is little Eleanor Parker can do with her meager assignment, though, and the treatment she receives from director Richard C. Sarafian is more than somewhat insulting to a star who has won three best-actress Academy Award nominations.   She has no sustained scenes in probably the smallest, least rewarding role of her starring career.   Without dialogue, she is glimpsed early in the film peering from a distant window, then stalking a dim hallway, and later on has a few lines inexplicably, grainily photographed from so far across the room that she is almost unrecognizable.   Her voice still has the old ring of authority, but Sarafian has not deemed it important for viewers to be able to see the artist to whom it belongs. It was his worst decision in a film scarcely filled with inspiration.

B. Television Films

1. HANS BRINKER. NBC. Dec. 13, 1969. Color. 120 Mins.

An MMM Production, in cooperation with the NBC-TV Network, produced in association with Gyula-Trebitsch Studio, Hamburg, Germany;
executive producer, Allan A. Buckhantz; producer for NBC and MMM
Productions, Inc., Ted Kneeland; director, Robert Scheerer; teleplay, William Manhoff; based on the book by Mary Mapes Dodge;
music, lyrics, Moose Charlap; music supervisor-conductor-arranger,
Harper McKay; ice choreography, Ted Shuffle; camera, Guenther
Haase; art director, Mathies Matthes; editor, Fred Srp.

Cast: Eleanor Parker, Richard Basehart, John Gregson, Cyril
Ritchard, Robin Askwith, Roberta Tovey, Sheila Whitmill, Jane An-
thony, Julian Barnes, Michael Wennink, David Auker, Colin Pilditch,
Ivan Butler, Liam Redmond, Jason Kindsey.

    Eleanor Parker is the mother of Hans Brinker (Askwith) and
wife of brain-injured Gregson in this musical version of Hans Brinker,
Or the Silver Skates filmed in Holland, Norway, and Hamburg, Germany.

2. MAYBE I'LL COME HOME IN THE SPRING. ABC. Feb. 16, 1971.
    Color. 90 Mins.

Metromedia Productions; executive producer, Charles Fries; producer-
director, Joseph Sargent; teleplay, Bruce Feldman; camera, Russell
Metty; music, Earl Robinson; editor, Pem Herring.

Cast: Sally Field, Eleanor Parker, Jackie Cooper, Lane Bradbury,
David Carradine.

    Parker plays the mother of a runaway daughter (Field) who
forsakes the hippie drug culture to return home.

3. VANISHED. NBC. March 8, 1971/March 9, 1971. Color. 240
    Mins.

Universal; executive producer, David Victor; producer, David J.
O'Connell; director, Buzz Kulik; teleplay, Dean Riesner; based on the
novel by Fletcher Knebel; camera, Lionel Lindon; music, Leonard
Rosenman; assistant director, Jim Fargo; art director, John J. Lloyd;
editor, Robert Watts.

Cast: Richard Widmark, Skye Aubrey, Tom Bosley, James Farentino,
Larry Hagman, Murray Hamilton, Arthur Hill, Robert Hooks, E. G.
Marshall, Eleanor Parker, William Shatner, Robert Young, Chet Huntley,

Betty White, Stephen McNally, Sheree North, Robert Lipton, Michael
Strong, Jim Davis, Christine Belford, Catherine McLeod, Denny
Miller, Don Pedro Colley, Russell Johnson, Susan Kussman, Neil
Hamilton, Martin Agronsky, Herbert Kaplow, Judy Jordan, Richard
Dix, Nancy Lee Dix, Athena Lorde, Stacy Keach, Sr., Kevin Hagen,
Herb Vigran, Ilka Windish, Randolph Mantooth, Dick Kleiner, Vernon
Scott, Fred Holliday, Carleton Young, Helen Kleeb.

Parker enacts the alcoholic wife of a missing advisor (Hill)
to the President of the United States (Widmark) in the longest film
made for television up to that time. Said Tom Mackin in the Newark
[N.J.] Evening News: "Eleanor Parker was marvelous."

4. HOME FOR THE HOLIDAYS. ABC. Nov. 28, 1972. Color. 90
    Mins.

ABC Circle Films; executive producers, Aaron Spelling, Leonard
Goldberg; producer, Paul Junger Witt; associate producer, Tony
Thomas; director, John Llewellyn Moxey; teleplay, Joseph Stefano;
camera, Leonard J. South; music, George Tipton; art director,
Rolland M. Brooks; editor, Allan Jacobs.

Cast: Sally Field, Jill Haworth, Julie Harris, Eleanor Parker, Jessica
Walter, Walter Brennan, John Fink, Med Flory.

Parker is the "mothering," actually homicidally insane older
sister of Field, Haworth, and Walter, who is trying (with some success) to murder them. "Julie Harris, Eleanor Parker Excellent in
TV Movie Thriller," read the headline for Jim Meyer's review in The
Miami Herald, which noted: "Miss Parker, restrained until the final
moments, superbly projected the torment of a woman who had every
reason to be distraught. We'll probably not see two such high-
powered actresses teamed again on TV this season, unfortunately."

5. THE GREAT AMERICAN BEAUTY CONTEST. ABC. Feb. 13,
    1973. Color. 90 Mins.

ABC Circle Films; executive producers, Aaron Spelling, Leonard
Goldberg; producer, Everett Chambers; director, Robert Day; teleplay, Stanford Whitmore; camera, James Crabe; music, Kennberg;
art director, Rolland M. Brooks; editor, James Mitchell.

Cast: Eleanor Parker, Bob Cummings, Louis Jourdan, Joanna Cameron,
Susan Damonte, Farrah Fawcett, Kathy Baumann, Tracy Reed, Larry
Wilcox, Patricia Barry, Ryan MacDonald, Christopher Norris, Barbi
Benton, Brett Somers, Will Tusher, Vernon Scott, Morton Moss, Joan
Crosby, Joe Pilcher, Norma Lee Browning.

Parker portrays the hostess of the fictional Miss American Beauty

Contest. Reported Judith Crist in <u>TV Guide</u>: "Eleanor Parker's performance as a past winner and present coordinator of <u>The Great American Beauty Contest</u> makes this schmaltzy five-contestants-and-how-they-make-out opera watchable."

6. FANTASY ISLAND. ABC. Jan. 14, 1977. Color. 120 Mins.

Spelling/Goldberg Productions; producers, Aaron Spelling, Leonard Goldberg; director, Richard Lang; teleplay, Gene Levitt; camera, Arch R. Dalzell; music, Laurence Rosenthal; art director, Paul Sylos; editor, John Woodcock.

Cast: Ricardo Montalban, Herve Villechaize, Bill Bixby, Sandra Dee, Peter Lawford, Carol Lynley, Hugh O'Brien, Victoria Principal, Christina Sinatra, Dick Sargent, John McKinney, Cedric Scott, Peter MacLean, Ian Abercrombie, Elizabeth Dartmoor, Eleanor Parker.

    Parker is the domineering millionaire who feigns death to observe what her loved ones really think of her. A "pilot" that was sold for series.

7. THE BASTARD. Operation Prime Time/MCA TV. May, 1978. Color. 240 Mins.

Executive producer, John Wilder; producer, Joe Byrne; director, Lee H. Katzin; teleplay, Guerdon Trueblood; from the novel by John Jakes; camera, Michel Hugo; art director, Lloyd Papez; set decorator, Richard Friedman; music, John Addison; editors, Bob Shugrue, Michael Murphy; costumes, Vincent Dee, Jean Pierre Dorleac, associate producer, Susan Lichtwardt.

Cast: Andrew Stevens, Noah Beery, Peter Bonerz, Tom Bosley, Kim Cattrall, John Colicos, William Daniels, Buddy Ebsen, Lorne Greene, James Gregory, Olivia Hussey, Herbert Jefferson, Jr., Cameron Mitchell, Harry Morgan, Patricia Neal, Eleanor Parker, Donald Pleasence, William Shatner, Barry Sullivan, Keenan Wynn, Jim Antonio, William Bassett, George Chandler, Ike Eisenman, Alan Napier, Charles Haid, Russell Johnson, Claude Earl Jones, Monte Landis, Mark Neely, John Mark Robinson, Elizabeth Shepherd, Carol Tru Foster, James Whitmore, Jr.

    Parker plays the ruthless English duchess who endures a loveless marriage to gain her husband's inheritance for herself and her son (Neely).

8. SHE'S DRESSED TO KILL (later televised as SOMEONE'S KILLING THE WORLD'S GREATEST MODELS). NBC. Dec. 10, 1979. Color. 120 Mins.

Barry Weitz Productions/Grant, Case, McGrath Enterprises; executive in charge of production, William C. Snyder; producers, Weitz, Merrill Grant; director, Gus Trikonis; teleplay, George Lefferts; costumes, Travilla.

Cast: Eleanor Parker, Jessica Walter, John Rubinstein, Corinne Calvet, Joanna Cassidy, Clive Revill, James McMullen, Connie Sellecca, Gail Joy, Cathee Shiriff, Casey Brown.

Parker is a one-time noted fashion designer who attempts a comeback with a showing at her mountaintop retreat, where her models are systematically murdered--by her.

9. ONCE UPON A SPY. ABC. Sept. 19, 1980. Color. 120 Mins.

David Gerber Productions/Columbia Pictures Television; executive producer, Gerber; producer, Jay Daniel; director, Ivan Nagy; teleplay, Jimmy Sangster; story, Lemuel Pitkin, Sangster; camera, Dennis Dalzell; editors, Bob Fish, William Neel; art director, Ross Bellah; production designer, Duane Alt; music, John Cacavas.

Cast: Eleanor Parker, Ted Danson, Mary Louise Weller, Christopher Lee, Leonard Stone, Jo McDonnell, Yuliis Ruval, Irena Ferris, Burke Byrnes, Gary Dontzig, Bobb Hopkins, Vicky Perry.

Parker essays "The Lady," the elegant head of a secret investigative unit. A pilot for a series that did not sell.

10. MADAME X. NBC. March 16, 1981. Color. 120 Mins.

Lavenback-Riche Productions/Universal Television; producers, Wendy Riche, Paula Levenback; director, Robert Ellis Miller; teleplay, Edward Anhalt; based on a play by Alexandre Bisson and the 1966 screenplay by Jean Holloway; camera, Woody Omens; editor, Skip Lusk; art director, William McAllister; music, Angela Morley.

Cast: Tuesday Weld, Granville Van Dusen, Eleanor Parker, Jeremy Brett, Len Cariou, Martina Deignan, Robert Hooks, Jerry Stiller, Robin Strand, Norman Bartold, Raleigh Bond, Stanley Brock, Camilla Carr, Pola Miller, Tony Planer, John Rose, William Wintersole, Wendy Cutler, Meg Sargent, Bridget Sienna, Ellen Snortland, Deanna Deignan, Bennett Foster, Susan Lanier, Beverly Hay, Ramon Menendez, John Madison, Randi Martin, Tom Tully, Edward Anhalt.

Parker is the wealthy matriarch who banishes her errant daughter-in-law (Weld). In Daily Variety, "Tone." wrote:

Eleanor Parker gets that choice mother-in-law role (last time out played to the teeth by Constance Bennett), and she

brings out all the plausible malevolence of the class conscious matron; it's as strong as Weld's perf, and, at the
same time, understandable: This mother-in-law demands
suitability, and her son married beneath his station.

C. Series Television

1. THIS IS YOUR LIFE. Subject: Marjorie Lawrence. NBC. May
    18, 1955. 30 Mins.

A Ralph Edwards Production; producer-director, Axel Gruenberg;
script editor, Paul Phillips; research, Jan Boehme, Don Malmberg.

Cast: Ralph Edwards, host; Marjorie Lawrence, honoree; Eleanor
Parker, Lawrence Tibbett, Lauritz Melchior.

    Eleanor Parker appears as herself, a surprise guest, in a live
show honoring polio-stricken opera singer Lawrence, whom Parker
was portraying on theater screens in Interrupted Melody.

2. CHECKMATE. Episode: "The Renaissance of Gussie Hill." CBS.
    Jan. 17, 1962. 60 Mins.

Producer, Dick Berg; director, Ron Winston; teleplay, Oliver Gard,
Mark Rodgers; original story, Gard.

Cast: Anthony George, Doug McClure, Sebastian Cabot, Jack Betts,
Eleanor Parker, Herschel Bernardi, Cliff Norton, Sam Hearn, Harriet
MacGibbon, Annette Cabot.

    Parker portrays the regal beauty farm owner who turns out
to be a retired stripper with an ex-convict boyfriend (Bernardi).

3. THE ELEVENTH HOUR. Episode: "Why Am I Grown So Cold?"
    NBC. Feb. 6, 1963. 60 Mins.

Executive producer, Norman Felton; producer, Sam Rolfe; director,
Byron Paul; creator, Harry Julian Fink; teleplay, Dick Nelson; music,
Harry Sukman.

Cast: Wendell Corey, Jack Ging, Eleanor Parker, Dan Duryea,
Arthur Petersen, Ed Peck, Lori March, Jan Peters.

    Parker guest-stars as a frigid drinker involved with a medical
quack (Duryea). Most harrowing scene: the actress running down a
street and throwing herself through a plate glass window. Parker

was nominated for the "Outstanding Single Performance by an Actress in a Leading Role" Emmy Award, but Kim Stanley won for an appearance on Ben Casey.

4. BOB HOPE PRESENTS THE CHRYSLER THEATRE. Episode: "Seven Miles of Bad Road." NBC. Oct. 18, 1963. Color. 60 Mins.

Director-writer, Douglas Heyes.

Cast: Eleanor Parker, Jeffrey Hunter, Neville Brand, James Anderson, Bernie Hamilton.

Parker, the drawling wife of a sadistic small-town sheriff (Brand), goes on the make for a handsome vagrant (Hunter).

5. BREAKING POINT. Episode: "A Land More Cruel." ABC. Jan. 27, 1964. 60 Mins.

Creator, George Lefferts; producers, Morton Fine, David Friedkin; director, Paul Stanley; teleplay, George Bellak; music, David Raksin.

Cast: Paul Richards, Eduard Franz, Eleanor Parker, Barry Livingston, Robert Brubaker, William Stevens, Bek Nelson.

Parker plays a fashion designer compelled to pick up the wrong kind of men, eventually seeking psychiatric help.

6. KRAFT SUSPENSE THEATER. Episode: "Knight's Gambit." NBC. March 26, 1964. Color. 60 Mins.

Producer, Robert Bless; director, Walter Grauman; teleplay, Lorenzo Semple, Jr., Halsted Welles; music, Johnny Williams.

Cast: Roger Smith, Eleanor Parker, Chester Morris, Murray Matheson, Erika Peters, Vito Scotti, H. M. Wynant, Ted de Corsia.

Parker is the devoted secretary-companion to a drunken expatriate (Morris) with unsavory connections. A pilot for a projected series to star Smith that did not sell.

7. CONVOY. Episode: "Lady on the Rock." NBC. Oct. 15, 1965. 60 Mins.

Executive producer, Frank Price; producer, Cy Chermak; director, Richard Sarafian; teleplay, Chermak, Don Brinkley.

Cast: John Gavin, John Larch, Linden Chiles, Sean McClory, John
Marley, Peter Mamakos, Brendan Dillon, James Doohan, Felipe Turich,
Lynne Beaulieu, Richard Angarola.

Parker is cast as an American woman on Gibralter who makes a
deal with the Germans during World War II.

8.   THE MAN FROM U.N.C.L.E. Episode: "The Seven Wonders of
the World Affair." NBC. Jan. 8, 1968/Jan. 15, 1968. Color.
120 Mins.

Executive producer, Norman Felton; producer, Anthony Spinner;
director, Sutton Roley; teleplay, Norman Hudis; camera, Robert
Hauser.

Cast: Robert Vaughn, David McCallum, Leo G. Carroll, Barry Sulli-
van, Eleanor Parker, Leslie Nielsen, Tony Bill, Mark Richman, Daniel
O'Herlihy, Albert Paulsen, Hugh Marlowe, Ruth Warrick, David Hurst,
Inger Stratton, Edgar Stehli, Richard Bull, Amy Thomson, Annella
Bassett, Arthur Hanson, Barbara Moore.

Parker appears as the scheming, ill-fated wife of the U.N.C.L.E.
agent (Sullivan) who kidnaps "the seven intellectual wonders of the
world" in the final show of this series. Released overseas by M-G-M
as an 89-minute theater film entitled, How to Steal the World.

9.   BRACKEN'S WORLD. NBC. Weekly Series Debut: Sept. 19,
1969. Color. 60 Mins.

Producer, Stanley Rubin; directors, writers, various; executive story
consultant, Del Reisner.

Cast: Eleanor Parker, Dennis Cole, Elizabeth Allen, Peter Haskell,
Linda Harrison, Laraine Stephens, Karen Jensen, Stephen Oliver,
Madlyn Rhue, Jeanne Cooper, Gary Dubin.

Parker is top-billed as the executive secretary to a movie
mogul, never shown. (At one time during the series' several years
of evolution, Spencer Tracy was said to have been interested in
playing the studio magnate.) Parker quit the short-lived series after
16 segments, stating that her role had dwindled in importance from
the original concept to which she had agreed. Bettye Ackerman replaced her. Reviewing the opening episode, Kay Gardella in the New
York Daily News:

> It remained to Eleanor Parker, who played the attractive,
> middle-aged Sylvia Caldwell, assistant to the unseen head
> of the studio, to give the hour class and distinction. She
> gave a forceful, intelligent portrayal and at the same time

proved that box office Hollywood stars can step into TV
without falling flat on their faces.

10. GHOST STORY. Episode: "Half a Death." NBC. Nov. 3,
     1972. 60 Mins.

Creator-executive producer, William Castle; producer, Joel Rogosin;
director, Les Martinson; teleplay, Henry Slesar; camera, Emmett
Bergholz; editor, John Sheets.

Cast: Eleanor Parker, Pamela Franklin, Signe Hasso, Stephen Brooks,
Taylor Lacher, Andrew Duggan, Tod Andrews, Louis Quinn. Host:
Sebastian Cabot.

     Parker portrays the mother of twin girls (Franklin), one of
whom returns from an early grave to claim her sibling.

11. HAWAII FIVE-O. Episode: "The Big Aloha." CBS. Jan. 12,
     1978. Color. 60 Mins.

Director, Marc Daniels; teleplay, Gerry Day; music, Morton Stevens,
Pete Rugolo.

Cast: Jack Lord, James MacArthur, Kam Fong, Herman Wedemeyer,
Eleanor Parker, Cal Bellini, Lara Parker, John Reilly, Scott Kingston,
Richard Denning, Irmgard Aluli.

     Parker is seen as the matriarch of a Hawaiian dynasty implicated
in the murder of a doctor.

12. FANTASY ISLAND. Episode: "Yesterday's Love." ABC. March
     17, 1979. Color. 60 Mins.

Executive producers, Aaron Spelling, Leonard Goldberg; producers,
Arthur Rowe, Michael Fisher; director, George McCowan; teleplay,
Skip Webster; story, Bill Keenan.

Cast: Ricardo Montalban, Herve Villechaize, Eleanor Parker, Craig
Stevens, Lew Ayres, Dennis Cole, Lou Frizzell, Guy Madison, Mary
Louise Weller.

     Parker and Stevens play an estranged married couple who re-
ceive a gift from their children: a recreation of their whirlwind romance.

13. THE LOVE BOAT. Episode: "The Wedding." ABC. Sept. 15,
     1979. Color. 60 Mins.

Executive producers, Aaron Spelling, Douglas S. Cramer; producers, Gordon, Lynne Farr, Henry Colman; director, Roger Duchowny; teleplay, Ben Joelson, Art Baer, Ray Jessel, Lee Aronsohn, Lan O'Kun; editors, Bob Moore, Norman Wallerstein.

Cast: Gavin McLeod, Bernie Kopell, Fred Grandy, Ted Lange, Lauren Tewes, Lorne Greene, Mark Harmon, Lisa Hartman, Caren Kaye, Audra Lindley, Ray Milland, Donny Most, Eleanor Parker, Tony Roberts, Robert Lussier, Stephanie Steele, Julie Duffy.

Parker and Milland enact the divorced parents of the groom (Harmon) on a wedding cruise to Alaska.

14. VEGA$. Episode: "A Deadly Victim." ABC. Dec. 3, 1980. Color. 60 Mins.

Executive producer, Aaron Spelling; producers, Herman Groves, Jeffrey Hayes; director, Ray Austin.

Cast: Robert Urich, Greg Morris, Phyllis Davis, Bart Braverman, Eleanor Parker, Victor Buono, Vincent Baggetta, Jason Evers, Bubba Smith.

Parker is a lawyer who becomes a bedraggled Skid Row wino.

15. THE LOVE BOAT. Episode: "A Dress to Remember." ABC. May 8, 1982. Color. 60 Mins.

Executive producers, Aaron Spelling, Douglas S. Cramer; producers, Art Baer, Ben Joelson; director, Robert Scheerer; teleplay, Howard Albrecht, Sol Weinstein.

Cast: Gavin McLeod, Bernie Kopell, Fred Grandy, Ted Lange, Lauren Tewes, Eleanor Parker, Catherine Parks, Brianne Leary, Bob Denver, Forrest Tucker, Markie Post, Lyle Waggoner, Kelly Monteith.

Parker plays a poor flower vendor who gets dressed up to meet her long-lost daughter (Parks).

16. FANTASY ISLAND. Episode: "Nurses' Night Out." ABC. Oct. 22, 1983. Color. 60 Mins.

Executive producers, Aaron Spelling, Leonard Goldberg; producers, Arthur Rowe, Don Ingalls; director, Philip Leacock; teleplay, Robert Sherman, Hollace White, Stephanie Green.

Cast: Ricardo Montalban, Christopher Hewitt, Peter Graves, Eleanor Parker, Joanna Cassidy, Patricia Klous, Monte Markham.

Parker is one of the nurses treated by grateful patient Graves to their "wildest fantasies."

17. HOTEL. Episode: "The Offer." ABC. Dec. 7, 1983. Color.
     60 Mins.

Executive producer, Aaron Spelling; producers, Bill, Jo LaMond, Joe Wallenstein; director, Don Chaffey; teleplay, Ross Teel, Geoffrey Fischer.

Cast: Anne Baxter, James Brolin, Connie Sellecca, Eleanor Parker, Margaret O'Brien, Donald O'Connor, Liberace, Craig Stevens, Lorenzo Lamas, Dianne Kay, Albert Hague.

Parker is seen as a hotelier who tries to steal the hotel manager (Brolin) from rival owner Baxter.

18. FINDER OF LOST LOVES. Episode: "A Gift." Dec. 8, 1984.
     Color. 60 Mins.

Executive producer, Aaron Spelling; producers, Liz Coe, Jeffrey Hayes; director, Cliff Bole; teleplay, Coe.

Cast: Tony Franciosa, Deborah Adair, Anne Jeffreys, Eleanor Parker, Barbara Rush, Wendy Smith, Grant Goodeve.

Parker plays a woman who resorts to lies in an effort to find her daughter (Smith).

19. MURDER, SHE WROTE. Episode: "Stage Struck." CBS. Dec.
     14, 1986. Color. 60 Mins.

Executive producer, Peter S. Fischer; producer, Robert F. O'Neill; director, John Astin; teleplay, Philip Gerson.

Cast: Angela Lansbury, Shea Farrell, Bob Hastings, Donald Most, Edward Mulhare, Christopher Norris, Dan O'Herlihy, Eleanor Parker, John Pleshette, John Schuck, Ann Turkel.

Parker portrays an alcoholic actress trying to make a stage comeback.

D. Television Specials

1. THE BUICK ELECTRA PLAYHOUSE. Episode: "The Gambler, the Nun and the Radio." CBS. May 19, 1960. 90 Mins.

Executive producer, A. E. Hotchner; producer, Gordon Duff; direct-
ors, Albert Marre, James Clark; teleplay, Hotchner; based on Ernest
Hemingway's short story; associate producer, Joe Scully; art director,
Robert Tyler Lee; lighting, Leard Davis; technical director, Bob
Stone; assistant director, George Turpin.

Cast: Eleanor Parker, Richard Conte, George Chandler, Charles
Bickford, L. Q. Jones, Frank Killmond, William Schallert, Jorge
Moreno, José Gonzales-Gonzales, Martin Garralaga, Mary Wickes,
Abel Fernandez, Stafford Repp, Miriam Colon, Rodolfo Acosta, Alan
Hale, Jr., Robert Burton.

    Eleanor Parker portrays the Irish nun in a 1932 Montana hospital
attending a Mexican gambler (Conte) who refuses to identify the person
who shot him. The taped show was not liked by critic Harriet Van
Horne in the New York World-Telegram and Sun, but she did call
Parker, in her dramatic television debut, "a lovely actress."

2. GUESS WHO'S COMING TO DINNER. ABC. July 4, 1975. Color.
    30 Mins.

Producer-director, Stanley Kramer; teleplay, Bill Idelson; based on
characters created in a screenplay by William Rose.

Cast: Leslie Charleson, Bill Overton, Richard Dysart, Eleanor Parker, Madge Sinclair, Lee Weaver, Rosetta LeNoire, William Callaway.

    Parker, as the mother of a white girl (Charleson) married to
a black man (Overton), plays the role originated by Katharine Hepburn in the 1967 film. A pilot for a series that did not sell.

3. ACADEMY AWARDS. Live coverage of the 50th annual Awards
    of the Academy of Motion Picture Arts and Sciences from the
    Dorothy Chandler Pavilion of the Los Angeles Music Center. ABC.
    April 3, 1978. Color.

Producer, Howard W. Koch; director, Marty Pasetta; writers, William
Ludwig, Leonard Spigelgass; musical director, Nelson Riddle; chore-
ographers, Rob Iscove, Patricia Birch; costume designer, Moss
Mabry; master of ceremonies, Bob Hope.

Performers: Sammy Davis, Jr., Marvin Hamlisch, Gene Kelly, Natalie
Wood, Karen Black, Susan Blakely, Stockard Channing, Cyd Charisse,
Joan Collins, Eleanor Parker, Camilla Sparv, Debby Boone, Aretha
Franklin, Gloria Loring, Jane Powell, Starr Danais.

    Parker is one of the actresses modeling clothes from collections
nominated for Academy Awards that year.

NEUROTIC. For her work as a frigid drinker in NBC-TV's The
Eleventh Hour series segment, "Why Am I Grown So Cold?", Eleanor
Parker won a 1963 "Outstanding Single Performance in a Leading Role"
Emmy Award nomination.

CHARISMATIC. During the summer of 1972, Eleanor Parker made her musical comedy debut starring as flamboyant actress Margo Channing in the national touring company of Broadway's <u>Applause</u>.

UNFORGIVING. Eleanor Parker was cast as Hannah Hunnicutt, an embittered Texas wife and mother, in the M-G-M film <u>Home from the Hill</u> (1960), directed by Vincente Minnelli.

ADULTEROUS. In a remake of W. Somerset Maugham's <u>The Painted Veil</u>, which first had starred Greta Garbo, Eleanor Parker played the errant wife of a doctor fighting cholera in China in M-G-M's <u>The Seventh Sin</u> (1957).

LICENTIOUS. Eleanor Parker as the title character, the floozie among three different personalities occupying the same body in <u>Lizzie</u> (1957), released by M-G-M.

SCHEMING. Seen as the larcenous wife of a desperado, Eleanor
Parker co-starred with "King of the Movies" Clark Gable in United
Artists' The King and Four Queens (1956).

SEDUCTIVE. Eleanor Parker as Delilah, one of her many operatic characters in M-G-M's <u>Interrupted Melody</u> (1955), in which she portrayed the life of crippled diva Marjorie Lawrence and earned her third best-actress nomination from the film Academy.

VIOLENT. In one of the decade's liveliest female roles, Eleanor Parker impersonated a gun-toting pioneer belle out to trap a man in Many Rivers to Cross (1955), an M-G-M film.

DESPERATE. Eleanor Parker enacted the hard-riding Confederate
spy in the M-G-M Western <u>Escape from Fort Bravo</u> (1954).

TEMPESTUOUS. As the fiery Lenore, traveling player of pre-French Revolution days, Eleanor Parker appeared in M-G-M's film swashbuckler from Rafael Sabatini's novel Scaramouche (1952).

HAPPY. Eleanor Parker holds the scroll proclaiming her "world's best actress" for <u>Caged</u> (1950) at the 11th International Film Festival in Venice, Italy.

PATHETIC. Eleanor Parker ran the gamut from guileless teen-ager to hardened ex-convict as star of Warners' Caged (1950), receiving the "world's best actress" honor at the Venice Film Festival and the first of three best-actress Academy Award nominations.

NAIVE. The somewhat zany young Broadway actress, Sally Middleton, was played by Eleanor Parker in the Warner Bros. film version of John van Druten's stage hit, The Voice of the Turtle (1947).

VICIOUS. As the Cockney slut Mildred Rogers, Eleanor Parker
starred in Of Human Bondage (1946), Warner Bros.' remake of the
W. Somerset Maugham story which 12 years before made a major star
of Bette Davis.

CHARMING. Eleanor Parker represented the all-American girl as war wife in <u>The Very Thought of You</u> (1944), the film which solidified the actress' position as a new star at Warner Bros.

PRE-TEEN. Eleanor Parker as young equestrienne in Cleveland, Ohio.

E. Stage Appearances

1. FORTY CARATS. By Jay Allen, adapted from a French play by
Pierre Barillet, Jean-Pierre Gredy; director, Barry Nelson;
scenery, John Pitts; lighting, James Riley; costumes, Sara Brook.
Opened on March 2, 1970, at the Royal Poinciana Playhouse,
Palm Beach, Fla.; other locations into 1971 included Atlanta, Ga.;
Miami, Fla.; Hollywood, Fla.; and Nyack, N. Y.

Cast: Eleanor Parker, Christopher Wines (replaced by Christopher
Reeve for later engagements), Raymond Hirsch, Nancy Cushman, Jane
Zachary, Eugene Smith, Ruth Kobart, Nancy Douglass, Milo Boulton,
Ruth Baker, Dwayne Early.

Eleanor Parker, for her professional stage debut, plays Ann
Stanley, a 40-year-old who loves a 22-year-old man (Wines) in a
romantic comedy that had starred Julie Harris on Broadway in 1968.
In the Ft. Lauderdale News, Bob Freund wrote:

> Star Eleanor Parker is so radiantly beautiful that it is diffi-
> cult to accept her as a successful businesswoman who is
> shy about love ... after two marriages. But the lady is
> such a consummate actress that she makes us believe every-
> thing she says and does, and laugh along with her when
> cracks are made about her age. The marvelous throaty voice
> projects extremely well, and her timing and stage presence
> are authoritative and entirely professional.

2. APPLAUSE. Producers, Joseph Kipness, Lawrence Kasha in association with Nederlander Productions, George M. Steinbrenner
III; book, Betty Comden, Adolph Green; music, Charles Strouse;
lyrics, Lee Adams; director-choreographer, Ron Field; scenery,
Robert Randolph; costumes, Ray Aghayan; lighting, Tharon
Musser; musical direction-vocal arrangements, Donald Pippin;
musical conductor, Jack Lee; orchestrations, Philip J. Lang;
dance and incidental music arranged by Mel Marvin; original
choreography restaged by Ed Nolfi. Opened on June 27, 1972,
at the San Diego, Calif., Civic Theatre; other locations that
summer included the Denver, Colo., Auditorium Theatre and the
National Theatre in Washington, D.C. With a different supporting
cast, Parker also starred in a summer, 1973, production at the
Dallas, Texas, Music Hall.

Cast: Eleanor Parker, George McDaniel, Norwood Smith, Beverly
Dixon, Ted Pritchard, Orrin Reiley, Candy Brown, John Anania,
Gil Gerard, Ray Thorne, Janice Lynde.

Parker, succeeding original star Lauren Bacall, portrays the
flamboyant, aging stage actress Margo Channing in the national

company of Broadway's 1970 Tony Award-winning "best musical,"
based on the Bette Davis film <u>All About Eve</u>. Despite rave reviews
("Miss Parker is smashingly fine": Richard L. Coe in <u>The Washington
Post</u>), the costly tour ended prematurely in Washington, D.C., due
to insufficient business.

3. FINISHING TOUCHES. By Jean Kerr; producer-director, Carl
    Stohn, Jr.; sets, W. Gates Denninger. Opened on Nov. 19, 1974,
    and played until Dec. 22, 1974, at the Pheasant Run Playhouse,
    St. Charles, Ill.

Cast: Eleanor Parker, Raymond Hirsch, Neil Patrick, Laura Jean
Devon, Richard Parker, Paul Clemens, Sharon Price, John Purcell.

    Parker is cast as Katy Cooper, the wife of a middle-aged college
professor (Hirsch) infatuated with a student (Price) in this family
comedy. Parker is supported by members of her real-life family:
husband Raymond Hirsch and three of her children, Richard Parker,
Paul Clemens, and Sharon (Friedlob/Clemens) Price. "Miss Parker's
performance in <u>Finishing Touches</u> was up to my expectations," wrote
Jerry Bennett in the St. Charles, Illinois, <u>Free Press</u>. "She is a
great actress who could have carried the entire play by herself. She
did not have to, though, because the cast she had behind her was
excellent." Barbara Bel Geddes and Robert Lansing starred in the
Broadway original which opened on February 8, 1973, and ran for
164 performances.

4. THE NIGHT OF THE IGUANA. By Tennessee Williams; managing
    director of the Center Theatre Group, Robert Fryer; director,
    Joseph Hardy; setting, lighting, H. R. Poindexter; costumes,
    Noel Taylor; production associate, Robert Linden. Opened on
    Dec. 19, 1975, and played until Jan. 31, 1976, at the Center
    Theatre Group/Ahmanson Theatre, Los Angeles, California.

Cast: Richard Chamberlain, Dorothy McGuire, Raymond Massey,
Eleanor Parker, Allyn Ann McLerie, Benjamin Stewart, Matt Bennett,
Susan Lanier, Norma Connolly, Ricardo Landeros, José Marin, Jennifer
Savidge, Ben Van Vackter, Michael Ross Verona.

    Parker appears as the lusty, boozing hotel keeper Maxine Faulk,
a role created on Broadway in 1961 by Bette Davis. In his syndicated
newspaper review, Rex Reed opined:

> Eleanor Parker is probably not bawdy enough for the cheap
> demands of Maxine. No matter how you camouflage her, she
> is still a lady and not a predatory bird gnawed by the un-
> pleasant prospect of oncoming menopause. Still, she's an
> accomplished actress whose command of the stillness around
> her inspires confidence. Swaggering boldly in rubber soles,

barking commands at her guests and servants, muttering and
grumbling to cover passions that threaten to erupt inside
her, she tosses her short-cropped horse's mane as though
she had been out in a storm. She gives the play a strong
sense of survival spirit and aids it enormously.

5. PAL JOEY. Artistic director of Circle in the Square, Theodore
Mann; director, Mann; managing director, Paul Libin; book, John
O'Hara; music, lyrics, Richard Rodgers, Lorenz Hart; musical
direction, vocal and dance arrangements, Gene Palumbo; scenery,
John T. Moore; costumes, Arthur Boccia; lighting, Thomas Skelton;
choreography, Margo Sappington. Previewed in late May-early
June 1976, at Circle in the Square, New York, starring Eleanor
Parker and Edward Villella. Because of "artistic differences,"
both left the show along with other personnel before it officially
opened on June 27, then starring understudies Joan Copeland
and Christopher Chadman. It ran 73 performances.

Cast: Eleanor Parker, Edward Villella, Janie Sell, Dixie Carter,
Harold Gary, Boni Enten, Austin Colyer, Adam Petrowski, Joe Sirola.

    Parker plays Vera Simpson, the wealthy patroness lover of a
punk nightclub hoofer (Villella) in this revival of the 1940 Broadway
musical that had featured Vivienne Segal and Gene Kelly.

                            F. Radio

1. THE LUX RADIO THEATRE. "Pride of the Marines." CBS. Dec.
   31, 1945.

Cast: John Garfield, Eleanor Parker, Dane Clark.

    Eleanor Parker, recreating her film role, is Ruth, sweetheart
of a blinded Marine (Garfield).

2. SCREEN DIRECTORS PLAYHOUSE. "Caged." NBC. Aug. 2,
   1951.

Cast: Eleanor Parker, Hope Emerson.

    Parker, recreating her film role, is Marie, a naive prison inmate.

HOLLYWOOD SOUND STAGE. "The Postman Always Rings Twice."
CBS. Jan. 24, 1952.

Cast: Eleanor Parker, Richard Widmark.

   Parker is Cora, a conspirator in murder.

4. THE LUX RADIO THEATRE.   "September Affair."   CBS.   Feb.
    22, 1954.

Cast: Eleanor Parker, Dana Andrews.

   Parker is Manina, a concert pianist.

5. THE LUX RADIO THEATRE.   "Detective Story."   CBS.   April
    26, 1954.

Cast: Kirk Douglas, Eleanor Parker.

   Parker, recreating her film role, is Mary, wife of a detective
(Douglas).

G. Miscellany

1. NBC: THE FIRST 50 YEARS--A CLOSER LOOK, PART TWO.
    NBC-TV. Jan. 31, 1978. 120 Mins.

Executive producer, director of new sequences, Greg Garrison;
producer, Lee Hale; narration writer, Jess Oppenheimer; additional
material, Bill Angelos, Bill Box, Orson Welles.

Cast: Orson Welles, narrator; hosts, Peter Falk, Alfred Hitchcock,
James Stewart.

   Eleanor Parker is shown and identified in a flash from the TV
movie Vanished in this television special.

2. STARBLOOPERS. A Novelty Production from Ray Self, John
    Gregory. Thorn EMI Video. 1979. 47 Mins.

Cast: Eve Arden, Lauren Bacall, Humphrey Bogart, George Brent,
James Cagney, Dane Clark, Joan Crawford, Bette Davis, Ann Dvorak,
Errol Flynn, Kay Francis, John Garfield, Miriam Hopkins, Leslie
Howard, Viveca Lindfors, Joel McCrea, Dennis Morgan, Paul Muni,
Merle Oberon, Pat O'Brien, Eleanor Parker, Dick Powell, George
Raft, Claude Rains, Ronald Reagan, Edward G. Robinson, Ann Sheri-
dan, Shirley Temple, Jane Wyman.

Parker is shown at work on <u>The Voice of the Turtle</u> in this home video collection mostly comprised of outtakes (fluffed scenes) from 1930s and 1940s Warner Bros. films. Reagan, heard to exclaim "goddamn" many times, is pictured botching several attempts to unzip Parker's dress for their movie.

3. THE SUPER DUPER BLOOPER REEL (formerly PRESIDENTIAL BLOOPER REEL). Mizzell Films. Hollywood Home Theatre. 1980. 55 Mins.

Cast: Eve Arden, Lauren Bacall, Humphrey Bogart, George Brent, James Cagney, Dane Clark, Joan Crawford, Bette Davis, Ann Dvorak, Errol Flynn, Kay Francis, John Garfield, Miriam Hopkins, Leslie Howard, Priscilla Lane, Viveca Lindfors, Jayne Mansfield, Joel McCrea, Dennis Morgan, Paul Muni, Merle Oberon, Pat O'Brien, Janis Paige, Eleanor Parker, Dick Powell, George Raft, Claude Rains, Ronald Reagan, Edward G. Robinson, Mickey Rooney, Ann Sheridan, Jane Wyman.

Parker and Reagan appear in numerous fluffs from <u>The Voice of the Turtle</u> in this home video featuring outtakes from old Warner Bros. films.

4. GOING HOLLYWOOD: THE WAR YEARS. A Castle Hill Production. Disney Cable TV Channel. June 6, 1988. 80 Mins.

Production supervisor, Milly Sherman; producer-director, Julian Schlossberg; associate producers, Jonathan Kaplan, Anthony Potenza; creative consultant, Phillip Schopper; writer, Charles Badaracco.

Cast: Van Johnson, host; Vivian Blaine, Dane Clark, Jackie Cooper, Gloria De Haven, Douglas Fairbanks, Jr., Evelyn Keyes, Joan Leslie, Roddy McDowall, Tony Randall, Sylvia Sidney.

Parker is seen and identified in film clips from <u>Pride of the Marines</u> in this TV documentary.

III. ARTICLES ON ELEANOR PARKER

A. Magazines

Asher, Jerry. "Miss Paradox." Photoplay, Feb. 1946

Asher, Jerry. "She Wishes on a Star." Photoplay, Aug. 1950

Bailey, Audrey. "Flowers in Your Hair." Movie Life, Aug. 1943

Balcom, Ted. "Letters: Eleanor Parker." Films in Review, April 1960

Batsford, Cecil. "Readers Inc.: 'Oscar's Overdue for Eleanor'." Photoplay, March 1955

Benedetta, Mary. "The Amazing Miss Parker." Picturegoer (England), Oct. 21, 1950

Brent, Gloria. "The Voice You Love to Hear." Motion Picture, Nov. 1944

Chez Nous (Belgium). Cover. Nov. 1954

Cinegrafico (Cuba). Cover. April 1952

Ciné-Roman (Belgium). Cover. April 25, 1948

Cooper, Marion. "Nice Girl." Movieland, Jan. 1945

Cottom, J. V. "Eleanor Parker: Une Sensitive Qui S'Emancipe...." Ciné Revue (France), Jan. 12, 1967

Dahl, Arlene. "From Now on I'm a Redhead Says Eleanor Parker." Picturegoer (England), Aug. 31, 1957

Delville, Olivier. Cover/"Eleanor Parker: Première ambassadrice du cinéma Américain au Festival de Bruxelles." Le Soir Illustré (Belgium), June 1947

De Rig, Marie. "Puzzle Worth Solving." Silver Screen, Oct. 1945

Downing, Hyatt. "Changeable Lady." Photoplay, April 1955

Downing, Hyatt. "Please, Miss Parker: Look the Same Girl--Just Once!" Photoplay (England), June 1955

Dreier, Hans. "House Dutiful." Photoplay, March 1950

Dunne, Jane. "Portrait in Dots...." Screen Stars, March 1947

Eiga No Tomo (Japan). Cover. Oct. 1954

Eiga No Tomo (Japan). "Eleanor Parker Turns to Egyptian Princess." Dec. 1954

Estampa (Argentina). Covers. Sept. 8, 1947; Oct. 6, 1947; Jan. 5, 1948; March 28, 1949; Jan. 1, 1951

Festival (France). Cover. Nov. 21, 1951

Franchey, John. "Bound for Glory ... The Girl." Screen Stars, Nov. 1944

G. Brans Kleine Romans (Holland). Cover/"Eleanor Parker." Sept. 29, 1950

Hammond, John. "Never a Dull Moment." Movie Show, Jan. 1946

Hendricks, Helen. "My 3 Great Desires." Silver Screen, May 1953

Holland, Jack. "Hollywood's Mystery Girl." Screenland, July 1954

Holliday, Kate. "Let's Do That Again!" Motion Picture, Oct. 1948

Irwin, Louise. "Shy Girl with Nerve." Photoplay, June 1945

Kessner, Jane. "Eleanor Parker's Memory Chest." Movieland, Apr. 1950

Komori, Kazuko. "The Life Story of Eleanor Parker." Eiga No Tomo (Japan), April 1953

Life. "Eleanor Parker: Actress Plays 'Of Human Bondage'." Apr. 30, 1945

Life Romances. Cover. March 1947

Lindner, Cecilia. "Readers Inc ... 'Soap Box'." Photoplay, Jan. 1953

Look. "Eleanor Parker." April 3, 1945

MacArthur, Mildred. "You've Got to Lend Fate a Hand." Silver Screen, Sept. 1951

Mac Trevor, Joan. "Une étoile pas comme les autres: la belle et pudique Eleanor PARKER!" Cine Tele Revue (France), March 2, 1989

McClelland, Douglas. "Eleanor Parker." Films in Review, March 1962

McClelland, Douglas. "Eleanor Parker: Lady in a Cage." Hollywood Studio Magazine, Sept. 1984

McClelland, Douglas. "Eleanor Parker on TV." Films in Review, Oct. 1965

McClelland, Doug. "Why Eleanor Parker?" Quirk's Reviews, July 1989

Meyer, Jim. "Eleanor Parker: Above and Beyond." Hollywood Studio Magazine, May 1979

Miller, Cynthia. "Constant Nymph." Modern Screen, Nov. 1945

Mooring, W. H. "What Price Eleanor Among the New Stars?" Picturegoer (England), Jan. 19, 1946

Morris, Ronald. "Rosy Parker." Picturegoer (England), May 29, 1954

Motion Picture. "City Slickers"/"Tall Toppers." Oct. 1945

Motion Picture. "Two Piece Prints." May 1944

Motion Picture Star Album #3. "Eleanor Parker." 1947

Movie Fan. "Eleanor Parker." July 1946

Movie Glamour. Cover. 1945

Movie Life. "Come Spring." April 1946

Movie Life. "Intimate Close-Ups: Eleanor Parker." May 1955

Movie Pix. "Eleanor Parker: Trouble Made Her Fortune." Aug. 1954

Movie Play. "Midwestern Miss." Jan. 1947

Movie Play. Three-photo layouts. Winter 1944; May 1946

Movie Show. "Break for Eleanor." Jan. 1948

Movie Spotlight. "Catching Up with History." Feb. 1955

Movie Spotlight. "Hollywood at Home: Eleanor Parker." Nov. 1951

Movie Spotlight. "Pretty Perfect." Jan. 1952

Movie Stars Parade. "Heading Up." Sept. 1944

Movies. "Scrapbook Portraits." April 1952

Movies. "Something New...." Jan. 1948

Movies. "Yokel Dokel." June 1946

New Stars over Hollywood. "Eleanor Parker." Oct. 1945

Novak, Mickell. "The Kid with a Catch in Her Voice." Screenland, June 1945

O'Leary, Dorothy. "Perils of Parker." Movie Stars Parade, March 1950

Pageant. "A Star Comes Unstrung in a Mad New Movie." Oct. 1966

Parker, Eleanor. Cover/"En vérité les glamour girls me tapent sur les nervs." Ciné Revue (France), Sept. 16, 1949

Parker, Eleanor. "I Learned About Women from Women." Screenland, May 1950

Parker, Eleanor. "Love Walked In." Motion Picture, Oct. 1955

Parker, Eleanor. "Steps Every Girl Should Take." Screen Stars, Feb. 1952

Parker, Eleanor. "The Role I Liked Best (Mildred in Of Human Bondage)...." Liberty, no date

Parker, Eleanor. "What a Modern Girl Needs to say 'No!'" Screenland, Dec. 1951

Pedelty, Donovan. "Things Are Perking Up for Parker." Picturegoer (England), June 20, 1953

Photoplay. "Parker's Progress." April 1948

"Pic." "The Girl with a Dual Personality." Sept. 1945

Picturegoer (England). Covers. Feb. 3, 1945; June 5, 1948

Rapper, Irving. "Director's Pet ... Eleanor Parker." Screen Guide, March 1948

Romances (Cuba). Covers. July 1947; Oct. 1947; Sept. 1951

Ruuskanen, Lauri-Juhani. Letter. Photoplay, Aug. 1955

Saglimbeni, Gaetano. "I grandi di Hollywood: Eleanor Parker." Gente (Italy), Feb. 18, 1988

Screen Album. "Eleanor Parker." Summer 1945

Screen Album. "Eleanor Jean Parker." Winter 1946

Screen & TV Album. "Eleanor Parker." May-July 1971

Screen Guide. "How to 'Unmake' a Bed." Jan. 1948

Screen Guide. "The Year's Toughest Role." Feb. 1946

Screen (Japan). "Eleanor Parker." Nov. 1954

Screen Life. "Screen Life Feature: Favorites, Eleanor Parker--
Cliché Twister." July 1953

Screen Parade (New Zealand). "Eleanor Parker: She Still Prefers
Cheeseburgers to Crêpe Suzettes." June 1952

Screen Stars. "Career Mother." Dec. 1949

Screen Stars. "Parker Paradise." June 1947

Screen Stars. Photo. March 1945

Screen Stories. "Eleanor Parker." Nov. 1951

Screen Stories. "Eleanor Parker ... Girl of a Thousand Faces."
March 1955

Screen World. "Crusading Beauty." Dec. 1950

Screenland. "Dressed to Thrill." Aug. 1945

Screenland. "Forward-Looking Fashions." Oct. 1945

Shelley, Elizabeth. "Was It Ever 'Perfect'?" Movie Stars Parade,
Oct. 1953

Silver Screen. "Pertinent Points on Parker." June 1943

Silver Screen. Photo. Jan. 1947

Silver Screen. "Wife with a Past." Nov. 1951

V Magazine (France). Cover. July 1948

Who's Who in Hollywood: 1958. "On the Marquee (Stars)." 1958

Who's Who in Hollywood: 1966. "Starring." 1966

Who's Who in Hollywood: 1967. "On the Marquee (The Stars)."
1967

Who's Who in Movies. "Curtain Calls." 1971

Woman (Australia). "Gallery of Stars: Eleanor Parker." March 18, 1946

Woman (Australia). "Gallery of Stars: Eleanor Parker." Aug. 30, 1948

Yates, Bruce. "Letters: Additions & Corrections--Eleanor Parker." Films in Review, April 1962

B. Newspapers

ABC Television press release. "Eleanor Parker Eyes Broadway." Nov. 16, 1972

Alpert, Don. "Eleanor: How American Dreams Are Made." Los Angeles Times, April 24, 1966

American Weekly, The. Cover: Magazine section. June 18, 1950

Anderson, Jack E. "What's It All About, Eleanor? Your New TV Show, That Is." The Miami Herald, Aug. 12, 1969

Belser, Lee. "Eleanor Can Prove 'Drive' Over-rated." Los Angeles Mirror, Nov. 28, 1960

Berg, Louis. "Shady Lady: Eleanor Parker is an Undercover Girl When the Sun's Out." This Week, Nov. 4, 1956

Buffalo Courier-Express. "Don't Look Now, But--Eleanor Doesn't Stand Out in Crowd." Feb. 21, 1965

Cedrone, Lou. "Miss Parker." The Baltimore Sun, July 9, 1969

Chicago Sunday Tribune. Cover: Magazine section. March 30, 1947

Cleveland News, The. "Secret War Bride." May 19, 1943

Cleveland News, The. "School friends." Nov. 19, 1943

Cleveland News, The. "Starlet Will Sell Bonds Here Friday." Aug. 18, 1943

Cleveland Press, The. Cover: "Show Time" section. Oct. 7, 1966

Cleveland Press, The. "Eleanor Parker ... has landed her best screen role...." March 24, 1943

Cleveland Press, The. "Eleanor Parker, (Young and Beautiful) Cleveland Film Actress, Home on Visit." Dec. 16, 1941

Cleveland Press, The. "Hollywood Discovers Beautiful Clevelander and Signs Her Up!" July 11, 1941

Coe, Richard L. "'She's One of the Best Actresses in the Movies'." The Washington Post, July 23, 1972

Cuskelly, Richard. "Around LA: A Lady Who Likes Not to Play One." Los Angeles Herald-Examiner, Dec. 14, 1975

Dahl, Arlene. "Beauty Spot." London Standard (England), May 9, 1966

Dayton [Ohio] Journal Herald, The. "Busy Eleanor." Oct. 16, 1953

Dayton [Ohio] Journal Herald, The. "Civic Participation." Sept. 3, 1951

Dayton [Ohio] Journal Herald, The. "Eleanor Parker, Greene (County) Native. Seeks Divorce." July 3, 1953

Dayton [Ohio] Journal Herald, The. "First Cowboy Film." May 28, 1953

Dayton [Ohio] Journal Herald, The. "New Indian Name." June 4, 1953

Dayton [Ohio] Journal Herald, The. "Parker Homecoming." Aug. 22, 1951

Dayton [Ohio] Journal Herald, The. "USO Lounge to Open: Movie Star to Dedicate It." Sept. 18, 1951

Detroit News Pictorial Magazine, The. "Make-Up Magic." March 27, 1955

Fort Lauderdale News. "Children's Classic Filmed for Special." Nov. 28, 1969

Freund, Bob. Cover: "Show Time" section/"Stage Attracts Movie Superstar." Fort Lauderdale News, March 27, 1970

Freund, Bob. "Eleanor Parker Will Star Here." Fort Lauderdale News and Sun-Sentinel, Jan. 10, 1970

Gamester, George. "Names in the News." Toronto Star (Canada), May 14, 1980

Gardella, Kay. "Eleanor Parker 'Chained' to Bracken's World TVer." N.Y. Daily News, Aug. 15, 1969

Gebhart, Myrtle. "Eleanor Parker Is the Favorite Girl of Movie Directors." Boston Sunday Post, July 16, 1944

Graham, Sheilah. "Babies Play Key Part in Eleanor Parker's Career, Private Life." The Indianapolis Star, Feb. 24, 1952

Graham, Sheilah. "Eleanor Parker Started Her Career with a Shock." Atlanta Constitution, March 9, 1952

Graham, Sheilah. "Marriage, House Make Eleanor Parker Happy." North American Newspaper Alliance, Jan. 9, 1947

Hayes, Ronald. "Miss Parker to Play Role Sans Glamour." Ft. Wayne [Ind.] News-Sentinel, July 30, 1949

Hayes, Ronald Q. "Actress Finds Work Easier Sans Make-up." Ft. Wayne [Ind.] News-Sentinel, Aug. 15, 1949

Heffernan, Harold. "Actress Cuts Costs, Keeps Closer Ties." The Toledo Blade, Aug. 3, 1960

Heffernan, Harold. "Eleanor Parker Getting Tired of Violence in Her Film Roles." The Newark [N.J.] Evening News, Feb. 5, 1963

Hollywood Reporter, The. "Eleanor Parker for L.A. Stage Debut in 'Iguana'." Aug. 28, 1975

Hollywood Reporter, The. "Eleanor Parker Gets 'Applause'." March 24, 1972

Hollywood Reporter, The. "Eleanor Parker in 'Music'." March 5, 1964

Hollywood Reporter, The. "Eleanor Parker Quits 20th-Fox's 'Bracken's World'." Sept. 29, 1969

Holt, Ernie. "Eleanor Parker Says ... I Want to be a Temptress But Hollywood Says No, No." The National Enquirer, June 25, 1961

Hopper, Hedda. "She Loves to Act!" Chicago Sunday Tribune, Nov. 11, 1951

Kany, A. S. "Let's Go Places." The Dayton [Ohio] Journal Herald, Aug. 21, 1951

Kany, A. S. "Let's Go Places." The Dayton [Ohio] Journal Herald, Sept. 17, 1951

Lane, Lydia. "A Great Change in Personality." Miami Daily News, Feb. 2, 1957

Lane, Lydia. "Hollywood Beauty: Star Finds Beauty More Than Skin Deep." Miami Daily News, June 15, 1954

London Daily Herald (England). Separation from Paul Clemens. May 14, 1964

London Evening News (England). "--And Family Girl." May 4, 1948

London Evening Standard (England). "Eleanor Parker--'Humiliated'." March 10, 1965

MacPherson, Virginia. "Actress Bars Bikini Swim Suit, Even for Loving Mate." The Boston Traveler, Feb. 20, 1951

Manners, Dorothy. "Even Eleanor's Name Authentic." Los Angeles Examiner, Jan. 11, 1953

Manners, Dorothy. "Snappy Shots." Pictorial Living, April 2, 1950

Marsh. "Cleveland's Own Film Star Home on Month's Holiday." The [Cleveland] Plain Dealer, Aug. 13, 1943

Miami Daily News. "Eleanor Parker's Face Is Unfamiliar." April 24, 1955

Miami Herald, The. "Eleanor Parker, Hubby Reconcile." Feb. 6, 1961

Miami News, The. "Eleanor Parker Set for 'Wylie' (Eye of the Cat)." April 20, 1968

Miami Sunday News. Cover: Magazine section. Feb. 3, 1957

Mosby, Aline. "Paul Clemens' Favorite Model is His Wife." Fort Wayne [Ind.] News-Sentinel, Nov. 24, 1956

Muir, Florabel. "Eleanor: 'I Don't Feel I Stooped'." Detroit Free Press, Oct. 16, 1966

New York Post. "Eleanor Parker, 43, Takes 4th Husband." April 18, 1966

New York Times, The. "Eleanor Parker Divorced." March 10, 1965

New York Times, The. "Eleanor Parker Is Married." April 19, 1966

New York Times, The. "Eleanor Parker Resigns from 'Pal Joey'." June 9, 1976

New York Times, The. "Studio Suspends Eleanor Parker." June 31, 1948

New York Daily News. Collapse and hospitalization in Los Angeles "from overwork." Dec. 8, 1954

New York Daily News. "Goes to the Unhitching Post." March 10, 1965

New York Morning Telegraph. "The Girl Nobody Knows." Dec. 27, 1951

New York Sunday Mirror. Covers: Magazine section. Feb. 4, 1951; June 27, 1954

New York Sunday Mirror. Cover: Magazine section/"Our Cover Girl." March 25, 1945

New York Sunday Mirror. Cover: Magazine section/"This Week's Cover." June 11, 1950

New York Sunday News. Cover: Magazine section. Aug. 24, 1952

New York Sunday News. "That Parker Girl Made Good." Oct. 14, 1951

Parker, Eleanor. "Nobody Wants to Hear About Your Travels." The Boston Globe, July 11, 1961

Parsons, Louella. "Director Labels Eleanor Parker 'Best Actress Since Greta Garbo'." The Miami Herald, Oct. 21, 1945

Parsons, Louella O. "Eleanor Parker: Portrait of a Happy Wife." New York Journal-American, March 12, 1961

Parsons, Louella O. "In Hollywood with Louella O. Parsons: Eleanor Parker." Pictorial Living, June 25, 1950

Parsons, Louella O. "Louella O. Parsons in Hollywood: Eleanor Parker." Seattle Post-Intelligencer Pictorial Review, Nov. 11, 1951

Pearson, Ruth S. "Family Comes First with Eleanor Parker ... And They're a Happy, Handsome Lot at PRP." St. Charles, Ill., Chronicle, Nov. 20, 1974

Philadelphia Inquirer, The. Cover: "Picture Parade" section. June 7, 1945

Plain Dealer, The (Cleveland). "Baby Girl for Parkers." March 8, 1948

Plain Dealer, The (Cleveland). "Eleanor Parker." Oct. 31, 1944

Plain Dealer, The (Cleveland). "Ex-Classmates Having Reunion with Film Star." Sept. 10, 1951

Pullen, Glenn C. "Eleanor Parker, Here for 'Christy' Premiere at
Hipp, Becomes Sparkling Blonde." The Cleveland Press, Sept. 11,
1951

Rau, Neil. "Visiting the Studios with Neil Rau." Los Angeles Examiner, Aug. 6, 1944

Rosenfield, John. "The New Bette Davis with Old's Blessing." The
Dallas Morning News, Sept. 20, 1944

Schallert, Edwin. "Eleanor Parker in Lively Return." Los Angeles
Times, May 15, 1949

Scott, John L. "Eleanor Parker Goes 'Uncaged' in Comedy." Los
Angeles Times, Feb. 11, 1950

Scott, John L. "Eleanor Parker Nearing Turning Point of Career."
Los Angeles Times, Jan. 4, 1948

Shain, Percy. "Night Watch: Eleanor's Daughter to Wed Israeli."
The Boston Globe, July 7, 1969

Shain, Percy. "That's Bracken's Ex-secretary." Boston Sunday
Globe, Dec. 14, 1969

Shales, Tom. "Eleanor Parker: Career Hazards." The Washington
Post, July 12, 1972

Shull, Richard K. "TV Series Lies Ahead for Eleanor Parker."
The [Baltimore] Evening Sun, July 28, 1969

Skolsky, Sidney. "Hollywood Is My Beat: 'Call Her Miss, Mister'."
New York Post, May 17, 1947

Skolsky, Sidney. "Hollywood Is My Beat: 'Hard to Recognize....'"
New York Post, May 2, 1954

Skolsky, Sidney. "Hollywood Is My Beat: 'Princess'." New York
Post, July 11, 1950

Star-Ledger, The (Newark, N.J.). "Eleanor Parker Returns to
Films." Aug. 7, 1968

Star Weekly (Toronto, Canada). Cover. Aug. 18, 1951

Swaebly, Frances. "Eleanor Here 'To Get Feet Wet'." The Miami
Herald, March 15, 1970

Thomas, Bob. "Eleanor Parker Plays First Scene in Nude." Hollywood
(Fla.) Sun-Tattler, April 1, 1966

Thompson, Howard. "Miss Parker Plots a Placid Career." The New York Times, Jan. 11, 1953

Toledo Blade, The. "Star Sheds Mate 'Blind' to Her Films." Dec. 5, 1944

Variety. "Eleanor Parker in 'Hole'." Sept. 3, 1958

Variety. "She-Spy Saga." Sept. 27, 1961

Wallace, Inez. "Cleveland's Eleanor Parker Gave 'Everything' to Films." The Cleveland News, June 4, 1944

Wilson, Jean Sprain. "Eleanor's Not Sensational--She's Just Terrific!" The Miami News, Nov. 12, 1958

Woods, Sherry. "Eleanor Parker Enjoys First Stage Role." Palm Beach Post, March 6, 1970

IV. PUBLISHED MENTIONS

A. Books

Aaronson, Charles S., ed. 1966 International Television Almanac
New York: Quigley, 1965, p. 226

Adams, Les, and Buck Rainey. Shoot-Em-Ups. New Rochelle, N.Y.:
Arlington House, 1978, pp. 429, 443, 453, 470

Adamson, Joe. Byron Haskin. Metuchen, N.J.: Scarecrow Press,
1984, pp. 220-22, 258

Agan, Patrick. Whatever Happened To--. New York: Ace, 1974,
pp. 158-59

Alexander, Diane. Playhouse. Los Angeles: Dorleac-MacLeish,
1984, p. 1

Alicoate, Jack, ed. The 1956 Film Daily Year Book of Motion Pictures.
New York: The Film Daily, 1956, pp. 86, 127, 184, 189, 258, 261,
512W

Amberg, George. The New York Times Film Reviews: 1913-1970.
New York: Arno/Quadrangle, 1971, pp. 301-302

Anderegg, Michael A. William Wyler. Boston: Twayne, 1979, pp.
175, 177, 257

Anderson, Janice. Ronald Reagan. New York: Exeter, 1982, pp.
35, 44-45, 80

Arden, Eve. Three Phases of Eve. New York: St. Martin's, 1985,
p. 70

Astor, Mary. A Life on Film. New York: Delacorte, 1971, p. 237

Aumont, Jean-Pierre. Sun and Shadow. New York: Norton, 1977,
p. 180

Aylesworth, Thomas G. The Best of Warner Bros. New York:
Gallery, 1986, p. 84

Bahn, Chester B., ed. The 1961 Film Daily Year Book of Motion Pictures. New York: The Film Daily, 1961, pp. 231, 474

Barbour, Alan G. Humphrey Bogart. New York: Pyramid, 1973, pp. 114-15, 151

Barris, Alex. Hollywood According to Hollywood. So. Brunswick, N.J.: Barnes, 1978, pp. 28, 30, 149

Barris, Alex. Hollywood's Other Women. So. Brunswick, N.J.: Barnes, 1975, pp. 31, 33

Baxter, John. Hollywood in the Sixties. New York: Barnes, 1972, p. 146

Baxter, John. The Gangster Film. New York: Barnes, 1970, p. 41

Beaver, James N., Jr. John Garfield: His Life and Films. So. Brunswick, N.J.: Barnes, 1978, pp. 124-25, 127-28, 132-33, 194

Behlmer, Rudy, and Tony Thomas. Hollywood's Hollywood. Secaucus, N.J.: Citadel, 1975, pp. 26-28, 31, 195, 296-97, 307, 333

Belton, John. Cinema Stylists. Metuchen, N.J.: Scarecrow Press, 1983, p. 207

Belton, John. Robert Mitchum. New York: Pyramid, 1976, pp. 104-5, 149

Bergan, Ronald. The United Artists Story. New York: Crown, 1986, pp. 161, 170, 192

Bergen, Polly. Polly's Principles. New York: Wyden, 1974, pp. 14, 103

Bessie, Alvah. Inquisition in Eden. New York: Macmillan, 1965, pp. 2, 74-75

Blum, Daniel, ed. Screen World: 1951. New York: Greenberg, 1951, pp. 34, 80, 144

Blum, Daniel, ed. Screen World: 1952. New York: Greenberg, 1952, pp. 33, 78, 105

Blum, Daniel, ed. Screen World: 1953. New York: Greenberg, 1953, p. 57

Blum, Daniel, ed. Screen World: 1954. New York: Greenberg, 1954, pp. 10, 144

Blum, Daniel, ed. Screen World: 1955. New York: Greenberg, 1955, pp. 7, 53, 80

Blum, Daniel, ed. Screen World: 1956. New York: Greenberg,
1956, pp. 27, 88

Blum, Daniel, ed. Screen World: 1957. New York: Greenberg,
1957, pp. 11, 153

Blum, Daniel, ed. Screen World: 1958. New York: Greenberg,
1958, pp. 26, 69

Blum, Daniel, ed. Screen World: 1960. Philadelphia: Chilton,
1960, p. 67

Blum, Daniel, ed. Screen World: 1961. Philadelphia: Chilton,
1961, pp. 28-29

Blum, Daniel, ed. Screen World: 1962. Philadelphia: Chilton,
1962, p. 42

Blum, Daniel, ed. Screen World: 1963. Philadelphia: Chilton,
1963, p. 18

Blum, Daniel, ed. Screen World: 1965. New York: Crown, 1965,
p. 32

Blum, Daniel, with John Kobal. A New Pictorial History of the Talkies.
New York: Putnam, 1968, pp. 215, 217, 231, 260, 282, 318

Booker, Phil. Jeanne Crain--The Beautiful Dreamer. New York:
Carlton, 1977, pp. 43, 58

Brooks, Tim, and Earle Marsh. The Complete Dictionary to Prime
Time Network TV Shows: 1946-Present. New York: Ballantine,
1981, p. 106

Brown, Jay A., ed. Rating the Movies. New York: Beekman, 1986,
pp. 86, 123, 142, 277, 352, 372, 391, 420

Brown, Peter H., and Jim Pinkston. Oscar Dearest. New York:
Harper & Row, 1987, p. 79

Brown, Peter Harry. Kim Novak: Reluctant Goddess. New York:
St. Martin's, 1986, pp. 68, 71, 74, 263

Bull, Clarence, and Raymond Lee. The Faces of Hollywood. Cranbury, N.J.: Barnes, 1968, p. 202

Cadden, Tom Scott. What a Bunch of Characters! Englewood Cliffs,
N.J.: Prentice-Hall, 1984, pp. 17, 97, 119, 151, 159, 232, 248, 261-
62, 284-85

Cameron, Ian. Adventure in the Movies. New York: Crescent,
the 1970s, p. 131

Cameron, Ian and Elisabeth. Dames. New York: Praeger, 1969, pp. 99-100

Canham, Kingsley. The Hollywood Professionals, Volume I. New York: Barnes, 1973, pp. 46, 71, 127, 135

Capra, Frank. The Name Above the Title. New York: Macmillan, 1971, p. 459

Carey, Gary. Judy Holliday. New York: Seaview, 1982, p. 117

Carney, Raymond. American Vision: The Films of Frank Capra. New York: Cambridge University Press, 1986, pp. 487, 500

Carpozi, George, Jr. Clark Gable. New York: Pyramid, 1961, p. 145

Cawkwell, Tim, and John M. Smith, eds. The World Encyclopedia of Film. London: Studio Vista, 1972, p. 209

Cohen, Daniel, and Susan Cohen. Encyclopedia of Movie Stars. New York: Gallery, 1985, p. 191

Cohen, Daniel, and Susan Cohen. History of the Oscars. London: Bison, 1986, pp. 73, 76, 85

Collins, Joan. Past Imperfect. New York: Simon & Schuster, 1984, pp. 355, 358

Crist, Judith. The Private Eye, The Cowboy and the Very Naked Girl. New York: Holt, Rinehart & Winston, 1967-68, p. 108

Crowther, Bosley. The Lion's Share. New York: Dutton, 1957, p. 305

Culbert, David, ed. Mission to Moscow. Madison: University of Wisconsin, 1980, pp. 26, 43, 46, 243

David, Nina. TV Season: 74-75. Phoenix, Ariz.: Oryx, 1976, p. 69

David, Nina. TV Season: 76-77. Phoenix, Ariz.: Oryx, 1978, p. 88

David, Nina. TV Season: 77-78. Phoenix, Ariz.: Oryx, 1979, pp. 7, 26

Denton, Clive, and Kingsley Canham. The Hollywood Professionals, Volume V. New York: Barnes, 1976, pp. 76, 108, 129

Donovan, Paul. Roger Moore. London: W. H. Allen, 1983, pp. 56,

Douglas, Kirk. The Ragman's Son. New York: Simon & Schuster,
1988, p. 262

Druxman, Michael B. Charlton Heston. New York: Pyramid, 1976,
pp. 47-49, 146

Druxman, Michael B. Make It Again, Sam. So. Brunswick, N.J./
New York: Barnes, 1975, pp. 259, 261, 284-85

Druxman, Michael B. One Good Film Deserves Another. So. Brunswick, N.J.: Barnes, 1977, pp. 87-88

Eames, John Douglas. The MGM Story. New York: Crown, 1975, pp.
210, 250-51, 259, 264, 271, 280, 283, 299, 342

Eames, John Douglas. The Paramount Story. New York: Crown,
1985, pp. 201, 210, 257, 303

Edwards, Anne. Early Reagan. New York: William Morrow, 1987,
p. 322

Essoe, Gabe. The Films of Clark Gable. Secaucus, N.J.: Citadel,
1970, pp. 59, 239

Essoe, Gabe, and Ray Lee. Gable: A Complete Gallery of His Screen
Portraits. Los Angeles: Price Stern Sloan, 1967, p. 121

Fans' Own Manual, The. London: Award, 1960, p. 86

Finch, Christopher, and Linda Rosenkrantz. Gone Hollywood. Garden
City, N.Y.: Doubleday, 1979, p. 82

Finler, Joel. All-Time Box-Office Hits. New York: Gallery, 1985,
p. 122

Finler, Joel W. The Movie Directors Story. New York: Crescent,
1985, pp. 24, 130

Fitzgerald, Michael G. Universal Pictures. Westport, Conn.: Arlington House, 1977, p. 717

Fordin, Hugh, ed. Film Daily 1970 Yearbook of Motion Pictures and
Television. New York: Film TV Daily, 1970, pp. 881, 940

Francisco, Charles. You Must Remember This.... Englewood Cliffs,
N.J.: Prentice-Hall, 1980, p. 200

Fraser, George MacDonald. The Hollywood History of the World.
New York: Beech Tree/William Morrow, 1988, p. 129

Frazee, Steve. Many Rivers to Cross. Greenwich, Conn.: Gold
Medal, 1955. Movie edition of novel

Freedland, Michael. The Two Lives of Errol Flynn. New York:
William Morrow, 1979, p. 167

Gable, Kathleen. Clark Gable: A Personal Portrait. Englewood
Cliffs, N.J.: Prentice-Hall, 1961, p. 108

Garceau, Jean, with Inez Cocke. "Dear Mr. G--": The Biography
of Clark Gable. Boston: Little, Brown, 1961, p. 266

Garland, Brock. War Movies. New York: Facts on File, 1987, pp.
16, 56, 118, 162

Garnett, Tay, with Fredda Dudley Balling. Light Your Torches and
Pull Up Your Tights. New Rochelle, N.Y.: Arlington House, 1973,
p. 179

Gehman, Richard. Bogart. New York: Gold Medal, 1965, p. 138

Gelman, Howard. The Films of John Garfield. Secaucus, N.J.:
Citadel, 1975, pp. 117, 119, 121-24, 129

Gertner, Richard, ed. 1986 International Motion Picture Almanac.
New York: Quigley, 1986, p. 206

Godfrey, Lionel. The Life and Crimes of Errol Flynn. New York:
St. Martin's, 1977, pp. 163-64

Goldstein, Ruth M., and Edith Zornow. Movies for Kids. New York:
Ungar, 1980, p. 238

Gow, Gordon. Hollywood in the Fifties. New York: Barnes, 1971,
pp. 59-60

Green, James E., ed. The Greatest American Films. Washington,
D.C.: The American Film Institute, 1978, p. 57

Hajdu, David, ed. Best on Home Video. New York: Doubleday,
1985, pp. 210-11

Halliwell, Leslie. The Filmgoer's Companion: 4th Edition. New York:
Hill & Wang, pp. 554, 596

Hans Brinker, Or the Silver Skates. Winona, Wisc.: Hal Leonard
Music, 1969, pp. 2, 6 of photo spread. Moose Charlap's songs arranged for organ by Chester Nordman

Hardy, Phil, ed. The Encyclopedia of Horror Movies. New York:
Harper & Row, 1984, p. 204

Hardy, Phil. The Encyclopedia of Westerns. Minneapolis: Woodbury,
1984, p. 223

Harman, Bob. Hollywood Panorama. New York: Dutton, 1971, pp. 57-58

Haun, Harry. The Movie Quote Book. New York: Lippincott & Crowell, 1980, pp. 308, 350-51

Haver, Ronald. A Star Is Born. New York: Alfred A. Knopf, 1988, p. 15

Head, Edith, and Paddy Calistro. Edith Head's Hollywood. New York: Dutton, 1983, pp. 206, 212, 226-27

Hemming, Roy, ed. Video Review's Movies on Video. New York: Viare, 1983, pp. 27, 44, 73, 86, 88, 129-30, 136, 152, 180, 193, 203, 231, 246, 296

Hemming, Roy. The Melody Lingers On. New York: Newmarket, 1986, pp. 184, 252, 361, 370

Henreid, Paul, with Julius Fast. Ladies' Man. New York: St. Martin's, 1984, pp. 166, 172

Heston, Charlton. The Actor's Life. New York: Dutton, 1978, p. 473

Higham, Charles. Errol Flynn: The Untold Story. Garden City, N.Y.: Doubleday, 1980, p. 358

Higham, Charles. Warner Brothers. New York: Scribner's, 1975, p. 197

Higham, Charles, and Joel Greenberg. Hollywood in the Forties. New York: Barnes, 1968, pp. 106, 114

Hirschhorn, Clive. The Hollywood Musical. New York: Crown, 1981, pp. 250, 303, 345, 348, 384

Hirschhorn, Clive. The Universal Story. New York: Crown, 1983, p. 301

Hirschhorn, Clive. The Warner Bros. Story. New York: Crown, 1979, pp. 234, 238, 241, 244-45, 249, 257, 260-61, 266, 270, 273, 278, 282, 286, 289, 371

Holtzman, Will. Judy Holliday. New York: Putnam, 1982, p. 146

Holtzman, Will. William Holden. New York: Pyramid, 1976, pp. 100-101, 151

Humphrey, William. Home from the Hill. New York: Perma, 1959. Movie edition of novel

Hyams, Jay. War Movies. New York: Gallery, 1984, pp. 102, 112

Jackson, Shirley. Lizzie (The Bird's Nest). New York: Signet, 1957. Movie edition of novel

Jeavons, Clyde. A Pictorial History of War Films. Secaucus, N.J.: Citadel, 1974, pp. 159-60, 244

Jones, Ken D., and Arthur F. McClure. Hollywood at War. So. Brunswick, N.J.: Barnes, 1973, pp. 111, 145, 164-65, 275, 279, 313

Jordan, René. Clark Gable. New York: Pyramid, 1973, pp. 127, 153

Kael, Pauline. 5001 Nights at the Movies. New York: Holt, Rinehart & Winston, 1982, pp. 144, 363, 423, 437, 546

Kael, Pauline. Kiss Kiss Bang Bang. Boston: Little, Brown, 1965, p. 134

Kaplan, Mike, ed. Variety Presents: The Complete Book of Major U.S. Show Business Awards. New York: Garland, 1985, pp. 33, 35, 42, 114

Kaplan, Mike, ed. Variety Who's Who in Show Business. New York: Garland, 1985, p. 261

Karr, Kathleen, ed. The American Film Heritage. Washington, D.C.: Acropolis, 1972, pp. 40-41

Katz, Ephraim. The Film Encyclopedia. New York: Perigee, 1979, p. 895

Kaufman, Dave. TV 70. New York: Signet, 1969, pp. 23-25

Kelley, Kitty. His Way. New York: Bantam, 1986, pp. 517-18, 520

Kiersch, Mary. Curtis Bernhardt. Metuchen, N.J.: Scarecrow Press, 1986, pp. 96, 106, 171-72

Kinnard, Roy, and R. J. Vitone. The American Films of Michael Curtiz. Metuchen, N.J.: Scarecrow Press, 1986, p. 135

Kleno, Larry. Kim Novak on Camera. La Jolla, Calif.: Barnes, 1980, pp. 65-66, 68-69, 183, 316, 264

Knight, Arthur, intro. The New York Times Directory of the Film. New York: Arno/Random House, 1971, pp. 88, 109-10, 191, 261, 904

Kobal, John. Gotta Sing Gotta Dance. New York: Hamlyn, 1970,
pp. 283, 285

Koch, Howard. As Time Goes By. New York: Harcourt Brace
Jovanovich, 1979, p. 112

LaGuardia, Robert, and Gene Arceri. Red: The Tempestuous Life
of Susan Hayward. New York: Macmillan, 1985, p. 115

Lamour, Dorothy, with Dick McInnes. My Side of the Road. Englewood Cliffs, N.J.: Prentice-Hall, 1980, p. 120

Lawton, Richard, with Hugo Leckey. Grand Illusions. New York:
McGraw-Hill, 1973, p. 218

Leigh, Janet. There Really Was a Hollywood. Garden City, N.Y.:
Doubleday, 1984, p. 146

Leighton, Frances Spatz. The Search for the Real Nancy Reagan.
New York: Macmillan, 1987, p. 49

Lemza, Douglas, ed. Rediscovering the American Cinema. New
York: Films Incorporated, 1977, pp. 78, 98, 178, 215

Libby, Bill. They Didn't Win the Oscars. Westport, Conn.: Arlington House, 1980, pp. 126, 186

Lieberman, Susan, and Frances Cable. Memorable Film Characters.
Westport, Conn.: Greenwood Press, 1984, pp. 4, 119, 138, 281

Likeness, George. The Oscar People. Mendota, Ill.: Wayside, 1965,
pp. 150, 260, 263

Linet, Beverly. Susan Hayward: Portrait of a Survivor. New York:
Atheneum, 1980, p. 205

Lloyd, Ann, and David Robinson, eds. Movies of the Fifties. London:
Orbis, 1982, pp. 88-89

Lloyd, Ann, and David Robinson, eds. Movies of the Forties. London: Orbis, 1982, p. 30

Lloyd, Ann, and Graham Fuller. The Illustrated Who's Who of the
Cinema. New York: Macmillan, 1983, p. 339

Madsen, Axel. William Wyler. New York: Crowell, 1973, pp. 304,
322, 434

Mailer, Norman. An American Dream. New York: Dell, 1966. Movie
edition of novel

Maltin, Leonard, ed. The Real Stars. New York: Curtis, 1973,
pp. 116, 121, 241, 307

Maltin, Leonard, ed. The Real Stars #2. New York: Curtis, the
1970s, pp. 122-23, 126-28, 212, 224

Maltin, Leonard, ed. The Real Stars. New York: Popular Library,
1979, pp. 93, 106, 201, 207, 242, 266

Maltin, Leonard, James Robert Parish, and Florence Solomon, eds.
TV Movies. New York: Signet, 1969, pp. 10, 21, 45, 74, 83, 102,
119, 140, 210-11, 231, 251, 262, 273, 287, 297-98, 307, 310, 323,
325, 328, 347, 352, 368, 385, 402, 412, 473, 476, 498-500, 503, 524

Mank, Gregory William. The Hollywood Hissables. Metuchen, N.J.:
Scarecrow Press, 1989, p. 444

Marill, Alvin H. Movies Made for Television. Westport, Conn.:
Arlington House, 1980, pp. 55, 57, 116, 130, 250, 278, 325

Marill, Alvin H. Robert Mitchum on the Screen. So. Brunswick,
N.J.: Barnes, 1978, p. 164

Marshall, J. D. Blueprint on Babylon. Tempe, Ariz.: Phoenix
House, 1978, p. 307

Martin, Mick, and Marsha Porter. Video Movie Guide: 1987. New
York: Ballantine, 1986, pp. 183, 554, 804

Martin, Mick, Marsha Porter, and Ed Remitz. Video Movie Guide
for Kids. New York: Ballantine, 1987, pp. 257, 334

Massey, Raymond. A Hundred Different Lives. Boston: Little,
Brown, 1979, pp. 410-414

Maugham, W. Somerset. The Painted Veil (The Seventh Sin).
New York: Pocket Books, 1957. Movie edition of novel

McBride, Joseph, ed. Frank Capra. Washington, D.C.: The
American Film Institute, 1982, p. 60

McBride, Joseph. Kirk Douglas. New York: Pyramid, 1976, pp.
57-59, 149

McCarty, Clifford. Bogey: The Films of Humphrey Bogart. New
York: Citadel, 1965, pp. 136, 152-53

McClelland, Doug. The Golden Age of "B" Movies. Nashville, Tenn.:
Charter House, 1978, pp. 13, 65-67

McClelland, Doug. Hollywood on Hollywood: Tinsel Town Talks. Winchester, Mass.: Faber & Faber, 1985, pp. x, 55 100, 100, 100,100, 000

McClelland, Doug. Hollywood on Ronald Reagan: Friends and Enemies Discuss Our President, The Actor. Winchester, Mass.: Faber & Faber, 1983, pp. 8, 129, 131, 134, 208, 243

McClelland, Doug. StarSpeak: Hollywood on Everything. Winchester, Mass.: Faber & Faber, 1987, pp. 65-66, 74-75, 241

McClelland, Doug. Susan Hayward: The Divine Bitch. New York: Pinnacle, 1973, pp. 129, 178

McClelland, Doug. The Unkindest Cuts: The Scissors and the Cinema. So. Brunswick, N.J.: Barnes, 1972, pp. 79-80, 191

McClure, Arthur, and Ken D. Jones. Star Quality. So. Brunswick, N.J.: Barnes, 1974, p. 91

McClure, Arthur F., Alfred E. Twomey, and Ken Jones. More Character People. Secaucus, N.J.: Citadel, 1984, p. 71

McNeil, Alex. Total Television: 1948-Present. New York: Penguin, 1984, pp. 93, 761

Mellen, Joan. Big Bad Wolves: Masculinity in the American Film. New York: Pantheon, 1977, pp. 16, 194

Meyer, William R. Warner Brothers Directors. New Rochelle, N.Y.: Arlington House, 1978, pp. 95-96, 108, 139, 319, 321

Michael, Paul. The Academy Awards: A Pictorial History. New York: Crown, 1982, pp. 211, 429-30

Michael, Paul. Humphrey Bogart: The Man and His Films. New York: Bobbs-Merrill, 1965, pp. 150-51

Michael, Paul, and James Robert Parish. The American Movies Reference Book: The Sound Era. Englewood Cliffs, N.J.: Prentice-Hall, 1969, pp. 28, 178, 194-95, 248, 312, 367-69, 381, 418, 495

Michael, Paul, and James Robert Parish. The Emmy Awards. New York: Crown, 1970, p. 327

Miller, Don. "B" Movies. New York: Curtis, 1973, pp. 268-70

Miller, Maud M., ed. Winchester's Screen Encyclopedia. London: Winchester, 1948, p. 151

Minnelli, Vincente, with Hector Arce. I Remember It Well. New York: Doubleday, 1974, p. 332

Moix, Terenci. Hollywood Stories. Barcelona, Spain: Lumen, 1971. Photo with Robert Taylor.

Monaco, James. Who's Who in American Film Now. New York: Zoetrope, 1981, p. 140

Montgomery, Elizabeth Miles. The Best of MGM. New York: Gallery,
1986, pp. 125, 137

Morella, Joe, and Edward Z. Epstein. Lana: The Public and Private
Lives of Miss Turner. New York: Citadel, 1971, pp. 119, 152

Morella, Joe, and Edward Z. Epstein. Rebels: The Rebel Hero in
Films. New York: Citadel, 1971, pp. 23-26

Morella, Joe, and Edward Z. Epstein. Jane Wyman. New York:
Delacorte, 1985, pp. 100, 166

Morella, Joe, Edward Z. Epstein, and Eleanor Clark. Those Great
Movie Ads. New Rochelle, N.Y.: Arlington House, 1972, pp. 8,
49, 94, 126, 160

Morella, Joe, Edward Z. Epstein, and John Griggs. The Films of
World War II. Secaucus, N.J.: Citadel, 1973, pp. 122, 211, 226-28

Moreno, Eduardo. The Films of Susan Hayward. Secaucus, N.J.:
Citadel, 1979, p. 210

Morino, Marianne. The Hollywood Walk of Fame. Berkeley, Calif.:
Ten Speed Press, 1987, p. 278

Morris, George. John Garfield. New York: Jove, 1977, pp. 98-99,
101-102, 104-105, 152

Munn, Michael. Charlton Heston. New York: St. Martin's, 1986,
pp. 57, 210

National Board of Review, The. 500 Best American Films to Buy,
Rent or Videotape. New York: Pocket Books, 1985, pp. 102, 293,
332, 397

Neal, Patricia, with Richard DeNeut. As I Am. New York: Simon
& Schuster, 1988, pp. 117-18, 345

Nobile, Philip, ed. Favorite Movies: Critics' Choice. New York:
Macmillan, 1973, p. 246

Nowlan, Robert A., and Gwendolyn Wright Nowlan. Cinema Sequels
and Remakes, 1903-1987. Jefferson, N.C.: McFarland, 1988, pp.
117-18, 227-28, 556-58, 575, 579, 592, 660, 838

Osborne, Robert. Academy Awards Illustrated. Hollywood: Marvin
Miller, 1965, pp. 175, 183, 215

Ottoson, Robert. A Reference Guide to the American Film Noir.
Metuchen, N.J.: Scarecrow Press, 1981, pp. 31-32, 59

Parish, James Robert. Actors' Television Credits: 1950-1972.
Metuchen, N.J.: Scarecrow Press, 1973, p. 647

Parish, James Robert. Good Dames. Cranbury, N.J.: Barnes,
1974, pp. 45-47, 74, 100, 102, 129-30, 223, 239

Parish, James Robert, and Alvin H. Marill. The Cinema of Edward
G. Robinson. So. Brunswick, N.J.: Barnes, 1972, pp. 206-207

Parish, James Robert, and Don E. Stanke. The All-Americans.
New Rochelle, N.Y.: Arlington House, 1977, pp. 71, 160, 278,
305, 333-34, 359-60

Parish, James Robert, and Don E. Stanke. The Forties Gals. Westport, Conn.: Arlington House, 1980, pp. 98, 131, 158-59, 188-89,
292, 405, 431-32, 435

Parish, James Robert, and Don E. Stanke. The Glamour Girls.
New Rochelle, N.Y.: Arlington House, 1975, pp. 529, 556, 566, 573

Parish, James Robert, and Don E. Stanke. The Leading Ladies.
New Rochelle, N.Y.: Arlington House, 1977, pp. 66, 90, 133, 143,
151, 172, 192, 264, 463, 485

Parish, James Robert, and Don E. Stanke. The Swashbucklers.
New Rochelle, N.Y.: Arlington House, 1976, pp. 306, 308-9, 343,
345, 377, 409

Parish, James Robert, and Gregory Mank. The Best of MGM. Westport, Conn.: Arlington House, 1981, pp. 104, 126

Parish, James Robert, and Lennard DeCarl. Hollywood Players:
The Forties. New Rochelle, N.Y.: Arlington House, 1976, pp. 44,
202, 279, 521-22

Parish, James Robert, and Michael R. Pitts. The Great Gangster
Pictures. Metuchen, N.J.: Scarecrow Press, 1976, pp. 73-74

Parish, James Robert, and Michael R. Pitts. The Great Spy Pictures.
Metuchen, N.J.: Scarecrow Press, 1974, p. 324

Parish, James Robert, and Michael R. Pitts. The Great Spy Pictures
II. Metuchen, N.J.: Scarecrow Press, 1986, p. 52

Parish, James Robert, and Michael R. Pitts. The Great Western
Pictures. Metuchen, N.J.: Scarecrow Press, 1976, pp. 96-97

160   Eleanor Parker

Parish, James Robert, and Michael R. Pitts with Gregory Mank.
Hollywood on Hollywood. Metuchen, N.J.: Scarecrow Press, 1978,
pp. 165, 201, 275-76, 389-90

Parish, James Robert, and Ronald L. Bowers. The MGM Stock Company. New Rochelle, N.Y.: Arlington House, 1973, pp. 123, 271,
297

Parish, James Robert, and Vincent Terrace. Actors' Television
Credits: Supplement II, 1977-1981. Metuchen, N.J.: Scarecrow
Press, 1982, p. 240

Parish, James Robert, and William T. Leonard. The Funsters. New
Rochelle, N.Y.: Arlington House, 1979, pp. 54, 299

Parish, James Robert, with Gregory W. Mank. The Hollywood Relia-
bles. Westport, Conn.: Arlington House, 1980, pp. 25-26, 42

Parish, James Robert, with Mark Rost. Actors' Television Credits:
Supplement I. Metuchen, N.J.: Scarecrow Press, 1978, p. 310

Parish, James Robert, with Vincent Terrace. Actors' Television
Credits: Supplement III, 1982-1985. Metuchen, N.J.: Scarecrow
Press, 1986, p. 322

Peary, Danny, ed. Close-Ups. New York: Workman, 1978, p. 349

Peary, Danny. Guide for the Film Fanatic. New York: Fireside,
1986, p. 263

Perry, Jeb. H. Universal Television: The Studio and Its Programs,
1950-1980. Metuchen, N.J.: Scarecrow Press, 1983, pp. 9-10,
237-38

Pettigrew, Terence. Bogart. New York: Proteus, 1978, pp. 131-32,
142

Pickard, Roy. Who Played Who in the Movies. New York: Schocken,
1981, p. 128

Picturegoer Film Annual: 1951-52. London: Odhams, pp. 8, 109

Pitts, Michael R. Western Movies: A TV and Video Guide to 4200
Genre Films. Jefferson, N.C.: McFarland, 1986, pp. 119, 186, 207,
253

Pratley, Gerald. The Cinema of Otto Preminger. New York: Barnes,
1971, p. 111

Prichard, Susan Perez. Film Costume: An Annotated Bibliography.
Metuchen, N.J.: Scarecrow Press, 1981, pp. 439, 463

Quigley, Martin, Jr., and Richard Gertner. Films in America: 1929-1969. New York: Golden, 1970, pp. 57, 239, 311

Quinlan, David. Quinlan's Illustrated Directory of Film Stars. London: Batsford, 1986, p. 339

Quirk, Lawrence J. The Films of Joan Crawford. New York: Citadel, 1968, pp. 155, 172

Quirk, Lawrence J. The Films of Robert Taylor. Secaucus, N.J.: Citadel, 1975, pp. 20-21, 126-28, 140-41, 145-46, 221

Quirk, Lawrence J. The Films of William Holden. Secaucus, N.J.: Citadel, 1973, pp. 146-49

Quirk, Lawrence J. Jane Wyman: The Actress and the Woman. New York: Dembner, 1986, pp. 74, 209

Ragan, David. Who's Who in Hollywood. New Rochelle, N.Y.: Arlington House, 1976, p. 345

Reagan, Nancy, with Bill Libby. Nancy. New York: Berkley, 1981, p. 111

Reagan, Ronald, with Richard G. Hubler. Where's the Rest of Me? New York: Duell, Sloan & Pearce, 1965, p. 193

Reed, Rex. Do You Sleep in the Nude? New York: New American Library, 1968, p. 183

Ringgold, Gene, and Clifford McCarty. The Films of Frank Sinatra. New York: Citadel, 1971, pp. 102-103, 151-52, 217

Ringgold, Gene, and DeWitt Bodeen. Chevalier: The Films and Career of Maurice Chevalier. Secaucus, N.J.: Citadel, 1973, pp. 221, 224

Rivkin, Allen, and Laura Kerr. Hello, Hollywood! New York: Doubleday, 1962, p. 314

Rose, Helen. Just Make Them Beautiful. Santa Monica, Calif.: Dennis-Landman, 1976, pp. 48, 99-100, 130

Rosen, Marjorie. Popcorn Venus. New York: Coward, McCann & Geoghegan, 1973, p. 294

Rovin, Jeff. The Films of Charlton Heston. Secaucus, N.J.: Citadel, 1977, pp. 50-52

Sadoul, Georges. Dictionary of Films. Berkeley: University of California Press, 1972, p. 210

Sarris, Andrew. The American Cinema. New York: Dutton, 1968, p. 174

Schary, Dore. Heyday. New York: Berkley, 1981, pp. 241, 257

Scherle, Victor, and William Turner Levy. The Films of Frank Capra. Secaucus, N.J.: Citadel, 1977, pp. 50-52

Scheuer, Steven H., ed. The Complete Guide to Videocassette Movies. New York: Henry Holt, 1987, pp. 157, 189, 369, 427, 494, 529

Scheuer, Steven H. TV Movie Almanac & Ratings: 1958 & 1959. New York: Bantam, 1958, pp. 16, 27, 33, 40, 57, 113, 134, 136, 143, 145, 151, 165, 229

Schoell, William. Stay Out of the Shower. New York: Dembner, 1985, p. 118

Schulman, Arnold. A Hole in the Head. Greenwich, Conn.: Gold Medal, 1959. Novelization of film

Schuster, Mel. Motion Picture Performers: A Bibliography of Magazine and Periodical Articles, 1900-1969. Metuchen, N.J.: Scarecrow Press, 1971, p. 512

Schuster, Mel. Motion Picture Performers: A Bibliography of Magazine and Periodical Articles, Supplement No. 1, 1970-1974. Metuchen, N.J.: Scarecrow Press, 1976, p. 568

Sennett, Ted. Great Movie Directors. New York: Abrams, 1986, pp. 34, 96, 206

Sennett, Ted. Hollywood Musicals. New York: Abrams, 1981, pp. 310-11

Sennett, Ted. Masters of Menace: Greenstreet and Lorre. New York: Dutton, 1979, pp. 115, 135-36, 139, 205-206

Sennett, Ted, ed. The Movie Buff's Book. New York: Pyramid, 1975, pp. 26, 53, 184

Sennett, Ted. Warner Brothers Presents. New Rochelle, N.Y.: Arlington House, 1971, pp. 48, 113, 196, 202, 217, 222, 252, 257-58, 268, 314, 395, 399, 401-402, 404-408, 411

Server, Lee. Screenwriter: Words Become Pictures. Pittstown, N.J.: Main Street, 1987, p. 228

Sinatra, Nancy. Frank Sinatra: My Father. Garden City, N.Y.: Doubleday, 1985, pp. 143, 339

Shaheen, Jack G. Nuclear War Films. Carbondale-Edwardsville:
Southern Illinois University Press, 1978, p. 179

Shale, Richard. Academy Awards. New York: Ungar, 1978, pp.
395, 400, 421

Shay, Don. Conversations. Albuquerque, N.M.: Kaleidoscope,
1969, pp. 113, 195

Sherk, Dr. Warren. Agnes Moorehead: A Very Private Person.
Philadelphia: Dorrance, 1976, pp. 36-37

Shipman, David. The Great Movie Stars: The Golden Years. New
York: Crown, 1970, pp. 201, 365, 487, 541

Shipman, David. The Great Movie Stars: The International Years.
New York: St. Martin's, 1972, pp. 14, 312, 384-85

Shipman, David. The Story of Cinema. New York: St. Martin's.
1982, pp. 684, 850, 905

Slide, Anthony, ed. Selected Film Criticism: 1941-50. Metuchen,
N.J.: Scarecrow Press, 1983, p. 155

Slide, Anthony, ed. Selected Film Criticism: 1951-60. Metuchen,
N.J.: Scarecrow Press, 1985, p. 73

Spada, James. Grace: The Secret Lives of a Princess. New York:
Doubleday, 1987, p. 88

Speed. F. Maurice. Film Review: 1951-52. London: MacDonald,
p. 14

Speed. F. Maurice. Film Review: 1958-59. London: MacDonald,
p. 116

Springer, John. Forgotten Films to Remember. Secaucus, N.J.:
Citadel, 1980, pp. 125, 134-35, 200, 218-19

Steen, Mike. Hollywood Speaks. New York: Putnam, 1974, pp. 197-
98

Steinberg, Cobbett S. Film Facts. New York: Facts on File, 1980,
pp. 97, 219-20, 226, 332

Stine. Whitney, with Bette Davis. Mother Goddam. New York:
Berkley Medallion, 1974, pp. 60, 259, 376, 384

Strick, Philip. Great Movie Actresses. New York: Beech Tree.
1982, p. 153

Swanson, Gloria. <u>Swanson on Swanson</u>. New York: Random House, 1980, pp. 249, 251, 258

Swindell, Larry. <u>Body and Soul: The Story of John Garfield</u>. New York: William Morrow, 1975, pp. 188, 192-93, 198, 278

Swindell, Larry. <u>The Last Hero: A Biography of Gary Cooper</u>. Garden City, N.Y.: Doubleday, 1980, pp. 267, 273

Taylor, John Russell, and Arthur Jackson. <u>The Hollywood Musical</u>. New York: McGraw-Hill, 1971, p. 142

Terrace, Vincent. <u>The Complete Encyclopedia of Television Programs: 1947-1949</u>. So. Brunswick, N.J.: Barnes, 1979, p. 136

Terrace, Vincent. <u>Encyclopedia of Television: The Index--Who's Who 1937-1984</u>. New York: Zoetrope, 1986, p. 292

Thomas, Bob. <u>Golden Boy: The Untold Story of William Holden</u>. New York: St. Martin's, 1983, pp. 83, 101-102, 145, 268

Thomas, Tony. <u>The Films of Kirk Douglas</u>. Secaucus, N.J.: Citadel, 1972, pp. 80, 82-83

Thomas, Tony. <u>The Films of Ronald Reagan</u>. Secaucus, N.J.: Citadel, 1980, pp. 153-55, 168

Thomas, Tony. <u>The Great Adventure Films</u>. Secaucus, N.J.: Citadel, 1976, pp. 172, 174-75

Thomas, Tony. <u>Music for the Movies</u>. So. Brunswick, N.J.: Barnes, 1973, p. 137

Thomas, Tony, and Aubrey Solomon. <u>The Films of 20th Century-Fox</u>. Secaucus, N.J.: Citadel, 1979, pp. 226, 331, 339, 356

Thomas, Tony, Rudy Behlmer, and Clifford McCarty. <u>The Films of Errol Flynn</u>. New York: Citadel, 1969, pp. 144-45, 148-50, 160

Thompson, Howard, ed. <u>The New York Times Guide to Movies on TV</u>. Chicago: Quadrangle, 1970, pp. 17, 41, 45, 58, 66, 93, 102, 109, 123, 127, 138, 171, 207, 211

Tomkies, Mike. <u>The Robert Mitchum Story: "It Sure Beats Working."</u> Chicago: Regnery, 1972, p. 264

Tornabene, Lyn. <u>Long Live the King</u>. New York: Putnam, 1976, p. 352

Trent, Paul, and Richard Lawton. <u>The Image Makers</u>. New York: McGraw-Hill, 1972, p. 183

Tucker, Rob, and Les Adams. Ronald Reagan: From the Silver
Screen to the White House. Lubbock, Tex.: Nickelodeon, 1981,
pp. 58-59

Turner, Adrian. Hollywood 1950s. New York: Gallery, 1986, p.
24

Tuska, Jon. The Detective in Hollywood. Garden City, N.Y.:
Doubleday, 1978, pp. 364-65

Twomey, Alfred E., and Arthur F. McClure. The Versatiles. So.
Brunswick, N.J.: Barnes, 1969, p. 90

Valenti, Peter. Errol Flynn: A Bio-Bibliography. Westport, Conn.:
Greenwood Press, 1984, pp. 39, 90, 136, 139, 143

Valentino, Lou. The Films of Lana Turner. Secaucus, N.J.: Citadel, 1976, pp. 215, 264

Van Daalen, Nicholas. The Complete Book of Movie Lists. Toronto,
Ont.: Pagurian, 1979, pp. 97, 193

Vermilye, Jerry. Bette Davis. New York: Pyramid, 1973, pp. 99,
106, 129, 139, 145

Vermilye, Jerry. The Films of the Thirties. Secaucus, N.J.:
Citadel, 1982, p. 127

Vermilye, Jerry. Ida Lupino. New York: Pyramid, 1977, pp. 58,
84, 93, 102, 151

Warman, Eric, ed. Preview 1955. London: Dakers, 1955, pp. 156-57

Warner, Alan. Who Sang What on the Screen. No. Ryde, NSW,
Australia: Angus & Robertson, 1984, p. 21

Wayne, Jane Ellen. Crawford's Men. New York: Prentice-Hall,
1988, pp. xii, 192

Wayne, Jane Ellen. Gable's Women. New York: Prentice-Hall, 1987,
pp. 249, 258, 294

Wayne, Jane Ellen. The Life of Robert Taylor. New York: Warner,
1973, pp. 166-69

Wayne, Jane Ellen. Stanwyck. Toronto, Canada-New York: Paper-
Jacks, 1987, pp. 142, 146-47

Weaver. John T. Forty Years of Screen Credits, Vol. 2: K-Z.
Metuchen, N.J.: Scarecrow Press, 1970, pp. 1080-81

Wiley, Mason, and Damien Bona. Inside Oscar. New York: Ballantine, 1986, pp. 205, 213-14, 258, 261, 264-65

Williams, Chester. Gable. New York: Fleet, 1968, pp. 123, 154

Willis, Donald C. The Films of Frank Capra. Metuchen, N.J.: Scarecrow Press, 1972, p. 121

Willis, Donald C. Horror and Science Fiction Films: A Checklist. Metuchen, N.J.: Scarecrow Press, 1972, pp. 151, 283, 341

Willis, John, ed. Screen World: 1966. New York: Crown, 1966, pp. 34-35, 228

Willis, John, ed. Screen World: 1967. New York: Crown. 1967, pp. 7, 22-23, 67, 228

Willis, John, ed. Screen World: 1968. New York: Crown, 1968, pp. 8, 213, 224

Willis, John, ed. Screen World: 1969. New York: Crown, 1969, p. 227

Willis, John, ed. Screen World: 1970. New York: Crown, 1970, pp. 42, 229

Willis, John, ed. Screen World: 1971. New York: Crown, 1971, p. 232

Willis, John, ed. Screen World: 1972. New York: Crown, 1972, p. 231

Willis, John, ed. Screen World: 1974. New York: Crown, 1974, p. 226

Willis, John, ed. Screen World: 1980. New York: Crown, 1980, p. 112

Willis, John. Theatre World: 1971-1972. New York: Crown, 1973, p. 145

Wills, Garry. Reagan's America: Innocents at Home. Garden City, N.Y.: Doubleday, 1987, p. 156

Wilson, Arthur, ed. The Warner Bros. Golden Anniversary Book. New York: Dell, 1973, pp. 117, 119, 121-28, 132-34, 164

Wilson, Ivy Crane, ed. Hollywood in the 1940s. New York: Ungar, 1980, pp. 78, 159

Wood, Michael. America in the Movies. New York: Basic Books, 1975, p. 41

Zinman, David. 50 from the 50's. New Rochelle, N.Y.: Arlington House, 1979, pp. 91-92, 94-96, 187-88, 193

B. Magazines

Addison, George. "Above and Beyond." Film Index (Australia), no date

Asher, Jerry. "The Reformation of Ronnie." Screenland, Sept. 1947

Balling, Fredda Dudley. "We Remember Hollywood." Movie Digest, Jan. 1972

Balling, Fredda Dudley. "We Remember Hollywood." Movie Digest, Sept. 1972

Balling, Fredda Dudley. "We Remember Hollywood." Movie Digest, Jan. 1973

Barnett, Hoyt. "The Winner, Joe Palooka!" Motion Picture, June 1946

Bawden, James. "Ronald Neame." Films in Review, Jan. 1987

Behlmer, Rudy. "Erich Wolfgang Korngold." Films in Review, Jan. 1967

Bodeen, DeWitt. "Rex Ingram and Alice Terry." Films in Review, March 1975

Bowers, Lynn. "What Hollywood Itself Is Talking About!" Screenland, Sept. 1949

Bowers, Lynn. "What Hollywood Itself Is Talking About!" Screenland, May 1954

Bowers, Ronald. "The 50th Academy Awards." Films in Review, May 1978

Bowers, Ronald L. "Joan Blondell." Films in Review, April 1972

Brew, Alice. Letter. Picturegoer (England), Oct. 30, 1954

Briggs, Colin. "Bad Girls in Prison." Hollywood Studio Magazine, Sept. 1984

Briggs, Colin. "Andrea King: A Career Profile." Hollywood Studio Magazine, May 1985

Britannicus, Cato. "Why the Stars Shine." Films in Review, Oct. 1955

Brown, Barry. "Henry Travers." Films in Review, June-July 1974

Brunas, John. "Gladys George." Film Fan Monthly. March 1972

Buckley, Michael. "Gig Young." Films in Review, Feb. 1971

Buckley, Michael. "Irving Rapper." Films in Review, Aug.-Sept. 1986

Buckley, Michael. "Lee Grant." Films in Review, Aug.-Sept. 1987

Buckley, Michael. "Patricia Neal." Films in Review, April 1983

Buckley, Michael and Marie. "And the Nominees Are." Films in Review, May 1978

Cameron, Ian, Mark Shivas, Paul Mayersberg, and V. F. Perkins. "Richard Brooks." Movie, Spring 1965

Caylor, Ron. "How Reagan's Leading Ladies Rate Him in the White House." National Enquirer, Feb. 16, 1982

Chic (Cuba). Cover with Anthony Dexter. Nov. 1951

Churchill, Reba and Bonnie. "Hollywood Earfuls." Silver Screen, Sept. 1950

Churchill, Reba and Bonnie. "Hollywood Earfuls." Silver Screen, June 1952

Ciné-Miroir (France). "Never Say Goodbye." July 20, 1948

Ciné Revue (France). Cover with Errol Flynn. May 23, 1946

Cinémonde (France). Cover with Anthony Dexter. Aug. 23, 1951

Cinémonde (France). "Histoire de Detective (Detective Story)." Aug. 1, 1952

Cinémonde (France). Photo. Oct. 1, 1954

Cinémonde (France). "'Scaramouche' Fait Mouche." Christmas, 1952

Cinévie (France). Photo with Errol Flynn. Oct. 31, 1945

Clarens, Carlos. "Clark Gable: 1901-1960." Films in Review, Dec. 1960

Connolly, Mike. "Hollywood Report." Modern Screen, April 1952

Connor, Edward. "The Sound Track." Films in Review, May 1955

Cooper, Marion. "Guns and Music ... " Screen Stars, Jan. 1945

Crivello, Kirk. "The Fate of the Warner Bros. Actresses." Hollywood Studio Magazine, June 1979

Davies, Joseph E. "Why We Must Understand Russia!" Photoplay, July 1943

Demchek, Jim. "Letters: Memorable Performances." Films in Review, Feb. 1958

Dickens, Homer. "Sydney Greenstreet." Screen Facts 1964

Druesne, Maeve. "Tuesday Weld." Films in Review, Feb. 1986

East, Weston. "Here's Hollywood." Screenland, July 1947

Ecran (Chile). Cover with Anthony Dexter. 1951

Eiga No Tomo (Japan). "Detective Story." Feb. 1942

Eiga No Tomo (Japan). "Scaramouche." Oct. 1952

Eliason, Richard. "Letters: Unforgotten Movie Moments." Films in Review, April 1959

Ellis, Lester. "StarSpeak: Book Is a Funfest!" Hollywood Studio Magazine, June 1987

Esquire. "ME? A movie about me? Manny, it's a natural." Jan. 1967

Fangoria. "The Pit and the Pen of Alex Gordon." June 1985

Film Complet (France). Cover with Humphrey Bogart/"Pilot de Diable (Chain Lightning)." July 19, 1951

Film Complet (France). Cover with Ronald Reagan/"Aventure à Deux (The Voice of the Turtle)." Dec. 30, 1948

FilmJournalen (Sweden). Photo with Bert Friedlob. Jan. 27, 1952

Films and Filming (England). Cover with George Hamilton. Feb. 1960

Films in Review. Cover with Glenn Ford. April 1955

Films in Review. Cover with Stewart Granger. June-July 1952

Films in Review. "Hors D'Oeuvres." Dec. 1955

Frolick, Billy. "Notes on 'The Oscar'." Premiere, April 1988

G. Brans Kleine Romans (Holland). "Caged." Sept. 29, 1950

Griffiths, J. Letter. Picturegoer (England), Jan. 22, 1954

Gwynn, Edith. "Hollywood Party Line." Photoplay, July 1953

Gwynn, Edith. "Hollywood Party Line." Photoplay, Aug. 1954

Hagan, Ray. "What All the Shouting Was About." Screen Facts, May-June 1963

Haspiel, James Robert. "Kim Novak: Yesterday's Superstar." Films in Review, Feb. 1978

Hawk, Bob. "Photoquiz." Look, May 14, 1946

Hebdo Roman (France). Cover with Clark Gable, Jean Willes/"Le Roi et Quatre Reines (The King and Four Queens)." May 18, 1959

Holland, Jack. "Let's Visit the Sets." Silver Screen, Aug. 1947

Holland, Jack. "Let's Visit the Sets." Silver Screen, Dec. 1949

Hollywood Studio Magazine. "Movie Trivia." June 1984

Hollywood Studio Magazine. "The Warner Women." Jan.-Feb. 1986

Hollywood Studio Magazine. "What Makes a Lady and What Makes a Broad?" May 1985

Horsfall, Bunty. Letter. Picturegoer (England), Oct. 1, 1955

Hunter, Jack F. "Ronald Reagan." Films in Review, April 1967

Hurd, Reggie, Jr. "Academy Award Mistakes." Films in Review, May 1955

Jason, Johnny. "Joan Collins and the 'B' Movie Queens!" Hollywood Studio Magazine, Dec. 1987

Jones, Russ. "En Garde!" Flashback, June 1972

King, Toni. "Readers Inc...." Photoplay, July 1952

Kinskey, Leonid. "As Time Goes By...." Movie Digest, Sept. 1972

Kreuger, Miles. "Dubbers to the Stars." High Fidelity, July 1972

Lee, Mary. "The Feature Attraction." Silver Screen, April 1948

Lee, Mary. "A Head for Beauty." Silver Screen, July 1942

Le film du coeur (France). Cover with Liana Orfei/"La Femme dans
Les Tenèbres (Lizzie)." Dec. 5, 1964

Life. "Lustre Creme Movie Star Sweepstakes." Sept. 17, 1956

Life. "A Peak for Portraits." Aug. 13, 1956

Lippe, Richard. "Kim Novak: A Resistance to Definition." Cine-
Action!, Dec. 1986

Look. Ad for Lustre Creme Shampoo. June 15, 1954

Look. "Hollywood Keeps Fit, Too." Feb. 19, 1946

Look. "Look's Film Forecast for 1944." Jan. 25, 1944

Look. "Mrs. Gable keeps her eye on the KING while he makes a
movie with four queens." Sept. 4, 1956

Loutzenhiser, James K. "Hugo Haas." Films in Review, Feb. 1978

Macklin, F. Anthony. "Charlton Heston: 'I Like to Think of Myself
as a Professional'." Film Heritage, Fall 1974

Madden, David. "Marble Goddesses and Mortal Flesh." The Film
Journal, Sept. 1972

Malone, John. "Five Great Bad Movies." The Dial, Feb. 1981

Maltin, Leonard. "John Cromwell." Action, May-June 1973

Maltin, Leonard, Jim Meyer, Doug McClelland, and Herman G. Weinberg.
"My 10 Favorite Films." Filmograph, 1970

Mank, Gregory. "Josephine Hutchinson." Films in Review, Nov. 1980

Marill, Alvin H. "Films on TV." Films in Review, Feb. 1978

Marill, Alvin H. "Films on TV." Films in Review, Aug.-Sept. 1975

Marill, Alvin H. "Stanley Kramer's Films ... on Television." Films
in Review, March 1985

Marill, Alvin H. "The Television Scene." Films in Review, Nov. 1980

Marshack, Laddie. "Moviemaking on Sutton Street." TV Guide,
Jan. 30, 1971

Maynard, John. "They Took Their Love to Las Vegas." Modern Screen, April 1951

McCarty, Clifford. "Letters: 'Men of the Sky'." Films in Review, Jan. 1966

McClelland, Doug. "Book Reviews: Hollywood Musicals, by Ted Sennett." Films in Review, Dec. 1981

McClelland, Doug. "Books & Periodicals: 'The Films of World War II,' by Joe Morella, Edward Z. Epstein and John Griggs." Filmograph, 1973

McClelland, Doug. "Jean Sullivan." Hollywood Studio Magazine, Jan. -Feb. 1986

McClelland, Doug. "Merande of the Movies ... Reluctantly." After Dark, Nov. 1973

McClelland, Doug. "Paul Clemens, Hollywood Thoroughbred." Hollywood Studio Magazine, July 1988

McClure, Donald. "Hollywood Earfuls." Silver Screen, Dec. 1949

McClure, Donald. "Hollywood Earfuls." Silver Screen, May 1950

Meyer, Jim. "A Conversation with Martha Hyer." Filmograph, 1972

Meyers, Malcolm F. "Letters: Beauties." Films in Review, Jan. 1959

Miller, Mark A., with Sharon Lind Williams. "Virginia Karns Is MOTHER GOOSE." Filmfax, Oct. 1988

Modern Screen. Ad for Lustre Creme Shampoo. June 1954

Modern Screen. Ad for Lustre-Net Hair Spray. May 1957

Mon Film (France). Cover with Charlton Heston/"Quand la Marabunta Gronde (The Naked Jungle)." Dec. 15, 1954

Mon Film (France). Cover with Errol Flynn, Patti Brady/"Ne Dites Jamais Adieu (Never Say Goodbye)." Feb. 2, 1949

Mon Film (France). Cover with Robert Taylor/"Le Grand Secret (Above and Beyond)." Dec. 23, 1953

Mon Film (France). "Scaramouche." May 6, 1953

Monsees, Robert A. "Maurice Chevalier: 1888-1972." Films in Review, May 1972

Morrison, Charlie. "The Mocambo Affair." Modern Screen, Jan. 1949

Motion Picture. Ad for book Many Rivers to Cross. March 1955

Motion Picture Herald. "Star Power in New 20th-Fox Productions."
May 13, 1964

Motion Picture. Photos. Dec. 1941; Sept. 1943; April 1946

Motion Picture. Photo with Errol Flynn. Nov. 1945

Motion Picture. Photo with William Bendix, Kirk Douglas. Feb. 1952

Movie Life. Rehearsal photos for The Man with the Golden Arm.
March, 1956

Movie Life Yearbook # 12. Photo with daughters Susan, Sharon and
her mother Mrs. Lola Parker. 1951

Movie Play. "Birthdays." March 1950

Movie Show. "Mission to Moscow." June 1943

Movie Show. Photo. Oct. 1945

Movie Show. Photo with Paul Henreid. Oct. 1945

Movie Show. "Pride of the Marines." Oct. 1945

Movie Spotlight. Photo with Kirk Douglas. Jan. 1952

Movie Spotlight. Photos with Miriam Rogers. Dec. 1949; April 1950

Movie Stars Parade. "Green Room Groups: Between Two Worlds
Cast Mix 'n' Shop Talk." July 1944

Movie Stars Parade. Item: Parker and deer. March 1950

Movie Stars Parade. Photo with Bert Friedlob. Aug. 1946

Movie Stars Parade. Photo with Robert Taylor. April 1954

Movie Stars Parade. "Too Many Santas." Dec. 1946

Movie Story. Fictionization of Caged. May 1950

Movie Story. Fictionization of Chain Lightning. Nov. 1949

Movie Story. Fictionization of Escape Me Never. April 1947

Movie Story. Fictionization of Of Human Bondage/"On the Set of
'Of Human Bondage'." Sept. 1946

Movie Story. Fictionization of Pride of the Marines. Oct. 1945

Movie Story. Photo with daughters Susan and Sharon. Sept. 1950

Movie Time. "Movie Time Takes You on Location in Egypt." Dec. 1954

Movie Time. Photo with Robert Taylor. Oct. 1954

Movieland. Item: Helping colleagues. June 1954

Movieland. Photo. April 1946

Movies. "Career Fashions that Double for Dates." Nov. 1943

Movies. Photo. Dec. 1954

Movies. Photo with Joe Kirkwood, Jr. Jan. 1952

Movies Then and Now. "Film Fandom in the Southwest--Where Do We Go From Here?" Second issue, 1989

Nogueira, Rui. "Robert Wise at Fox." Focus on Film, Spring 1973

Nogueira, Rui. "Writing for the Movies: Walter Newman." Focus on Film, Autumn 1972

Nolan, Jack Edmund. "Films on TV." Films in Review, May 1970

Nolan, Jack Edmund. "Films on TV." Films in Review, June-July 1973

Nolan, Jack Edmund. "Jerry Wald." Films in Review, Aug.-Sept. 1961

Novelle Film (Italy). Cover with Stewart Granger. May 26, 1956

O'Dowd, Brian. "Movies of '55." Hollywood Studio Magazine, Oct. 1987

O'Dowd, Brian. "Patricia Neal: A Great Actress Won't Give Up." Hollywood Studio Magazine, Sept. 1983

O'Dowd, Brian. "So Young ... So Beautiful!" Hollywood Studio Magazine, Dec. 1988

O'Leary, Dorothy. "End of Fantasy." Silver Screen, Nov. 1946

O'Leary, Dorothy. "His Life Is Unbelievable!" Silver Screen, April 1951

Parsons, Louella. "Good News." Modern Screen, Dec. 1953

Patterson, Charles. "Hollywood Talks!" Hollywood Studio Magazine,
March 1985

Photoplay. Ad for Woodbury Cold Cream. Nov. 1953

Photoplay. "Hollywood Clothes Line." Aug. 1949

Photoplay. "Inside Stuff." Sept. 1950

Photoplay. Item: Getting Interrupted Melody. Aug. 1955

Photoplay. Photo. Aug. 1949

Photoplay. Photo with Frank Sinatra, Edward G. Robinson, Carolyn
Jones, Frank Capra, Thelma Ritter. March 1959

Photoplay. Photo with Kim Novak, Mr. and Mrs. Arnold Stang.
March 1956

Photoplay. Photo with Leo Genn, Jean Simmons. Aug. 1952

Photoplay. Photo with Ronald Reagan. July 1947

Photoplay. "Your Needlework." March 1960

Photoplay Annual. Photo with Bert Friedlob. 1954

Photoplay Annual. Photo with daughters Susan and Sharon and with
her mother. 1951

Picture Show (England). Cover with Fred MacMurray/"A Millionaire
for Christy." Dec. 6, 1952

Picture Show (England). Cover with Glenn Ford/"Interrupted
Melody." Sept. 1955

Picture Show (England). Cover with Humphrey Bogart/"Chain Lightning." Aug. 4, 1950

Picture Show (England). Cover with Paul Henreid/"Between Two
Worlds." Dec. 2, 1944

Picture Show (England). Cover with Robert Taylor/"Many Rivers
to Cross." June 11, 1955

Picturegoer (England). Cover with Anthony Dexter. Aug. 18, 1951

Picturegoer (England). Max Factor Lipstick Ad. Dec. 18, 1954

Picturegoer (England). "What's Cooking." Feb. 20, 1954

Picturegoer (England). "Who's Who of the Stars? Eleanor Parker."
May 12, 1956

Picturegoer (England). "Wyman's Second Win; Douglas--After a
Recount." March 8, 1952

Purvis, Harry. "Letters: Of Cabbages & Kings." Films in Review,
March 1964

Quirk's Reviews. "Doug McClelland's 'Hollywood on Hollywood'."
March 1985

Ramsay, Hartley. "Letters: Casting Mistakes." Films in Review,
Nov. 1959

Record World. "Real-Life People Provide 3 Filmusicals, LPs in '64."
May 9, 1964

Reid, John Howard, others. "An American Dream." Film Index
(Australia), no date

Rexall Magazine, The. "Prize Winning Readers' Recipes to Help You
Save for Victory." Aug. 1943

Riley, Vicky. "Goodnight, Ladies." Photoplay, April 1951

Ringgold, Gene. "Robert Mitchum." Films in Review, May 1964

Roberts, John. "Who Were the 40's Most Beautiful?" Hollywood
Studio Magazine, May, 1984

Romances (Cuba). Cover with Gig Young. Feb. 1949

Rona Barrett's Hollywood. Photo with Raymond Hirsch. June 1973

Ross, Penelope. "John Garfield: The Rebel as Hero." Nostalgia
Illustrated, June 1975

Savage, Bill. "Letters: All-Time Bests." Films in Review, June-
July 1958

Schultz, Margie. "The Magic of Voice Dubbing." Hollywood Studio
Magazine, March 1988

Screen Facts. "The Academy Awards--Part Two: Best Actress."
1964

Screen Guide. Bio sketch. May 1951

Screen Guide. "Candids of the Month." Aug. 1947

Screen Guide. Photo with Robert Hutton, S. Z. Sakall. Feb. 1946

Screen Guide. Photo with Ronald Reagan. June 1947

Screen Hits Annual, 1952. Fictionization of Detective Story. 1952

Screen (Japan). "Interrupted Melody." Nov. 1957

Screen (Japan). "The Naked Jungle." July 1954

Screen (Japan). "Valentino." Feb. 1951

Screen (Japan). "Valley of the Kings." Nov. 1954

Screen Parade. Photo with Clark Gable. March 1957

Screen Romances. Fictionization of Between Two Worlds. July 1944

Screen Romances. Fictionization of Hollywood Canteen. Jan. 1945

Screen Romances. Fictionization of Never Say Goodbye. Aug. 1946

Screen Romances. Fictionization of The Very Thought of You. Dec. 1944

Screen Romances. Fictionization of The Voice of the Turtle. Jan. 1948

Screen Stars. "Angles on Ida." June 1947

Screen Stars. "Between Acts." Aug. 1946

Screen Stars. "Caught in the Act." June 1947

Screen Stories Annual, 1960. Fictionization of A Hole in the Head. 1960

Screen Stories. Fictionization of Detective Story. Nov. 1951

Screen Stories. Fictionization of Escape from Fort Bravo. Jan. 1954

Screen Stories. Fictionization of A Hole in the Head. Aug. 1959

Screen Stories. Fictionization of Home from the Hill. March 1960

Screen Stories. Fictionization of Interrupted Melody. March 1955

Screen Stories. Fictionization of The King and Four Queens. Dec. 1956

Screen Stories. Fictionization of The Man with the Golden Arm.
March 1956

Screen Stories. Fictionization of The Naked Jungle. April 1954

Screen Stories. Fictionization of Scaramouche. July 1952

Screen Stories. Fictionization of Valentino. Feb. 1951

Screen Stories. Fictionization of Valley of the Kings. July 1954

Screen Stories. Fictionization of The Woman in White. June 1948

Screen Stories. Photo. May 1948

Screen World. Photo with Jan Rubini, Anthony Dexter. April 1951

Screenland. Item: Filming The Naked Jungle. Oct. 1953

Screenland. Photo. Sept. 1944

Screenland. Photo with Bert Friedlob, Melvin Frank. May 1953

Screenland. Photo with Bette Davis, Gary Merrill. May 1953

Screenland. Photo with daughter Susan, parents Mr. and Mrs. Lester
D. Parker. Aug. 1950

Screenland. Photo with Dennis O'Keefe, Norman Millen, Steffi Duna.
June 1945

Show. "Screen Test." June 1963

Silver Screen. Item: Gets along with Robert Taylor. May 1954

Silver Screen. Item: On the set of The Mysterious Doctor. Dec.
1942

Silver Screen. Item: Parker writes from Egypt. Feb. 1954

Silver Screen. "New Fashions with a Smile." July 1943

Silver Screen. Photo. Jan. 1947

Silver Screen. Photo with Bert Friedlob. Dec. 1946

Silver Screen. Photo with Dane Clark, John Garfield. April 1946

Silver Screen. Photo with Ernest Borgnine. June 1956

Silver Screen. Photo with hairdresser. Jan. 1952

Silver Screen. Photo with Humphrey Bogart. Jan. 1950

Silver Screen. Photo with Humphrey Bogart. Nov. 1949

Silver Screen. Photo with Joe Kirkwood, Jr. Nov. 1945

Silver Screen. Photo with Robert Taylor. April 1954

Silver Screen. "Topics for Gossip." April 1943

Silver Screen. "Unlimited Affection." Sept. 1946

Stacy, Dorothy M. Letter. Screen Stars. Feb. 1963

Stanke, Don. "Ruth Roman." Film Fan Monthly, April 1973

Stark, Samuel. "Robert Wise." Films in Review, Jan. 1963

Stipanic, Pfc. Sam V. "Interesting Letters: 'Pride of the Marines'."
Motion Picture, Nov. 1945

Super-Star 1960-61 Information Chart. Modern Screen, 1960

Swisher, Viola Hegyi. "Center Theater Group's 'The Night of the
Iguana'." After Dark, March 1976

Thompson, George. "The Crumpled Marriage." Motion Picture,
Dec. 1963

Tildesley, Alice L. "Animal Actors." Movieland, Dec. 1945

Time. "Staten Island Soprano." Jan. 2, 1956

Townsend, Richard. "Bonzo's Buddy Plays the Political Arena."
After Dark, Aug. 1976

Uselton, Roi A. "Opera Singers on the Screen: 3." Films in
Review, June-July 1967

Vermilye, Jerry. "Ida Lupino." Films in Review, May 1959

Vermilye, Jerry. "Walter Huston." Films in Review, Feb. 1960

Virzi, John. "Letters: Eleanor Parker's Second Husband." Films
in Review, May 1962

Vogue. Biographical sketch. March 15, 1945

Walker, Derek. "Films Coming: This Will Raise the Rows." Picturegoer (England), Dec. 24, 1955

Weatherly, Joan Evans. "From the Editor's Desk." Hollywood
Studio Magazine, Sept. 1984

Whitney, Dwight. "In This Case, Creation Took Seven Years." TV
Guide, Nov. 8, 1969

York, Cal. "Inside Stuff." Photoplay, Aug. 1944

C. Newspapers

Adams, Cindy. "Cindy Adams." New York Post, Dec. 10, 1987

Alexander, Ronald. "Money Is Better Than Frostbite." New York
Herald Tribune, April 30, 1961

American Weekly, The. Ad for Lux Soap. March 27, 1955

Archerd, Army. "Just for Variety." Daily Variety, March 1, 1978

Asbury Park Press, The. "Marilyn Monroe's Gown Featured." Dec.
9, 1979

Bahrenburg, Bruce. "'Romantic' Films to Counteract Hard Times."
Newark [N.J.] Sunday News, Jan. 17, 1971

Barney, Phil. "Eleanor Parker Has Lead in 'Lizzie'." Tampa Sunday
Tribune, April 28, 1957

Beck, Marilyn. "Hollywood Hotline: Studios Are Running After
'Sammy'." The Newark [N.J.] Star-Ledger, Aug. 13, 1981

Beneckson, S. S. "'Hole in the Head'." Hollywood [Fla.] Sun-Tattler,
July 8, 1959

Bolton, Whitney. "Has Artist Changed His Perspective?" N.Y.
Morning Telegraph, Dec. 3, 1954

Bradford, Jack. "Metro on Rush Schedule—Liz Only Works 21 Days."
Hollywood [Fla.] Sun-Tattler, Aug. 3, 1964

Bradford, Jack. "Parsons Role: Help from Oscar." Newark [N.J.]
Evening News, April 23, 1968

Bradford, Jack. "Rambling Reporter." The Hollywood Reporter,
Oct. 27, 1966

Bradford, Jack. "Rambling Reporter." The Hollywood Reporter, Jan.
6, 1967

Buck, Jerry. "Operation Prime Time Gives Networks a Worry."
The Asbury Park Press, April 16, 1978

Cameron, Kate. "New Faces in Peyton Place." N.Y. Sunday News,
April 30, 1961

Cameron, Kate. "News Picks 10 Best Films of '60." N.Y. Sunday
News, Jan. 1, 1961

Cameron, Kate. "Remake 'Of Human Bondage'." N.Y. Sunday News,
Sept. 20, 1964

Cameron, Kate. "'Sound of Music' on Screen." N.Y. Sunday News,
Feb. 28, 1965

Carmody, Jay. "Author of 'Caged' Declares All Its Shocks Authentic." The [Washington, D.C.] Evening Star, June 12, 1950

Charlotte [No. Carolina] Observer. Ad for Lux Soap. Feb. 22, 1948

Chicago Daily Tribune. "Movie Plays in Pictures: Above and Beyond."
Jan. 12, 1953

Chicago Herald American. "Hostess Fashions of the Week." March
5, 1950

Chicago Herald American. Sketch of Scaramouche principals. July
6, 1952

Chicago Sun-Times. "Name Oscar Winners." Feb. 25, 1952

Chicago Sun-Times. "Who Will Win the Oscar?" March 11, 1956

Chicago Tribune, The. Ad for Hollywood Bread. April 20, 1955

Christy, George. "The Great Life." The Hollywood Reporter, March
30, 1978

Cleveland Press, The. "Not Speaking." July 20, 1962

Coe, Richard L. "No 'Applause'." The Washington Post, July 18,
1972

Connolly, Mike. "Connolly's Mailbag." Newark [N.J.] Evening News,
April 24, 1966

Connolly, Mike. "Rambling Reporter." The Hollywood Reporter,
March 7, 1966

Connolly, Mike. "Rambling Reporter." The Hollywood Reporter,
June 14, 1966

Connolly, Mike. "Resumes Career: More Films for Eleanor Parker." Newark [N.J.] Evening News, Oct. 1, 1965

Corry, John. "Broadway." The New York Times, April 30, 1976

Crowther, Bosley. "Return of a Native: Mr. Capra Does It with 'A Hole in the Head'." The New York Times, July 26, 1959

Cummings, John. "Celluloid Heroes Revisited: Part 1/Al Schmid/ 'Pride of the Marines'." Long Island Newsday, April 13, 1965

Dahl, Arlene. "How Make-Up Man Makes Up Star." Chicago Daily Tribune, Oct. 22, 1952

Daily Variety. "MCA TV/Universal Puts 'The Bastard' in the Can." March 28, 1978

Daytona Beach Evening Star. Ad for Hollywood Bread. April 9, 1957

Dayton [Ohio] Journal Herald, The. "Dayton Friend to Help Greet Movie Star." Jan. 7, 1953

Dayton [Ohio] Journal Herald, The. "New Parker Role." Sept. 10, 1953

Dayton [Ohio] Journal Herald, The. "Parker-Gassman Team." Jan. 17, 1953

Detroit Free Press. "Names and Faces ... It's a Boy for Eleanor Parker." Jan. 9, 1958

Detroit Free Press. Photo with Clark Gable. Jan. 13, 1957

Detroit Free Press. "World Once Over ... Divorce Sought." Nov. 11, 1953

Detroit News. Photo with Navajo Indians. Dec. 7, 1953

Erdman, Richard. "Memoirs of a Warner Bros. Contract Player." Los Angeles Times, Sept. 7, 1980

Fidler, Jimmy. "Some of the Top Stars Spending Christmas in Far-Away Places." The Miami Herald, Dec. 24, 1953

Fields, Sidney. "Only Human: Coherence Out of Chaos." N.Y. Daily News, June 3, 1976

Film Daily, The. "Movies in the Magazines." Jan. 29, 1962

Film Daily, The. "Storks." Jan. 9, 1958

Fort Lauderdale News. "'Catman' Ray Berwick: Veteran Trainer
Rated Tops." May 16, 1969

Fort Wayne [Ind.] News-Sentinel. Photo with Jeffrey Hunter. July
18, 1964

Fort Wayne [Ind.] News-Sentinel. Photo with Robert Taylor, government officials. Jan. 10, 1953

Fraser, C. Gerald. "John Cromwell, 91; Directed 42 Movies." The
New York Times, Sept. 28, 1979

Gansberg, Alan L. "Levenback-Riche to Produce 7th 'Madame X'
for NBC." The Hollywood Reporter, Dec. 26, 1980

Gardella, Kay. "News Around the Dials: Tarzan Swings on TV."
N.Y. Daily News, Nov. 15, 1963

Gardella, Kay. "Television: Court Drama Tries Justice System."
N.Y. Daily News, March 1, 1978

Gilbert, Justin. "Mirror Critic's 10 Best of 1960." New York Mirror,
Jan. 8, 1961

Gottfried, Martin. "'Joey' Without a Joey Is a 'Pal' in Need." New
York Post, June 28, 1976

Gottfried, Martin. "Murder by Gossip." New York Post, July 3, 1976

Graham, Sheilah. "Battle Royal: Julie Vs. Audrey for 'Liza'." New
York Mirror, May 2, 1962

Graham, Sheilah. "Brando Wants to Play Chessman." New York
Mirror, May 18, 1960

Graham, Sheilah. "Chevalier, 74, Going Like 60." New York Mirror,
Oct. 21, 1962

Graham, Sheilah. "Dick Lavishes Jewels on Liz; Few on Wife." The
Miami News, July 26, 1962

Graham, Sheilah. "Hollywood: Jean Seberg Topcast in Harris-Shaw
Flick." New York Mirror, July 25, 1962

Graham, Sheilah. "Hollywood: Wayne to Africa?" Newark [N.J.]
Evening News, June 12, 1963

Graham, Sheilah. "Joan Fontaine Eyeing Broadway." New York
Mirror, Dec. 1, 1960

Graham, Sheilah. "Movies in Rome: Burton Moving Up." The Newark
[N.J.] Evening News, May 11, 1962

Graham, Sheilah. "Sandy Dennis Movie Off Till March." New York Post, Nov. 22, 1966

Graham, Sheilah. "Sheilah Graham Abroad: Sinatra Was Planning Musical to Help MM." New York Mirror, Aug. 11, 1962

Grant, Hank. "Off the Cuff." The Hollywood Reporter, Dec. 4, 1987

Grant, Hank. "Rambling Reporter." The Hollywood Reporter, July 9, 1968

Grant, Hank. "Rambling Reporter." The Hollywood Reporter, Nov. 19, 1973

Grant, Hank. "Rambling Reporter." The Hollywood Reporter, April 17, 1974

Griffith, Ann W. "On TV This Week: Summit Meeting." New York Herald Tribune, May 15, 1960

Groller, Ingrid. "Paul Clemens ... A Portrayal of a Traumatic Event." The [N.Y.] Trib, Feb. 17, 1978

Gross, Linda. "Ironies Abound in 1943 'Mission'." Los Angeles Times, July 6, 1983

Harmetz, Aljean. "'Orchestrating' Academy Awards." The New York Times, April 1, 1978

Harris, Radie. "Broadway Ballyhoo." The Hollywood Reporter, Feb. 24, 1971

Harris, Radie. "Broadway Ballyhoo." The Hollywood Reporter, Nov. 26, 1973

Hart, Alicia. "Of Interest to Women: Tweezing Eyebrows Strays." The Tacoma Sunday Ledger-News Tribune, Aug. 21, 1949

Hawkins, Robert F. "Seen Through a Venetian Screen." The New York Times, Aug. 5, 1962

Hislop, Alan. "'Is the Studio Your Whole Life?' She Asked." The New York Times, June 28, 1970

Hollywood Reporter, The. Photos. Oct. 23, 1944; Oct. 25, 1951

Hollywood Reporter, The. "W.B. Seven Arts Terminate Talks on 'Panic Button'." Sept. 23, 1963

Hopper, Hedda. "Dean Martin Is Sought as Star of 'Career' Film." The Chicago Tribune, Nov. 14, 1958

Hopper, Hedda. "Eleanor Parker Borrowed for Gable's Leading Lady."
Chicago Tribune, May 4, 1956

Hopper, Hedda. "Eleanor Parker Gets Role with Sinatra." Tampa
Morning Tribune, Aug. 13, 1955

Hopper, Hedda. "Eleanor Parker Lands 'Return to Peyton Place'."
The Chicago Tribune, Dec. 1, 1960

Hopper, Hedda. "Eleanor Parker to Be War Widow in 'One More
Time'." Chicago Tribune, Oct. 5, 1953

Hopper, Hedda. "Eleanor Parker to Play Belle." Miami Daily News,
March 3, 1953

Hopper, Hedda. "Eleanor's Taking Lana's Old Place." The Washington Post, Dec. 1, 1960

Hopper, Hedda. "Film to 'Wed' TV and Movies." Miami Daily News,
May 13, 1953

Hopper, Hedda. "Gable Looks at Film Making from a Producer's
Viewpoint." Chicago Tribune, June 20, 1956

Hopper, Hedda. "Hollywood." N.Y. Daily News, Feb. 8, 1961

Hopper, Hedda. "Hollywood." N.Y. Daily News, June 9, 1961

Hopper, Hedda. "Hollywood." N.Y. Daily News, Sept. 20, 1961

Hopper, Hedda. "Hollywood." N.Y. Daily News, Dec. 7, 1962

Hopper, Hedda. "Lancaster and Hecht to Need Four Stars in Diamond
Movie." Chicago Daily Tribune, March 8, 1955

Hopper, Hedda. "Looking at Hollywood." Chicago Daily Tribune,
Dec. 27, 1947

Hopper, Hedda. "Looking at Hollywood." The Chicago Tribune,
Sept. 16, 1949

Hopper, Hedda. "Maria Schell, Ford Will Co-Star Again." The
Chicago Tribune, Nov. 30, 1960

Hopper, Hedda. "Meredith to Direct Two Plays in New York." The
Chicago Tribune, March 5, 1964

Hopper, Hedda. "Miss Parker Seeks War Film Role." Chicago
Daily Tribune, May 15, 1959

Hopper, Hedda. "Parker Wants 'Country Girl'." Miami Daily News,
Jan. 22, 1954

Hopper, Hedda. "Peck Gets Role of Attorney in 'View from Pompey's Head'." The Chicago Tribune, Jan. 28, 1955

Hopper, Hedda. "Taylor, Parker Teamed Again." Miami Daily News, Feb. 19, 1954

Hopper, Hedda. "20th-Century Cancels 'Greatest Story Ever Told'." The Chicago Tribune, Sept. 5, 1961

Jacksonville [Fla.] Times-Union. "Feld Man Behind Insane Illusions." March 10, 1957

John, Frederick. "Movies: They Were the Stars of the Warner Galaxy." San Francisco Sunday Examiner & Chronicle, July 1, 1979

Jones, Marvene. "The V.I.P.'s." The Hollywood Reporter, Oct. 30, 1973

Kany, A. S. "Let's Go Places." The Dayton [Ohio] Journal Herald, March 10, 1953

Kaufman, Dave. "On All Channels: MCA's 'Bastard' Is the Different Kid on the Block of TV Sameness." Daily Variety, Feb. 2, 1978

Kelly, Herb. "Stars Fall on Beach." The Miami News, Nov. 2, 1958

Knight, Arthur. "Knight at the Movies: The Icing on the Cake." The Hollywood Reporter, April 11, 1980

Krupnick, Jerry. "Let's Get the TV Season on the Road!" Sunday [Newark, N.J.] Star-Ledger, Sept. 14, 1969

Landry, Robert J. "Actors, Directors & Miscasting." Variety, Jan. 10, 1962

Leogrande, Ernest. "Stars Are Out, Pal, and Here Comes the Sun." N.Y. Daily News, June 11, 1976

London Evening News (England). "Eleanor Parker Gets Venice Prize." Sept. 11, 1950

Los Angeles Mirror. "New Films Deal with Split Personalities." Feb. 26, 1957

Los Angeles Times. Sale of Reagan-Parker poster. Nov. 16, 1981

Mackin, Tom. "The Survivors Arrive." The [Newark, N.J.] Evening News, Sept. 30, 1969

Maksian, George. "Around the Dials: Hope's Series Signs 5 Stars." N.Y. Daily News, July 1, 1963

Maksian, George. "TV Movie Marquee." N.Y. Sunday News, Jan. 23, 1972

Maltin, Leonard. "Hollywood's 'Lost' Films--And Why They Can't Be Found." The New York Times, June 16, 1973

Manners, Dorothy. "Eleanor Parker Replaces Suzy; Crain for Collins." The Miami Herald, Oct. 31, 1960

Manners, Dorothy. "Eleanor Parker's New Career: Car Safety Crusader." The Washington Post, Nov. 18, 1966

Manners, Dorothy. Filming Panic Button. New York Journal-American, June 1, 1962

Manners, Dorothy. "Hollywood Chit-Chat: Eleanor Parker Gets Wifey Role." The [Newark, N.J.] Star-Ledger, Nov. 8, 1960

Manners, Dorothy. "Hollywood Chit-Chat: Jayne Fights Off Fear of Water to Complete Ski Shot." The [Newark, N.J.] Star-Ledger, June 1, 1962

Manners, Dorothy. "Hollywood Chit-Chat: Movie Audiences to Get a New Look at Nobility's Nudist." The [Newark, N.J.] Star-Ledger, July 2, 1962

Manners, Dorothy. "Hollywood Chit-Chat: Stu Whitman Replaces David Janssen." The [Newark, N.J.] Star-Ledger, March 1, 1966

Manners, Dorothy. "Hollywood in Focus." The [Newark, N.J.] Star-Ledger, May 31, 1968

Manners, Dorothy. "Hollywood in Focus." The [Newark, N.J.] Star-Ledger, June 26, 1969

Manners, Dorothy. "Hollywood in Focus." The [Newark, N.J.] Star-Ledger, Aug. 7, 1969

Manners, Dorothy. "Hollywood in Focus." The [Newark, N.J.] Star-Ledger, Nov. 21, 1969

Manners, Dorothy. "Return to 'Bounty' Is Brando's Idea." The Miami Herald, June 27, 1962

Marsh, Ward, and Noel Holmes. "Close-Up." The [Cleveland] Plain Dealer, Feb. 18, 1952

McCann, Richard Dyer. "'Scaramouche' on Way to the Screen." The Christian Science Monitor, no date

McHarry, Charles. "On the Town." N.Y. Daily News, Jan. 9, 1961

Meyer, Jim. "Passing Time Has Left Ruth Roman Untouched." The Miami Herald, Jan. 10, 1971

Miami Daily News. "Hollywood by Dallinger." Nov. 18, 1953

Miami Herald, The. Photo. Jan. 1, 1957

Miami Herald, The. Photo in Egypt. July 5, 1954

Miami Herald, The. Photo with Eileen Farrell. March 24, 1970

Michaels, Ken. "Journey to the Center of Bracken's World." Chicago Tribune Magazine, Feb. 1, 1970

Milberg, Doris J. "The Oscars, Part 2: The Haves and the Have-Nots." Movie Collector's World, April 19, 1985

Morallo, Richard. "Research Gave Writer's Scripts a Special Flair." Los Angeles Times, April 20, 1981

Motion Picture Daily. "Nominations for '62-'63 Emmy Awards." May 1, 1963

Muir, Florabel. "Hollywood: Scared of the Censor." N.Y. Daily News, March 28, 1966

Muir, Florabel. "Hollywood: 2001's a Dull Year." N.Y. Daily News, April 8, 1968

Neill, Frank. "Scribe Lists Notes About Movie People." Ft. Wayne [Ind.] News-Sentinel, Aug. 8, 1949

N.Y. Daily Mirror. Photo at granting of divorce from Bert Friedlob. Nov. 12, 1953

N.Y. Daily Mirror. Photo with five-day-old son Paul Day Clemens. Jan. 13, 1958

N.Y. Daily News. "Joey Revisited." May 5, 1976

N.Y. Daily News. Photo with five-day-old son Paul Day Clemens. Jan. 13, 1958

New York Herald Tribune. "Hollywood Cameras Penetrate Darkest Egypt." Feb. 28, 1954

New York Herald Tribune. "Graphic Skill and History in Movie Poster Exhibit." Dec. 25, 1960

New York Herald Tribune. Photo with Roger Smith. March 22, 1964

New York Journal-American. Photo with husband Paul Clemens, children Sharon, Susan, Richard after the children received permission from a Los Angeles court to adopt stepfather Clemens' surname. May 15, 1957

New York Journal-American. "Stage/Screen--Eleanor Parker prepares her St. Patrick's Day floral centerpiece ..." March 16, 1957

New York Journal-American. "Stars to Present Prizes to 18 at Stork Club Party." Jan. 29, 1953

New York Post. Photo with Otto Preminger. Jan. 29, 1956

N.Y. Sunday News. "Home from the Hill." March 13, 1960

N.Y. Sunday News. "Now Movie Stars Discover the Let's-Talk-It-Over Court." Nov. 15, 1953

N.Y. Sunday News. Photo with Anthony Dexter. Nov. 12, 1950

N.Y. Sunday News. Photo with Karen Jensen, Jay C. Flippen. Oct. 3, 1969

New York Times, The. Ad: "IBM Presents Movies to Remember, 1979 Season." June 11, 1979

New York Times, The. "Bert T. Friedlob Dies." Oct. 8, 1956

New York Times, The. Photo with Charles Bickford, Richard Conte. May 15, 1960

New York Times, The. "Public Views on Current Films." Aug. 9, 1959

New York Times, The. "Thomas F. Harari's Comedy to Be Made Film." Nov. 4, 1950

New York Times, The. "Villella Quits 'Pal Joey' Over 'Differences'." June 8, 1976

Newark [N.J.] Evening News. Photo with Bob Hope, Jeffrey Hunter. Aug. 23, 1963

Newark [N.J.] Evening News. Photo with Neville Brand, Jeffrey Hunter. July 24, 1964

Newark [N.J.] Sunday News. Photo. Sept. 14, 1969

Newark [N.J.] Sunday News. Photo with Jayne Mansfield, Maurice Chevalier, Mike Connors. July 1, 1962

Newhart, Bob. "June Allyson Never Kicked Anyone in the Shins."
The New York Times, July 23, 1967

O'Brian, Jack. "Jack O'Brian Says: Light as a Lead Balloon."
New York Journal-American, April 21, 1961

O'Brian, Jack. "Voice of Broadway." The [Newark, N.J.] Star-
Ledger, June 7, 1976

Ocean Grove and Neptune [N.J.] Times. "Doug McClelland Writes
'Blackface to Blacklist'." Jan. 28, 1988

Osborne, Robert. "On Location." The Hollywood Reporter, June
12, 1979

Osborne, Robert. "Rambling Reporter." The Hollywood Reporter,
March 17, 1987

Parsons, Louella O. "Another Triangle for Sybil?" New York Journal-
American, April 15, 1964

Parsons, Louella O. "Eleanor Stars in 'Lizzie'." The Detroit Times,
May 29, 1956

Parsons, Louella O. "Film Scenes Keep Bob Taylor, Eleanor Parker
Dripping Wet." The Miami Herald, June 18, 1954

Parsons, Louella O. "Hollywood Chit-Chat: Charles Addams' Get
Well Card to Carolyn Jones was Wild." The [Newark, N.J.] Star-
Ledger, Nov. 27, 1964

Parsons, Louella O. "Hollywood Chit-Chat: Eleanor Parker, Jim
Cagney Contrasts in 'Park Avenue'." The Newark [N.J.] Star-
Ledger, July 18, 1961

Parsons, Louella O. "Hollywood Headlines: Eleanor Parker Will
Act Double Personality Role." The Pontiac [Mich.] Press, May 30,
1956

Parsons, Louella O. "Hollywood Highlights: High Note for Julie."
New York Journal-American, Nov. 15, 1963

Parsons, Louella O. "Hollywood Highlights: Kelley Has a Heavenly
Team." New York Journal-American, Sept. 23, 1964

Parsons, Louella. Item: Plan to try New York stage. New York
Journal-American, March 15, 1956

Parsons, Louella O. "Kaye Signs for 'Merry Andrew'." The Chicago
American, March 15, 1956

Parsons, Louella O. "Life ... and Death in Hollywood, 1961." New York Journal-American, Dec. 31, 1961

Parsons, Louella O. "Speculating on Next Year's Oscars Starting Already." St. Petersburg [Fla.] Times, April 11, 1955

Parsons, Louella O. "Travers, Eleanor Star." The Detroit Times, June 15, 1956

Parsons, Louella O. "A Valentine to United Artists." The [Newark, N.J.] Star-Ledger, Feb. 7, 1961

Philadelphia Inquirer, The. Colorama section: Photo. Jan. 23, 1955

Pittsburgh Sun-Telegraph. Photo. March 16, 1955

Plain Dealer, The (Cleveland). "Scandal Threatens Beauty Contest." June 14, 1974

Pryor, Thomas M. "Somewhat Out of Focus." The New York Times, May 28, 1950

Querido, Phil. "Story of Hero Is Key to Success." The Louisville [Ky.] Times, March 23, 1955

Raidy, William A. "Revival of 'Pal Joey' Bewildering, Hardly Beguiling." Long Island Press, June 28, 1976

Ray, Herb. "Cover 'Boy'." Miami Sunday News, Jan. 6, 1957

Reed, Rex. "Joan Copeland Steals 'Pal Joey'." N.Y. Daily News, July 2, 1976

Rockwell, John. "Marjorie Lawrence, Wagnerian Soprano, Dead at 71." The New York Times, Jan. 15, 1979

Seattle Sunday Times Roto, The. Photo. Feb. 2, 1947

Sheehan, Henry. "The Hollywood Story: The Best Show in Town." The Hollywood Reporter, July 10, 1987

Skolsky, Sidney. "Hollywood Is My Beat." New York Post, Jan. 18, 1957

Smith, Bea. "June Lockhart's Casualness Brings New Sheen to 'Carats'." Union [N.J.] Leader, Feb. 3, 1972

Smith, Bea. "Movieland Book Shines." Union [N.J.] Leader, June 20, 1985

Smith, Bea. "'Retirement' Not for Carol Lynley." Newark [N.J.] Sunday News, May 28, 1961

Smith, Cecil. "There's No Bracken in 'Bracken's World'." The
[Newark, N.J.] Star-Ledger, May 21, 1969

Smith, Cecil. "Video Viewpoint: Cooper Returns to Actor's Role."
The [Newark, N.J.] Star-Ledger, Feb. 11, 1971

Smith, Liz. "Belushi's Widow Gets Comfort from Pals." N.Y. Daily
News, March 16, 1982

Smith, Liz. "Eleanor Parker Set to Role over 'Hotel'." N.Y. Daily
News, Oct. 7, 1983

Spero, Bette. "Author Spotlights Ron Reagan: Actor." The [Newark,
N.J.] Star-Ledger, July 7, 1983

Sullivan, Ed. "Little Old New York." N.Y. Daily News, Feb. 11,
1974

Sunday [Newark, N.J.] Star-Ledger. Cover "TV Time" section/
"The Gambler, The Nun and the Radio." May 15, 1960

Sunday [Newark, N.J.] Star-Ledger. "Girls Hold Their Own in a
Man's World." May 26, 1963

Sylvester, Bob. "Dream Street." N.Y. Daily News, March 30, 1973

Thomas, Bob. "Hollywood's Fast Changes Alter Series." Fort
Lauderdale News, July 23, 1970

Tusher, Will. "Reporter Hams Up ABC Movie of Week." The Hollywood Reporter, Dec. 29, 1972

Variety. "Chicago." Nov. 13, 1974

Variety. "Eleanor Parker, Edward Villella Set to Costar in 'Pal Joey'."
May 5, 1976

Variety. "Fashion Side of Acad." March 29, 1978

Variety. "Ginger Rogers as Mama; Judy Garland and Eleanor Parker
Pass Up 'Harlow' Role." March 31, 1965

Variety. "Hollywood." April 19, 1961

Variety. "International Sound Track." May 9, 1962

Variety. "International Sound Track." June 20, 1962

Variety. "New York Sound Track." Feb. 28, 1962

Variety. "Obituaries: Bert Friedlob." Oct. 10, 1956

Variety. "Realistic 'Oscar' Casting." Sept. 1, 1965

Wahls, Robert. "The Diva Everybody Digs." N.Y. Sunday News, Nov. 6, 1960

Wilson, Earl. "No Applause for Rita." New York Post, May 11, 1971

Winchell, Walter. "Cupid Busy on Broadway." The Miami Herald, Nov. 27, 1964

Winston, Carol H. "The New Valentino." N.Y. Sunday Mirror, Dec. 17, 1950

Wood, Thomas. "A Nice Place to Revisit!" New York Herald Tribune, Feb. 12, 1961

Wood, Thomas. "Pardon the Interruption in 'Interrupted Melody'." New York Herald Tribune, Feb. 20, 1955

Woods, Brenda. "Movie Star Buff Now Makes Money Writing Books About His Idols." N.Y. Sunday News, Feb. 23, 1975

Zeigler, Helen. "'Finishing Touches' Family Affair." DuPage County (Ill.) Times, Nov. 22, 1974

A. Theater Films

SOLDIERS IN WHITE

"Wear." "Soldiers in White." Variety, Feb. 11, 1942

BUSSES ROAR:

E.G. "'Buses [sic] Roar'--Palace." New York Herald Tribune, Sept. 25, 1942

Pryor, Thomas M. "At the Palace--'Busses Roar'." The New York Times, Sept. 25, 1942

V.K. "'Busses Roar': Sabotage Melodrama." Motion Picture Herald, Aug. 22, 1942

"Walt." "Busses Roar." Variety, Aug. 19, 1942

MISSION TO MOSCOW:

Cameron, Kate. "'Mission to Moscow' Controversial Film." N.Y. Daily News, April 30, 1943

Cook, Alton. "'Mission to Moscow' Superb Factual Film." New York World-Telegram, April 30, 1943

Corby, Jane. "'Mission to Moscow' Heads New Fox Bill." Brooklyn Eagle, July 10, 1943

Crowther, Bosley. "'Mission to Moscow,' Based on Ex-Ambassador Davies' Book, Stars Walter Huston. Ann Harding at Hollywood." The New York Times, April 30, 1943

Guernsey, Jr., Otis L. "On the Screen: 'Mission to Moscow'-- Hollywood." New York Herald Tribune, April 30, 1943

Platt, David. "Mission to Moscow." The [N.Y.] Daily Worker, May 16, 1943

THE MYSTERIOUS DOCTOR:

Cunningham, E. A. "'The Mysterious Doctor': Murder on the Moors."
Motion Picture Herald, Feb. 27, 1943

Guernsey, Otis L., Jr. "'The Mysterious Doctor'--Palace." New
York Herald Tribune, May 20, 1943

Pryor, Thomas M. "At the Palace." The New York Times, May 20,
1943

BETWEEN TWO WORLDS:

"Char." "Between Two Worlds." Variety, May 10, 1944

Crowther, Bosley. "Between Two Worlds." The New York Times,
May 6, 1944

Hale, Wanda. "'Between Two Worlds' Is 'Outward Bound' Remade."
N.Y. Daily News, May 6, 1944

Mishkin, Leo. "Screen Presents: Strand Offering Compelling Film."
N.Y. Morning Telegraph, May 6, 1944

Mortimer, Lee. "'Between Two Worlds' Splendidly Done." N.Y.
Daily Mirror, May 6, 1944

Movieland. "Movieland's Five Best Pictures of the Month: 'Between
Two Worlds'...." July 1944

Screen Stars. "Between Two Worlds." Aug. 1944

Sherburne, E. C. "'Between Two Worlds': 'Outward Bound' Reappears in a New Picture Version." The Christian Science Monitor,
May 5, 1944

Winsten, Archer. "Teetering Between Life and Death as Shown at
the Strand Theatre." New York Post, May 6, 1944

CRIME BY NIGHT:

"Sten." "Crime by Night." Variety, July 26, 1944

THE LAST RIDE:

Hale, Wanda. "Brooklyn Fox Shows Black Market Drama." N.Y.
Daily News, Sept. 30, 1944

"Jona."   "The Last Ride."   Variety, Sept. 13, 1944

Winsten, Archer.   "Gangsters in Tire Racket at Brooklyn Fox
Theatre."   New York Post, Sept. 30, 1944

THE VERY THOUGHT OF YOU:

Cameron, Kate.   "A Romantic Comedy on Strand's Screen."   N.Y.
Daily News, Nov. 18, 1944

Hollywood Reporter, The.   "W.B. 'Very Thought of You' Full of
Heart and Charm."   Oct. 16, 1944

Mishkin, Leo.   "Screen Presents: GI Meets Girl and Family, Too."
N.Y. Morning Telegraph, Nov. 21, 1944

Mortimer, Lee.   "'Very Thought of You' Is Good Fun."   N.Y. Daily
Mirror, Nov. 17, 1944

Movieland.   "Movieland's New Picture Guide: 'The Very Thought
of You'."   Jan. 1945

Pelswick, Rose.   "Dennis Morgan in New Film."   New York Journal-
American, Nov. 18, 1944

Photoplay.   "The Very Thought of You."   Jan. 1945

Pryor, Thomas M.   "The Very Thought of You."   The New York
Times, Nov. 18, 1944

Thirer, Irene.   "'The Very Thought of You'--of War Marriage, at
Strand."   New York Post, Nov. 18, 1944

"Walt."   "The Very Thought of You."   Variety, Oct. 18, 1944

HOLLYWOOD CANTEEN:

Cameron, Kate.   "'Hollywood Canteen' Has All-Star Cast."   N.Y.
Daily News, Dec. 16, 1944

Crowther, Bosley.   "'Hollywood Canteen,' Variety Show, Opens at
Strand."   The New York Times, Dec. 16, 1944

PRIDE OF THE MARINES:

Barnes, Howard.   "On the Screen: 'Pride of the Marines'--Strand."
New York Herald Tribune, Aug. 25, 1945

Crowther, Bosley. "'Pride of the Marines,' Based on War Career
of Al Schmid, in Which John Garfield Stars, at Strand." The New
York Times, Aug. 25, 1945

Family Circle. "Pride of the Marines." Sept. 14, 1945

Hale, Wanda. "Lest You Forget, See 'Pride of the Marines'." N.Y.
Daily News, Aug. 8, 1945

Hollywood Reporter, The. "'Pride of the Marines' Sets New Mark in
Film Achievement." Aug. 7, 1945

Life. "Movie of the Week: 'Pride of the Marines'." Aug. 6, 1945

Motion Picture. "Motion Picture Recommends 'Pride of the Marines'."
Oct. 1945

Photoplay. "Pride of the Marines." Oct. 1945

Silver Screen. "Pride of the Marines." Oct. 1945

Silver Screen. "We Point with Pride to John Garfield." Oct. 1945

OF HUMAN BONDAGE:

Ager, Cecelia. "Lightning Only Strikes Once." PM, July 7, 1946

"Brog." "Of Human Bondage." Variety, July 3, 1946

Cameron, Kate. "'Of Human Bondage' Somber Film Drama." N.Y.
Daily News, July 6, 1946

Commonweal, The. "Of Human Bondage." Aug. 9, 1946

Crowther, Bosley. "'Of Human Bondage,' a Remake of Film on Somerset Maugham Novel, Opens at the Strand." The New York Times,
July 6, 1946

Esquire. "Of Human Bondage." Sept. 1946

Grant, Jack D. "Of Human Bondage." The Hollywood Reporter,
July 2, 1946

Independent Film Journal, The. "Of Human Bondage." July 6, 1946

McCarten, John. "Of Human Bondage." The New Yorker, July 13,
1946

Motion Picture. "Of Human Bondage." Sept. 1946

Newsweek. "Movies: The New Bondage." July 22, 1946

Photoplay. "Of Human Bondage." Sept. 1946

Scheuer, Philip K. "Hollywood Tries Repeat with 'Of Human Bondage'." Los Angeles Times, July 20, 1946

Screen Album. "Screen Album's Oscar to ... Eleanor Parker." June-July 1946

Spies, Virginia. "Liberty Goes to the Movies: Of Human Bondage." Liberty, June 3, 1946

NEVER SAY GOODBYE:

"Brog." "Never Say Goodbye." Variety, Oct. 23, 1946

Crowther, Bosley. "Penalty--For Offside." The New York Times, Nov. 23, 1946

Guernsey, Otis L., Jr. "'Never Say Goodbye'--Strand." New York Herald Tribune, Nov. 23, 1946

Photoplay. "Never Say Goodbye." Feb. 1947

ESCAPE ME NEVER:

Crowther, Bosley. "Escape Me Never." The New York Times, Nov. 8, 1947

Film Daily, The. "Escape Me Never." Oct. 28, 1947

Newsweek. "Escape Me Ever [sic]." Nov. 17, 1947

Photoplay. "Escape Me Never." May 1947

Schallert, Edwin. "'Escape Me Never' Manages Escape from Real Impact." Los Angeles Times, Dec. 11, 1947

Tinée, Mae. "Baby in Film Steals Light of Its Stars." Chicago Daily Tribune, Dec. 19, 1947

Variety. "Escape Me Never." Oct. 28, 1947

THE VOICE OF THE TURTLE:

"Brog." "The Voice of the Turtle." Variety, Dec. 31, 1947

Evans, Delight. "Your Guide to Current Films: 'The Voice of the Turtle'." Screenland, Jan. 1948

Hale, Wanda. "Warners Reform 'Turtle'." N.Y. Daily News, Dec. 26, 1947

Motion Picture. "The Movie of the Month: 'The Voice of the Turtle'." March 1948

Movieland. "Movie of the Month: 'Voice of the Turtle'." Jan. 1948

Movie Stars Parade. "Performance of the Month [Eleanor Parker]." Jan. 1948

Newsweek. "Puritan Turtle." Feb. 25, 1948

Pathfinder. "Play into Picture." Feb. 25, 1948

Photoplay. "The Voice of the Turtle." Jan. 1948

Pryor, Thomas M. "The Voice of the Turtle." The New York Times, Dec. 26, 1947

Sullivan, Kay. "Voice of the Turtle." Parade, Feb. 8, 1948

Thompson, Jack. "Mirror Movie of the Week: 'The Voice of the Turtle'." N.Y. Sunday Mirror, Nov. 23, 1947

Time. "The Voice of the Turtle." Dec. 15, 1947

THE WOMAN IN WHITE:

Barnes, Howard. "On the Screen: Archaic Horror Film." New York Herald Tribune, May 8, 1948

"Brog." "The Woman in White." Variety, April 21, 1948

Cameron, Kate. "Classic Horror Tale Featured at Strand." N.Y. Daily News, May 8, 1948

Crowther, Bosley. "The Screen: 'The Woman in White,' Starring Eleanor Parker and Sydney Greenstreet, at Strand." The New York Times, May 8, 1948

Cue. "The Woman in White." May 8, 1948

Daily Variety. "The Woman in White." April 20, 1948

David, George L. "'Scudda' Feature Tiptop Fare at Paramount." Rochester Democrat and Chronicle, June 10, 1948

Hollywood Reporter, The. "'Woman in White' Shows Age in Plodding
Pace." April 20, 1948

Medow, Florence. "'Woman in White' Offers Welcome Change of Pace."
Chicago Sun-Times, May 16, 1948

Miami Herald, The. "Best Bets: 'The Woman in White'." Aug. 22,
1973

National Parent-Teacher. "The Woman in White." June 1948

Photoplay. "The Woman in White." June 1948

IT'S A GREAT FEELING:

"Brog." "It's a Great Feeling." Variety, July 27, 1949

Rhodes, Russell. "Entertainment: Strand Film Comedy Ribs Movie-
Makers." New York Journal of Commerce, Aug. 16, 1949

Weiler, A. H. "Gay Story Lampoons Studio." The New York Times,
Aug. 12, 1949

CHAIN LIGHTNING:

Guernsey, Otis L., Jr. "On the Screen: Whooosh!" New York
Herald Tribune, Feb. 19, 1950

Meyer, Jim. "Movies on Television: Bad Day Today, Two Good Films
Available Monday." The Miami Sunday News, Sept. 14, 1958

Newsweek. "Chain Lightning." March 6, 1950

Parsons, Louella O. "Movie Citations: Best Drama--'Chain Lightning'." Cosmopolitan, March 1950

Photoplay. "Chain Lightning." Feb. 1950

Weiler, A. H. "'Chain Lightning,' an Excursion by Warners into the
Jet Age, Arrives at Strand." The New York Times, Feb. 19, 1950

CAGED:

Arden, Doris. "Caged." Chicago Sun-Times, June 14, 1950

Bower, Helen. "Star Gazing: Prison Casts a Girl in Criminal's Mold."
Detroit Free Press, June 17, 1950

"Brog." "Caged." Variety, May 3, 1950

Carmody, Jay. "'Caged' a Passionate Tale of Women's Prison Life." The [Washington, D.C.] Evening Star, June 9, 1950

Guernsey, Otis L., Jr. "'Caged': Dames in the Hoosegow." New York Herald Tribune, May 20, 1950

Hollywood Reporter, The. "'Caged' Grim Prison Drama; Parker Triumphs in Fine Wald Prod'n." May 2, 1950

Masters, Dorothy. "Prison Movie an Impressive Strand Drama." N.Y. Daily News, May 20, 1950

Movieland. "Caged." July 1950

Newsweek. "Caged." June 19, 1950

Parents' Magazine. "Caged." June 1950

Parsons, Louella O. "Movie Citations: Best Feminine Performance-- Eleanor Parker in 'Caged'." Cosmopolitan, July 1950

Photoplay. "Caged." July 1950

Pryor, Thomas M. "Bleak Picture of a Woman's Prison." The New York Times, May 20, 1950

Screen Guide. "Caged." July 1950

Screen Stories. "Caged." July 1950

Time. "Caged." June 19, 1950

Tinée, Mae. "Film, 'Caged,' Hints Need of Prison Reform." Chicago Daily Tribune, June 13, 1950

Weitschat, Al. "'Caged' Gives Rugged Peek Inside Prison." The Detroit News, June 17, 1950

THREE SECRETS:

"Brog." "Three Secrets." Variety, Aug. 30, 1950

Croughton, Amy H. "Paramount Has Tense Melodrama." Rochester Times-Union, Sept. 29, 1950

Crowther, Bosley. "'Three Secrets,' Containing Some Absorbing, Dramatic Parts, Makes Bow at Strand." The New York Times, Oct. 21, 1950

V. Reviews   203

Daily Variety. "Three Secrets." Aug. 29, 1950

Elgutter, Ruth. "'Three Secrets' is Unusual in Plot, Well-Acted, Absorbing." _Toledo Times_, Oct. 13, 1950

Guernsey, Otis L., Jr. "'Three Secrets': Triple Agony." _New York Herald Tribune_, Oct. 21, 1950

Helming, Ann. "'Three Secrets' Emerges as Appealing Women's Picture." _Hollywood Citizen-News_, Sept. 29, 1950

Hollywood Reporter, The. "Femme Stars Score Under Wise's Meg." Aug. 29, 1950

Parsons, Louella O. "Movie Citations: Best Group Performance-- Eleanor Parker, Patricia Neal, Ruth Roman in 'Three Secrets'." _Cosmopolitan_, Sept. 1950

Photoplay. "Three Secrets." Oct. 1950

Robins, Frankie McKee. "This Month's Movies: 'Three Secrets'." _McCall's_, Aug. 1950

Schallert, Edwin. "Mothers Face Odd Issue in 'Secrets'." _Los Angeles Times_, Sept. 29, 1950

Screen Guide. "Three Secrets." Sept. 1950

Screenland. "Three Secrets." Aug. 1950

W. E. "'3 Secrets' Dramatic Saga." _Los Angeles Examiner_, Sept. 29, 1950

VALENTINO:

Alpert, Hollis. "Valentino." _The Saturday Review of Literature_, March 17, 1951

Cameron, Kate. "'Valentino' at Astor a Nostalgic Picture." _N.Y. Daily News_, April 20, 1951

Crowther, Bosley. "Anthony Dexter is Valentino in Film Version of Actor's Life Appearing at the Astor." _The New York Times_, April 20, 1951

Drake, Leah Bodine. "Film Version of Valentino Case of Mistaken Identity." _Evansville [Ind.] Courier_, March 23, 1951

Guernsey, Otis L., Jr. "'Valentino': Who?" _New York Herald Tribune_, April 20, 1951

Kane, Christopher. "Movie Reviews: Valentino." Modern Screen,
May 1951

Photoplay. "Valentino." May 1951

Time. "Valentino." May 7, 1951

A MILLIONAIRE FOR CHRISTY:

Barstow, James S., Jr. "A Millionaire for Christy." New York Herald
Tribune, Oct. 5, 1951

Family Circle. "A Millionaire for Christy." Nov. 1951

Hollywood Reporter, The. "A Millionaire for Christy." July 31, 1951

Newsweek. "A Millionaire for Christy." Oct. 15, 1951

New Yorker, The. "The Current Cinema." Oct. 13, 1951

Parsons, Louella O. "Movie Citations: Best Performance--Eleanor
Parker in 'A Millionaire for Christy'." Cosmopolitan, Nov. 1951

Scheuer, Philip K. "'Millionaire for Christy' Reminiscent But Merry."
Los Angeles Times, Oct. 13, 1951

Time. "A Millionaire for Christy." Oct. 22, 1951

Weiler, A. H. "At the Roxy." The New York Times, Oct. 5, 1951

DETECTIVE STORY:

Bower, Helen. "Star Gazing: The Past Catches Up in 'Detective
Story'." Detroit Free Press, Nov. 22, 1951

Cameron, Kate. "'Detective Story' a Superbly Made Film." N.Y.
Daily News, Nov. 7, 1951

Crowther, Bosley. "'Detective Story,' Film Based on Sidney Kingsley
Drama, Arrives at Mayfair." The New York Times, Nov. 7, 1951

F.G.S. "Douglas Fills Detective Role." So. Bend [Ind.] Tribune,
Jan. 14, 1952

Finlayson, John. "Kingsley's Play Makes Fine Movie." Detroit News,
Nov. 23, 1951

Guernsey, Otis L., Jr. "Detective Story." New York Herald Tribune, Nov. 7, 1951

"Herb." "Detective Story." <u>Variety</u>, Sept. 26, 1951

Jones, Paul. "'Detective Story' Called 'Sun's' Rival for Oscar." <u>Atlanta Constitution</u>, Dec. 6, 1951

Lesner, Sam. "'Detective Story' Great as Film." <u>The Chicago Daily News</u>, Dec. 26, 1951

<u>Look</u>. "Look Movie Review: 'Detective Story'." Dec. 4, 1951

<u>Modern Screen</u>. "Detective Story." Jan. 1952

Moon, Fred D. "'Detective Story' a Meaty Dish." <u>The Atlanta Journal</u>, Dec. 6, 1951

Mosdell, D. "Film Review." <u>The Canadian Forum</u> (Canada), Dec. 1951

<u>Movieland</u>. "The Reviewer's Box: <u>Detective Story</u>." Jan. 1952

<u>New Yorker, The</u>. "Detective Story." Nov. 11, 1951

Parsons, Louella O. "Movie Citations: Best Melodrama--'Detective Story'." <u>Cosmopolitan</u>, Dec. 1951

<u>Photoplay</u>. "Detective Story." Jan. 1952

<u>Redbook</u>. "Detective Story." Jan. 1952

<u>Screen Guide</u>. "Detective Story." Jan. 1952

<u>Screen Stories</u>. "Detective Story." Jan. 1952

<u>Screenland</u>. "Detective Story." Jan. 1952

<u>Time</u>. "Detective Story." Oct. 29, 1951

Tinée, Mae. "Crime Movie is Even Better Than the Play." <u>The Chicago Tribune</u>, Dec. 26, 1951

<u>SCARAMOUCHE</u>:

Cameron, Kate. "Music Hall Presents MGM's 'Scaramouche'." N.Y. <u>Daily News</u>, May 9, 1952

Crowther, Bosley. "'Scaramouche,' Metro Picture Based on Sabatini's Novel, Shown at Music Hall." <u>The New York Times</u>, May 9, 1952

Guernsey, Otis L., Jr. "'Scaramouche': En Garde!" <u>New York Herald Tribune</u>, May 9, 1952

"Herb." "Scaramouche." Variety, May 14, 1952

Hollywood Reporter, The. "'Scaramouche' Merry Epic; Wilson-Sidney Pic Sparkles with Wit." May 12, 1952

Parsons, Louella O. "Movie Citations: Best Adventure--'Scaramouche'." Cosmopolitan, Feb. 1953

Photoplay. "Scaramouche." Aug. 1952

Time. "Scaramouche." May 26, 1952

Vallee, William Lynch. "Scaramouche." Silver Screen, Aug. 1952

Zunser, Jesse. "Scaramouche." Cue, May 10, 1952

ABOVE AND BEYOND:

Bell, Eleanor. "The A-Bomb Versus Love." The Cincinnati Post, Jan. 16, 1953

Blake, Groverman. "Aisle Say: Above and Beyond." Cincinnati Times-Star, Jan. 16, 1953

"Brog." "Above and Beyond." Variety, Nov. 19, 1952

Cameron, Kate. "'Above and Beyond' Packs Terrific Punch." N.Y. Daily News, Jan. 31, 1953

Crowther, Bosley. "Domestic Trials of Atom Bomb Pilot Portrayed in 'Above and Beyond' at the Mayfair." The New York Times, Jan. 31, 1953

Guernsey, Otis L., Jr. "'Above and Beyond': Skyway to Hiroshima." New York Herald Tribune, Jan. 31, 1953

Hart, Henry. "Above and Beyond." Films in Review, Jan. 1953

Knight, Arthur. "Atom Bombs & Anti Communists." The Saturday Review of Literature, Jan. 24, 1953

Luban, Milton. "'Above and Beyond' Tense Drama Based on Atom Bomb." The Hollywood Reporter, Nov. 18, 1952

Martin, Mildred. "'Above and Beyond' is Bomb Drama at Stanley." The Philadelphia Inquirer, Jan. 30, 1953

New Yorker, The. "The Current Cinema: Two Misses, Not Very Near." Feb. 7, 1953

Parsons, Louella O. "Movie Citations: Best Drama--'Above and Beyond'." Cosmopolitan, Feb. 1953

Philadelphia Bulletin. "Above and Beyond." Jan. 30, 1953

Photoplay (England). "Above and Beyond." Sept. 1952

Time. "Above and Beyond." Jan. 5, 1953

Tinée, Mae. "Atom Bombing Story Becomes a Great Movie." Chicago Daily Tribune, Jan. 16, 1953

ESCAPE FROM FORT BRAVO:

Family Circle. "Escape from Fort Bravo." Jan. 1954

Guernsey, Otis L., Jr. "Screen: 'Escape from Fort Bravo." New York Herald Tribune, Jan. 23, 1954

Hale, Wanda. "The Mayfair Screens an Exciting Western." N.Y. Daily News, Jan. 23, 1954

Maughan, Rahna. "Escape from Fort Bravo." Silver Screen, Feb. 1954

McCarten, John. "Escape from Fort Bravo." The New Yorker, Jan. 30, 1954

Sarris, Andrew. "Tube Movies Rated PG (Pretty Good)--'Escape from Fort Bravo'." Village Voice, Sept. 26, 1977

Screenland. "Escape from Fort Bravo." Jan. 1954

Thompson, Howard. "'Escape from Fort Bravo,' Civil War Story Set in West, Opens at Mayfair." The New York Times, Jan. 23, 1954

Time. "Escape from Fort Bravo." Dec. 14, 1953

THE NAKED JUNGLE:

Bourke, George. "Love Blooms in 'Naked Jungle'." The Miami Herald, March 28, 1954

"Brog." "The Naked Jungle." Variety, Feb. 17, 1954

Churchill, Reba and Bonnie. "Your Guide to Current Films: 'The Naked Jungle'." Screenland, May 1954

Crowther, Bosley. "The Naked Jungle." The New York Times, April 3, 1954

Luban, Milton. "Pal-Haskin Film Suspense Jammed." The Hollywood Reporter, Feb. 10, 1954

McClay, Howard. "Parker, Heston Battle the Ants in 'Jungle'." Los Angeles Daily News, March 18, 1954

Newsweek. "New Films: 'The Naked Jungle'." March 29, 1954

Redelings, Lowell E. "'The Naked Jungle' in Bow: March of Soldier Ants Highlight of New Film." Hollywood Citizen-News, March 18, 1954

Schallert, Edwin. "Ants Stage Huge Drive on Humans." Los Angeles Times, March 18, 1954

Waterbury, Ruth. "'Naked Jungle' Suspenseful, Well Acted." Los Angeles Examiner, March 18, 1954

VALLEY OF THE KINGS:

Blackstone, Lillian. "'Valley of the Kings' Offers Armchair Tour of Nile." St. Petersburg [Fla.] Times, Sept. 3, 1954

Bourke, George. "'Valley of Kings' Eye-Catching." The Miami Herald, July 24, 1954

Brock, Bob. "Authentic Locale in 'Kings'." The Dallas Times Herald, Aug. 6, 1954

Cohen, Harold V. "Robert Taylor at the Penn in 'Valley of the Kings'." Pittsburgh Post Gazette, Sept. 18, 1954

De Schauennsee, Max. "'Valley of the Kings' Opens on Screen at Arcadia." The Philadelphia Bulletin, July 23, 1954

Krug, Karl. "Taylor is Penn Star." Pittsburgh Sun-Telegraph, Sept. 18, 1954

Lindeman, Edith. "'Valley of Kings' Story Not Interesting as Locale." Richmond [Va.] Times-Dispatch, Aug. 13, 1954

Martin, Mildred. "'Valley of the Kings' Opens in Color on Arcadia Screen." The Philadelphia Inquirer, July 23, 1954

McClelland, Douglas. "'Valley of the Kings' on Loew's Bill." Newark [N.J.] Evening News, Sept. 9, 1954

Parsons, Louella O. "Movie Citations: Best Film--'Valley of the Kings'." Cosmopolitan, Sept. 1954

Photoplay. "Valley of the Kings." Sept. 1954

Pihodna, Joe. "Valley of the Kings." New York Herald Tribune,
July 22, 1954

Stevens, Dale. "Same Plot, But the Freshness of Egypt Aids 'Valley
of the Kings'." The Dayton (Ohio) Daily News, Aug. 13, 1954

Time. "Valley of the Kings." July 26, 1954

Weiler, A. H. "Valley of the Kings." The New York Times, July 22,
1954

MANY RIVERS TO CROSS:

B.J.P. "Reviewing the Screen." The Milwaukee Journal, Feb.
17, 1955

Coe, Richard L. "Many Rivers, Many Laughs." The Washington Post,
Feb. 19, 1955

Lesner, Sam. "Eleanor Parker Kicks Robert Taylor Awake." Chicago
Daily News, Feb. 25, 1955

Masters, Dorothy. "Many Rivers to Cross." N.Y. Daily News, Feb.
23, 1955

Parents' Magazine. "Many Rivers to Cross." April 1955

Thompson, Howard. "The Screen: Detoured." The New York Times,
Feb. 24, 1955

INTERRUPTED MELODY:

Aitchison, Marion. "'Interrupted Melody' Blends Drama, Music." The
Miami Herald, March 16, 1957

Arden, Doris. "Inspiring Story About Singer." Chicago Sun-Times,
June 9, 1955

Branigan, Alan. "'Interrupted Melody' at Loew's." Newark [N.J.]
Evening News, June 9, 1955

Bruun, Paul M. "Bruun over Miami." The Miami Beach Sun, June
30, 1955

Cameron, Kate. "Tender Love Drama at Music Hall." N.Y. Daily
News, May 6, 1955

Crowther, Bosley. "Screen: The Defeat of Polio as Personal Drama."
The New York Times, May 6, 1955

Kelly, Herb. "Gentle and Warm Story in 'Interrupted Melody'."
Miami Daily News, June 30, 1955

Life. "Movies: Soprano's Second Comeback." May 16, 1955

Marsh, W. Ward. "Cheers for Eleanor Parker, Glenn Ford in 'Interrupted Melody,' Stillman Tomorrow." Cleveland Plain-Dealer, May
26, 1955

Martin, Mildred. "Trans-Lux Epic of Marjorie Lawrence." Philadelphia
Inquirer, June 9, 1955

Moffitt, Jack. "'Interrupted Melody' Has Artistry, Big B.O. Appeal."
The Hollywood Reporter, March 25, 1955

Movie Stars Parade. "Interrupted Melody." April 1955

Newsweek. "Sobs Set to Music." April 25, 1955

Parents' Magazine. "Interrupted Melody." May 1955

Parsons, Louella O. "Movie Citations: 'Interrupted Melody'." Cosmopolitan, April 1955

Pelswick, Rose. "'Interrupted Melody': Comeback of a Star." New
York Journal-American, May 6, 1955

Photoplay. "Interrupted Melody." April 1955

Quinn, Frank. "The New Movies: A-1 Musicals Bow in at Roxy,
Music Hall." N.Y. Daily Mirror, May 6, 1955

Ranney, Omar. "'Interrupted Melody' Brings Great Life Story to
Screen." The Cleveland Press, May 28, 1955

Sign Magazine, The. "Interrupted Melody." April 1955

Somers, Florence. "Redbook's Picture of the Month: 'Interrupted
Melody'." Redbook, May 1955

Spaeth, Arthur. "'Melody' Will Linger On." Cleveland News, May
26, 1955

Whitley, Reg. "Eleanor's 'Ghost' Steals the Picture." London Daily
Mirror (England), July 22, 1955

Windsor, Helen J. "Interrupted Melody." Films in Review, May 1955

Zinsser, William K.   "Interrupted Melody."   New York Herald Tribune,
May 6, 1955

THE MAN WITH THE GOLDEN ARM:

Bourke, George.   "'Man with the Golden Arm' Deals Out Raw, Sordid
Story of City Life."   The Miami Herald, Jan. 16, 1956

Bower, Helen.   "Melodrama Grips 'Golden Arm'."   Detroit Free Press,
Feb. 16, 1956

Cameron, Kate.   "The Man with the Golden Arm."   N.Y. Daily News,
Dec. 16, 1955

Crowther, Bosley.   "Narcotic Addict: 'Man with the Golden Arm'."
The New York Times, Dec. 16, 1955

Family Circle.   "The Man with the Golden Arm."   March 1956

Kelly, Herb.   "'Man with Golden Arm' Powerful Dope Story."   Miami
Daily News, Jan. 16, 1956

M. H.   "The Grimmest Film I've Ever Seen: 'The Man with the Golden
Arm'."   Picturegoer (England), Feb. 11, 1956

Motion Picture.   "The Man with the Golden Arm."   March 1956

Movie Mirror.   "The Man with the Golden Arm."   May 1956

Newsweek.   "Preminger's Inferno."   Dec. 26, 1955

Night and Day.   "A Night and Day Movie Best: 'The Man with the
Golden Arm'."   May 1956

Time.   "The Man with the Golden Arm."   Dec. 26, 1955

Willing, Diana.   "The Man with the Golden Arm."   Films in Review,
Jan. 1956

Zinsser, William K.   "Man with the Golden Arm."   New York Herald
Tribune, Dec. 16, 1955

Zunser, Jesse.   "The Man with the Golden Arm."   Cue, Dec. 17,
1955

THE KING AND FOUR QUEENS:

Bourke, George.   "'King, Four Queens' Is Good Hand."   The Miami
Herald, Feb. 18, 1957

Crowther, Bosley. "Screen: Ghost Town." The New York Times, Dec. 22, 1956

Kelly, Herb. "Cards Stacked Against Gable." Miami Daily News, Feb. 18, 1957

Picturegoer (England). "The King and Four Queens." Feb. 2, 1957

Stevenson, Walter. "'King' Gable Charms in 'Sexless' Western." The Detroit Times, Jan. 11, 1957

Zinsser, William K. "The King and Four Queens." New York Herald Tribune, Dec. 22, 1956

LIZZIE:

Aitchison, Marion. "Liz is a Triple-Threat Gal." The Miami Herald, March 16, 1957

Anderson, Stan. "Stillman's 'Lizzie' Stands Out as Excellent Psychiatric Film." The Cleveland Press, April 6, 1957

Crist, Judith. "This Week's Movies." TV Guide, March 31, 1973

Crowther, Bosley. "The Screen: 'Lizzie'." The New York Times, April 5, 1957

Kansas City Star, The. "At the Movies: 'Lizzie'." March 16, 1957

Kelly, Herb. "Eleanor Off Rocker Again." Miami Daily News, March 16, 1957

MacArthur, Harry. "Eleanor Parker Plays Triple-Threat Role." The [Washington, D.C.] Evening Star, June 22, 1957

Masters, Dorothy. "Three Girls in One in Mayfair's Picture." N.Y. Daily News, April 5, 1957

Mendlowitz, Leonard. "Penn Film Star Cast in 3 Roles." Pittsburgh Sun-Telegraph, March 16, 1957

Murphy, Anne F. "Lizzie." Films in Review, April 1957

Pelswick, Rose. "'Lizzie': Eleanor a Triple Threat." New York Journal-American, April 5, 1957

Photoplay. "Lizzie." May 1957

Pickering, Silas. "Lizzie." Pittsburgh Post-Gazette, March 16, 1957

Pittsburgh Times. "Lizzie." March 16, 1957

Powers, James. "Bresler-Haas Pic Has Fine Acting." The Hollywood
Reporter, March 5, 1957

Quinn, Frank. "Eleanor Parker is A-1 in 3-in-1 Role." N.Y. Daily
Mirror, April 5, 1957

Screen Stories. "Lizzie." April 1957

Sign Magazine, The. "Lizzie." May 1957

Spaeth, Arthur. "'Lizzie' Is a Gal with a Triple-Split Personality."
Cleveland News, April 5, 1957

Time. "Lizzie." March 25, 1957

Tinée, Mae. "Finds 'Lizzie' Weird Movie of 3 Persons." Chicago
Daily Tribune, March 19, 1957

Zinsser, William K. "Lizzie." New York Herald Tribune, April 5,
1957

THE SEVENTH SIN:

Beckley, Paul V. "The Seventh Sin." New York Herald Tribune,
June 29, 1957

Bourke, George. "'Seventh Sin' Is Forgiven; Late Reels Help to Save
It." The Miami Herald, May 31, 1957

Bower, Helen. "Star Gazing: She Atones for 7th Sin." Detroit Free
Press, July 20, 1957

Bruun, Paul M. "Bruun over Miami." Miami Beach Sun, May 30, 1957

Chicago Daily News. "The Seventh Sin." June 21, 1957

Cleveland Press, The. "Sincerity Marks 'Seventh Sin' at Stillman."
May 31, 1957

Cleveland News. "The Seventh Sin." May 31, 1957

Dayton [Ohio] News. "The Seventh Sin." June 10, 1957

Grant, Hank. "Lewis-Neame Pic Fine Adult Fare." The Hollywood
Reporter. May 13, 1957

Hinxman, Margaret. "Picturegoer Parade: The Seventh Sin."
Picturegoer (England), Sept. 7, 1957

J. H. "Miss Parker in Grim Tale at Columbia." The [Washington, D.C.] Evening Star, June 15, 1957

Kany, A. S. "Let's Go Places." The Dayton [Ohio] Journal Herald, June 10, 1957

Masters, Dorothy. "Eleanor Parker and Bill Travers: 'The Seventh Sin'." N.Y. Daily News, June 29, 1957

Movieland. "The Seventh Sin." Aug. 1957

Photoplay. "The Seventh Sin." Aug. 1957

Screen Stories. "The Seventh Sin." July 1957

Thompson, Howard. "'The Seventh Sin' Opens at the Palace." The New York Times, June 29, 1957

Tinée, Mae. "World Today Dates Movie 'Seventh Sin'." Chicago Daily Tribune, June 19, 1957

Waters, Bill. "'7th Sin' Tense Drama of Love and Adventure." Miami Daily News, May 30, 1957

"Whit." "The Seventh Sin." Variety, May 15, 1957

A HOLE IN THE HEAD:

Beckley, Paul V. "A Hole in the Head." New York Herald Tribune, July 16, 1959

Cook, Alton. "A Golden-Hearted Cynic with 'A Hole in the Head'." New York World-Telegram and Sun, July 16, 1959

Crowther, Bosley. "Screen: Capra's 'A Hole in the Head'." The New York Times, July 16, 1959

"Gene." "A Hole in the Head." Variety, May 20, 1959

Gilmour, Clyde. "A Hole in the Head." The Telegram (Toronto, Canada), Aug. 8, 1959

Ivers, James D. "A Hole in the Head." Motion Picture Daily, May 19, 1959

Lesner, Sam. "'A Hole in the Head' at the Oriental Magically Funny." The Chicago Daily News, June 18, 1959

Masters, Dorothy. "Sinatra Stars in Comedy at Loew's State." N.Y. Daily News, July 16, 1959

V. Reviews   215

Picturegoer (England). "A Hole in the Head." Aug. 22, 1959

Sennett, Ted. "A Hole in the Head." Films in Review, Aug.-Sept.
1959

Simon, Lynn. "'Hole in the Head' Heart-Warming." St. Petersburg
[Fla.] Times, June 30, 1959

Stewart, Evelyn. "Call This High Class Schmaltz." Detroit Free
Press, Aug. 7, 1959

Time. "A Hole in the Head." Aug. 3, 1959

Tinée, Mae. "This Newest Capra Film is Such Fun." Chicago Daily
Tribune, June 18, 1959

HOME FROM THE HILL:

American Weekly, The. "Movies: Home from the Hill." Feb. 28,
1960

Anderson, Stan. "A Real Star is Born in 'Home from the Hill'."
The Cleveland Press, March 18, 1960

Beckley, Paul V. "Home from the Hill." New York Herald Tribune,
March 4, 1960

Bourke, George. "Rich Production, Tastefully Done." The Miami
Herald, March 18, 1960

Coe, Richard L. "Purple Dust's Slow to Settle." The Washington
Post, March 19, 1960

Cook, Alton. "'Home from the Hill' Opens at Radio City." New York
World-Telegram and Sun, March 4, 1960

Crowther, Bosley. "Screen: 2½-Hour Drama." The New York Times,
March 4, 1960

E.D. "Home from the Hill." The Milwaukee Journal, March 17, 1960

Gilbert, Justin. "'Home from the Hill' is Powerful." N.Y. Daily
Mirror, March 4, 1960

Gilder, Rae. "'Home from the Hill' Has Drama, Suspense." The
Miami Beach Sun, March 18, 1960

Hale, Wanda. "'Home from the Hill' Distinguished Drama." N.Y.
Daily News, March 4, 1960

Hoekstra, Dick. "'Home from the Hill': Conflict Key to Exciting Film." Fort Lauderdale News, March 18, 1960

Kelly, Herb. "'Home from the Hill' Powerful." The Miami News, March 18, 1960

Lesner, Sam. "'Home from the Hill': A Tale of Texas Neurotics." The Chicago Daily News, March 28, 1960

Look. "Trouble in Texas." March 1, 1960

Marsters, Ann. "'Hill' Looms as '60 Hit." The Chicago American, March 29, 1960

Martin, Boyd. "'Home from the Hill' Quite Good." The [Louisville, Ky.] Courier-Journal, Aug. 2, 1960

McCall's. "Home from the Hill." April 1960

McCarten, John. "The Current Cinema: A Touch of Texas." The New Yorker, March 12, 1960

Mitchell, Gee. "'Home from the Hill' Absorbing Film Drama, Well Made, Acted." Dayton [Ohio] News, April 2, 1960

Newsweek. "New Film: Sex-Guns in the West." March 7, 1960

Oviatt, Ray. "'Home from the Hill' Colorful Melodrama." The Toledo Blade, March 31, 1960

Parents' Magazine. "Home from the Hill." March 1960

"Powe." "Home from the Hill." Variety, Feb. 10, 1960

St. Louis Post-Dispatch. "Red Meat and Good Acting." March 18, 1960

Screenland. "Home from the Hill." May 1960

Time. "Home from the Hill." April 11, 1960

Tinée, Mae. "Film's Guns and Gossip Both Lethal." Chicago Daily Tribune, March 28, 1960

RETURN TO PEYTON PLACE:

Beckley, Paul V. "The New Movie: 'Return to Peyton Place'." New York Herald Tribune, May 6, 1961

Bourke, George. "'Return' Loses Some of Impact." The Miami Herald, May 11, 1961

Cook, Alton. "'Return to Peyton Place' Opens at Paramount." New York World-Telegram and Sun, May 6, 1961

Crowther, Bosley. "Screen: A Selfish Mother." The New York Times, May 6, 1961

Gilbert, Justin. "'Return' is Reprise of 'Peyton Place'." N.Y. Daily Mirror, May 6, 1961

Hale, Wanda. "The Sequel is Here About Peyton Place." N.Y. Daily News, May 6, 1961

Lesner, Sam. "Sequel to 'Peyton Place' Proves 'Phony and Wasted'." The Chicago Daily News, May 10, 1961

Marsters, Ann. "'Peyton Place' Should Return Forever." The Chicago American, May 10, 1961

Mishkin, Leo. "Lucrative 'Return to Peyton Place'." N.Y. Morning Telegraph, May 6, 1961

Mitchell, Gee. "Further Adventures Among the Natives of Peyton Place." Dayton [Ohio] Daily News, May 31, 1961

Pelswick, Rose. "'Return to Peyton Place': More Dirt is Dug Up in a Staid N.E. Town." New York Journal-American, May 6, 1961

Vermilye, Jerry. "Return to Peyton Place." Films in Review, June-July 1961

Winsten, Archer. "'Return to Peyton Place' in Dual Bow." New York Post, May 6, 1961

MADISON AVENUE:

Beckley, Paul V. "Madison Avenue." New York Herald Tribune, March 29, 1962

Bourke, George. "'Madison Avenue' Movie Makes Point Pleasantly." The Miami Herald, Feb. 23, 1962

Butler, Charles A. "Madison Avenue." Films in Review, Dec. 1961

Cook, Alton. "'Madison Avenue' at Paramount." New York World-Telegram and Sun, March 29, 1962

F.H.G. "Madison Avenue." The Christian Science Monitor, March 27, 1962

Hale, Wanda. "Dana Andrews Stars in 'Madison Avenue'." N.Y. Daily News, March 29, 1962

Martin, Boyd. "Film Exploits Old Theme." The [Louisville, Ky.]
Courier-Journal, Feb. 9, 1962

Miami News, The. "Madison Avenue." Feb. 22, 1962

Pelswick, Rose. "Madison Avenue." New York Journal-American,
March 29, 1962

Quinn, Frank. "Four Movie Pros Take 'Madison Avenue' in Stride."

N.Y. Daily Mirror, March 29, 1962

Sign Magazine, The. "Madison Avenue." March 1962

Thirer, Irene. "'Madison Avenue' at the Paramount." New York Post,
March 29, 1962

Thompson, Howard. "'Madison Avenue' Seen at Paramount." The
New York Times, March 29, 1962

Toledo Blade, The. "Madison Avenue." Feb. 15, 1962

PANIC BUTTON:

Bourke, George. "'Panic' a Light Film." The Miami Herald, April
10, 1965

"Wear." "Panic Button." Variety, April 15, 1964

THE SOUND OF MUSIC:

Aaronson, Charles S. "The Sound of Music." Motion Picture Daily,
March 3, 1965

Bell, Joseph N. "Julie is the Joy in Saga of Singing Trapps." The
National Observer, March 8, 1965

Bourke, George. "'Sound of Music' a Great Film." The Miami Herald,
March 3, 1965

Cameron, Kate. "'The Sound of Music' a Heart-Lifting Film." N.Y.
Daily News, March 3, 1965

Chapin, Louis. "'Sound of Music' Filmic Splash." The Christian
Science Monitor, March 20, 1965

Coe, Richard L. "Julie Andrews: Alpine Skipper." The Washington
Post, March 18, 1965

Cook, Alton. "'Sound of Music' Comes in Sweetly." New York World-
Telegram and Sun, March 3, 1965

Crist, Judith. "Sugar and Spice, But Not Everything Nice." New
York Herald Tribune, March 3, 1965

Crowther, Bosley. "Screen: Julie Andrews and the Trapps." The
New York Times, March 3, 1965

Gertner, Richard. "Reviewing 'The Sound of Music'." Motion Picture
Herald, March 17, 1965

Hipp, Edward Sothern. "Trapp Saga." Newark [N.J.] Evening
News, March 3, 1965

Kelly, Herb. "'Sound of Music' Filled with Song, Beauty, Charm."
The Miami News, March 18, 1965

McClelland, Doug. "'Sound of Music' Musical Landmark." Record
World, March 6, 1965

Newsweek. "Ruritanian Reich." March 15, 1965

Pelswick, Rose. "Julie Andrews Is Wonderful." New York Journal-
American, March 3, 1965

Powers, James. "'Sound of Music' Restores Faith in the Art of Motion
Pictures." The Hollywood Reporter, March 1, 1965

Tozzi, Romano. "The Sound of Music." Films in Review, March
1965

"Whit." "The Sound of Music." Daily Variety, March 1, 1965

Winsten, Archer. "'The Sound of Music' at Rivoli." New York Post,
March 3, 1965

Wolf, William. "The Sound of Music." Cue, March 6, 1965

THE OSCAR:

Bourke, George. "Players Sparkle in Movie, 'Oscar'." The Miami
Herald, March 18, 1966

Cameron, Kate. "Bitter Drama Looks Inside Hollywood." N.Y. Daily
News, March 5, 1966

Cook, Alton. "'Oscar' Turns Trash into Cash." New York World-
Telegram and Sun, March 5, 1966

Crist, Judith. "'The Oscar' Deserves Booby Prize." New York
Herald Tribune, March 6, 1966

Crowther, Bosley. "Screen: 'Oscar' Arrives." The New York Times,
March 6, 1966

Freund, Bob. "'The Oscar' Is Slick, Artificial Film of Contenders
for Academy Award." The Fort Lauderdale News, March 19, 1966

Hart, Henry. "The Oscar." Films in Review, April 1966

Independent Film Journal, The. "The Oscar." Feb. 19, 1966

McClelland, Doug. "Tony Bennett's 'Oscar' Debut Auspicious."
Record World, Feb. 12, 1966

Pelswick, Rose. "Slick Drama of Filmland." New York Journal-
American, March 5, 1966

Powers, James. "'The Oscar' Realistic H'wood Drama Highlighted by
Top Performances." The Hollywood Reporter, Feb. 15, 1966

Time. "Prize Package." March 11, 1966

Winsten, Archer. "'The Oscar' at State & Festival." New York Post,
March 3, 1966

AN AMERICAN DREAM:

Boxoffice. "An American Dream." Sept. 5, 1966

Cameron, Kate. "'American Dream' Drama of Violence." N.Y. Daily
News, Sept. 1, 1966

Christie, Ian. "And I'll See You There, Too, Darlings." London
Daily Express (England), Sept. 30, 1966

Cue. "An American Dream." Sept. 3, 1966

DeVine, Larry. "'American Dream' Is Mixed-Up Mailer." The Miami
Herald, Oct. 17, 1966

Freund, Bob. "'An American Dream' Is More Like a Nightmare."
Fort Lauderdale News, Oct. 15, 1966

Gertner, Richard. "An American Dream." Motion Picture Herald,
Sept. 14, 1966

Greenberg, Abe. "'An American Dream'--A Smasher!" Hollywood
Citizen News, Aug. 26, 1966

Green Sheet, The. "An American Dream." Nov. 1966

Knight, Arthur. "An American Dream." *The Saturday Review of Literature*, Sept. 17, 1966

London Daily Mirror (England). "After Miss Parker, Everybody Dies." Sept. 30, 1966

Petersen, Clarence. "Film Tells Unsavory Story." *The Chicago Tribune*, Oct. 3, 1966

Photoplay. "An American Dream." Nov. 1966

Powers, James. "Warners' 'American Dream' Compelling, Absorbing Pic." *The Hollywood Reporter*, Aug. 25, 1966

Taylor, Harvey. "Mailer Movie: A Violent Tale, A Classic Fight." *Detroit Free Press*, Oct. 16, 1966

Thompson, Howard. "An American Dream." *The New York Times*, Sept. 1, 1966

Time. "Mailer Without Mailer." Sept. 5, 1966

Winsten, Archer. "'An American Dream' in Triple Bow." *New York Post*, Sept. 1, 1966

WARNING SHOT:

Bourke, George. "Janssen Is Slick in 'Shot'." *The Miami Herald*, Jan. 7, 1967

Frumkes, Roi. "Warning Shot." *Films in Review*, Feb. 1967

Green Sheet, The. "Warning Shot." Feb. 1967

Guarino, Ann. "Janssen Again is Man on the Run." N.Y. *Daily News*, June 8, 1967

Kelly, Herb. "David Janssen Still a Fugitive Even in Movie." *The Miami News*, Jan. 6, 1967

Mahoney, John. "'Warning Shot' Taut Drama, Janssen in Starring Role." *The Hollywood Reporter*, Jan. 3, 1967

Marsh, W. Ward. "'Warning' is Old-Time Blood 'n' Guts Melodrama." *The [Cleveland] Plain Dealer*, Feb. 11, 1967

Mastroianni, Tony. "'Fugitive' Finally Stops Running." *The Cleveland Press*, Feb. 10, 1967

Time. "Copy Cop: 'Warning Shot'." June 9, 1967

Winsten, Archer. "'Warning Shot,' a 'Sleeper,' with 'Busy Body' at RKO's." New York Post, June 8, 1967

THE TIGER AND THE PUSSYCAT:

Boxoffice. "The Tiger and the Pussycat." Aug. 28, 1967

Guarino, Ann. "Laughs in 'Pussycat' Not Roars." N.Y. Daily News, Sept. 21, 1967

Herridge, Frances. "'The Tiger' Takes a Look at the Middle-Aged Man." New York Post, Sept. 21, 1967

Powers, James. "'Tiger and Pussycat' Plays with Humor; Stars Should Help." The Hollywood Reporter, Sept. 22, 1967

Shepard, Richard F. "Neighborhoods' Pair." The New York Times, Sept. 21, 1967

EYE OF THE CAT:

Arnold, Gary. "Eye of the Cat." The Washington Post, July 30, 1969

Beacham, Rod. "Eye of the Cat." Films and Filming (England). Nov., 1969

Crist, Judith. "Eye of the Cat." New York, June 23, 1969

Freund, Bob. "Tabbies Star in Shocker as Evil Doers." Fort Lauderdale News, Aug. 12, 1969

Green Sheet, The. "Eye of the Cat." Aug. 1969

Guarino, Ann. "'Cat' Has No Bite in It." N.Y. Daily News, June 19, 1969

Herridge, Frances. "Cats Turn Menace in Suspense Film." New York Post, June 19, 1969

Independent Film Journal, The. "Eye of the Cat." June 10, 1969

London Telegraph (England). "Cold Plotters and Satanic Cats." Aug. 22, 1969

Meyer, James E. "Plenty of Pussyfooting in 'Eye of the Cat'." The Miami Herald, Aug. 12, 1969

Millar, Jeff. "Cats Are Only Cute in Latest Chiller." Houston
Chronicle, Aug. 22, 1969

Thompson, Howard. "Screen: Horror Tale Involving Felines." The
New York Times, Jan. 23, 1954

SUNBURN:

Champlin, Charles. "Critic at Large: 'Sunburn' Without Appeal."
Los Angeles Times, Aug. 10, 1979

Knight, Arthur. "Sunburn." The Hollywood Reporter, Aug. 10, 1979

Maslin, Janet. "Film: Acapulco 'Sunburn'." The New York Times,
Aug. 10, 1979

B. Television Films

HANS BRINKER:

Gould, Jack. "TV: Children's Classic." The New York Times,
Dec. 15, 1969

Gross, Ben. "'Hans Brinker' Skates to Success on TV Screen." N.Y.
Daily News, Dec. 15, 1969

Hull, Bob. "Hans Brinker." The Hollywood Reporter, Dec. 16, 1969

Mackin, Tom. "Cool to 'Hans Brinker'." The [Newark, N.J.] Evening
News, Dec. 15, 1969

"Tone." "Hans Brinker." Daily Variety, Dec. 15, 1969

Williams, Bob. "On the Air: Hans Brinker." New York Post, Dec.
15, 1969

MAYBE I'LL COME HOME IN THE SPRING:

Gardella, Kay. "TV Film with Sally Field Copout for Wayward Kids."
N.Y. Daily News, Feb. 17, 1971

VANISHED:

Adams, Val. "NBC's 'Vanished' Proves Movies Longer Than Ever."
N.Y. Daily News, March 10, 1971

Anderson, Jack. "Corny Ending Spoils TV Movie 'Vanished'." The Miami Herald, March 11, 1971

"Bok." "Vanished." Variety, March 17, 1971

"Daku." "Vanished." Daily Variety, March 9, 1971

Goff, John. "'Vanished,' Landmark Is Made for TV Films." The Hollywood Reporter, March 0, 1971

Mackin, Tom. "'Vanished' a Blockbuster." Newark [N.J.] Evening News, March 10, 1971

O'Connor, John J. "TV: Inside a Celluloid Washington, Clichés Intact." The New York Times, March 10, 1971

HOME FOR THE HOLIDAYS:

Mayer, Jim. "Julie Harris, Eleanor Parker Excellent in TV Movie Thriller." The Miami Herald, Nov. 30, 1972

Thomas, Kevin. "ABC Serves Up Some Seasonal Mystery." Los Angeles Times, Nov. 28, 1972

THE GREAT AMERICAN BEAUTY CONTEST:

Crist, Judith. "This Week's Movies." TV Guide, Feb. 10-16, 1973

Gardella, Kay. "The Quality of TV Movies Goes Down, Down." N.Y. Daily News, Feb. 15, 1973

Meyer, Jim. "Beauty Contest Film Is Good (When It Isn't Just Ghastly)." The Miami Herald, Feb. 15, 1973

Thompson, Howard. "TV Review: Beauty Contests Topic of ABC Film at 8:30." The New York Times, Feb. 13, 1973

FANTASY ISLAND

Thomas, Kevin. "Fantasizing for a Fee in 'Island'." Los Angeles Times, Jan. 14, 1977

"Tone." "Fantasy Island." Daily Variety, Jan. 14, 1977

THE BASTARD:

Coast-to-Coast Times. "The Bastard." May 17/30, 1978

O'Connor, John J. "'The Bastard' Winds Up Tonight." The New York Times, May 23, 1978

Rosenberg, Howard. "'The Bastard'--Misbegotten Mush." Los Angeles Times, May 22, 1978

"Tone." "The Bastard--Parts I & II." Daily Variety, May 22, 1978

SHE'S DRESSED TO KILL:

Flanders, Judy. "TV Choices." N.Y. Daily News, June 20. 1983

Hollywood Reporter, The. "She's Dressed to Kill." Dec. 10, 1979

ONCE UPON A SPY:

Thomas, Kevin. "Light Touch, Able Cast Perk Up 'Once Upon a Spy'." Los Angeles Times, Sept. 19, 1980

"Tone." "Once Upon a Spy." Daily Variety, Sept. 19, 1980

Williams, Gail. "Once Upon a Spy." The Hollywood Reporter, Sept. 19, 1980

MADAME X:

Brown, James. "The Tube Tonight: 'Madame X' Remake on NBC." Los Angeles Times, March 16, 1981

Gardella, Kay. "Madame X." N.Y. Daily News, March 16. 1981

Shales, Tom. "NBC's 'Madame X' is a Darn Good Yarn." Asbury Park Press, March 10, 1981

"Tone." "Madame X." Daily Variety, March 16, 1981

Williams. Gail. "Madame X." The Hollywood Reporter, March 13, 1981

C. Series Television

BRACKEN'S WORLD:

Amory, Cleveland. "Review: Bracken's World." TV Guide, Dec. 6, 1969

"Bill." "Bracken's World." Variety, Sept. 24, 1969

Gardella, Kay. "Bosoms, Bottoms & Broads Buttress Bracken's World." N.Y. Daily News, Sept. 20, 1969

Loynd, Ray. "Bracken's World." Entertainment World, Nov. 7, 1969

Time. "Parker in 'Bracken's World'." Sept. 26, 1969

"Daku." "The Love Boat." Daily Variety, Sept. 17, 1969

D. Television Specials

THE BUICK ELECTRA PLAYHOUSE (The Gambler, the Nun and the Radio):

Dube, Bernard. "Parker, Conte Shine in Hemingway Story." Montreal Gazette (Canada), May 19, 1960

O'Brian, Jack. "Jack O'Brian Says: Half-Baked Hemingway." New York Journal-American, May 20, 1960

Van Horne, Harriet. "Not His Cup of Tea." New York World-Telegram and Sun, May 19, 1960

GUESS WHO'S COMING TO DINNER:

"Bill." "Guess Who's Coming to Dinner." Variety, July 9, 1975

E. Stage Appearances

FORTY CARATS:

Freund, Bob. "Eleanor Parker Talents Brighten Comedy." Ft. Lauderdale News, March 31, 1970

Kelly, Herb. "Theater: 'Forty Carats'." The Miami News, March 18, 1970

Newman, Thelma. "'Forty Carats' Just Pure Fun with a Mod Switch." Palm Beach Post, March 3, 1970

Primak, Larry. "'Forty Carats' Is a Gem of a Play." Hollywood [Fla.] Sun-Tattler, April 2, 1970

Spencer, Lynne. "Play Obvious Bit of Advice." Palm Beach Times, March 3, 1970

Swaebly, Frances. "'Forty Carats' a Real Crowd-Pleaser." The Miami Herald, March 19, 1970

Vaughan, Elizabeth. "Eleanor Parker Charming; Brightens Playhouse Stage." Palm Beach News, March 3, 1970

Zelickson, Jill. "Cast Can't Rescue Unreal '40 Carats'." The Miami Herald (Palm Beach edition), March 4, 1970

APPLAUSE:

Coe, Richard L. "A Far Firmer 'Applause'." The Washington Post, July 13, 1972

"Don." "Applause." Variety, July 5, 1972

Downing, Robert. "Miss Parker Shines; 'Applause' Deserves Big Hand in Denver." The Denver Post, July 5, 1972

Lebherz, Richard. "Margo Channing in Love." Washington, D.C., Frederick News-Post, July 17, 1972

McIntyre, Dave. "Eleanor Parker in Spotlight: 'Applause' Scores Big as Solid, Lively Musical Show." San Diego Evening Tribune, June 28, 1972

FINISHING TOUCHES:

Bennett, Jerry. "'Finishing Touches' Displays the Beauty of a Well Written Play." St. Charles, Ill., Free Press, Nov. 27, 1974

Besser, Lu. "Eleanor Parker Cast Delightful at Pheasant Run." The West Chicago Press, Nov. 28, 1974

White, Charles A. "Finishing Touches' Is a Real-Life Family Affair." Barrington [Ill.] Courier, Nov. 28, 1974

THE NIGHT OF THE IGUANA:

Loynd, Ray. "Stalking Iguanas in Williams' Country." Los Angeles Herald-Examiner, Dec. 22, 1975

Reed, Rex. "'Iguana' Way Off Broadway, but Right on Target." N.Y. Sunday News, Jan. 25, 1976

Sullivan, Dan. "Talking Shannon Down in 'Iguana'." Los Angeles Times, Dec. 22, 1975

A. The 1940s

Blues in the Night. In the caption for a glamour portrait of Eleanor Parker published by Motion Picture magazine in December 1941, it was stated that she was in Warner Bros.' Blues in the Night, which featured Priscilla Lane, Richard Whorf and Betty Field. But Parker is not in any cast listings of this film, nor is it on any of her official résumés, and no one has ever mentioned seeing her in it. Therefore, it is probable that a resourceful Warner publicity department simply used her attractive likeness to get a plug for their new film.

Mr. Skeffington. Parker was announced for the small role of plain daughter to selfish beauty Fanny Skeffington (Bette Davis), but instead was given the feminine lead in the concurrent Between Two Worlds. She was replaced by Marjorie Riordan in the 1944 film.

Conflict. Parker was announced to play the young woman coveted by wife-murderer Humphrey Bogart, but when the 1945 release went into production Alexis Smith had the part.

Humoresque. Parker was first mentioned for the part of the heavy-drinking patroness of violinist John Garfield. The character eventually was played in the 1946 film by Joan Crawford.

The Jazz Singer. Parker and Dane Clark were announced for a remake of The Jazz Singer. It was done in the 1950s with Peggy Lee and Danny Thomas.

Stallion Road. Parker was suspended by Warner Bros. for refusing the feminine lead in Ronald Reagan's first postwar film, a story of modern horse ranching. Alexis Smith replaced her in the 1947 release.

Love and Learn. Parker was suspended by Warner Bros. for refusing the socialite role finally played by Martha Vickers in the 1947 film.

One Sunday Afternoon. Parker was announced to play the sweet young wife in the 1948 musical version of James Hagan's oft-filmed play, but was replaced by Dorothy Malone.

The Fountainhead. Parker wanted, and was talked about for, the role of the erratic heiress in Ayn Rand's story, but Patricia Neal got to co-star with Gary Cooper in the 1948 film.

Always Together. In several books, articles and even reviews, Parker is listed among the Warner guest stars in this 1948 release. She does not appear in the film.

The Girl from Jones Beach. Parker was mentioned for the school-teacher-model opposite Ronald Reagan, but did not want to cavort in a bathing suit, as required by the script; when the film was released in 1949 Virginia Mayo had the role.

The Hasty Heart. Warner Bros. wanted Parker to play the nurse with Ronald Reagan in the film of John Patrick's play, but it was to be made in England and she did not want to travel during winter with her infant daughter Susan. Patricia Neal took over in the 1949 film.

The Travelers. Planned in 1949 as a John Wayne Western to co-star Parker, it was filmed in 1951 by Warner Bros. as **Along the Great Divide** with Kirk Douglas and Virginia Mayo.

As We Are Today. Parker announced she would star for Warner Bros. in this Mildred Cram story, originally titled **Happiness**, but she did not do it.

Charge It. Although she hoped to star in this Warner Bros. property about a young couple's experiences with charge accounts, Parker never made it.

Somewhere in the City. Parker was suspended by Warner Bros. for refusing to play the nurse in this crime melodrama and was replaced by Virginia Mayo when the film was released as **Backfire** in 1950.

B. The 1950s

The Country Girl. Parker began campaigning to portray the wife of the alcoholic actor soon after Clifford Odets' drama opened on Broadway in 1950, and at one point columnist Hedda Hopper said she had the inside track. But when Paramount released the film in 1954, Grace Kelly had the part which won her the Academy Award.

Raton Pass. Parker turned down the feminine lead in this 1951 Western dealing with a married couple battling over a cattle empire. Patricia Neal accepted the role opposite Dennis Morgan, which ended her Warner contract.

My Most Intimate Friend. In 1953, M-G-M announced that Parker would play a TV commentator in this Sidney Sheldon screenplay subsequently mentioned as a co-starring vehicle for Lana Turner and Ava Gardner. It was never made.

Beau Brummell. Parker was announced to play Lady Patricia, a
Regency beauty, opposite Stewart Granger in the title role. But
when the British-filmed M-G-M production opened in 1954, Elizabeth
Taylor had the role.

One More Time. Under George Cukor's direction, Parker was sup-
posed to have played a young Korean-conflict widow in this original
comedy by Garson Kanin and Ruth Gordon, but the film was never
made.

Green Ice. Parker was mentioned for the role of the coffee plantation
owner; when the film was released in 1954 as Green Fire, Grace Kelly
was cast.

Untamed. Parker was among several stars said to have expressed
interest in portraying the Irish heroine who wound up in South
Africa fighting Zulus; Susan Hayward played the role in the 1955
film.

The Maverick. Parker was announced for the girl with a past in
this Western drama, but by the time it came out in 1957 as Three
Violent People, Anne Baxter was starring.

The Women. Parker was first announced for the gossiped-about wife
in M-G-M's musical remake of Clare Boothe's play. It finally went
to June Allyson in the 1956 release re-titled, The Opposite Sex.

Friendly Persuasion. Parker, Jane Wyman, Jane Russell, and Maureen
O'Hara were up for the Quaker spouse of Gary Cooper in this drama produced and directed by William Wyler, but Dorothy McGuire was cast in
the 1956 production.

Some Came Running. Parker was offered the part of the college
instructor with Frank Sinatra, Dean Martin, and Shirley MacLaine,
but turned it down. Martha Hyer accepted, won a 1958 best supporting actress Oscar nomination.

Bridge to the Sun. Parker was interested in playing the Southern
belle wife of a Japanese diplomat in the film of Gwen Terasaki's autobiography, but Carroll Baker starred in the 1961 film.

C. The 1960s

Away from Home. Parker was announced for the "nice wife" in the
proposed M-G-M film version of Rona Jaffe's novel, but it was never
made.

The Lady Takes the Floor. Parker was announced for the part of a
men's magazine editor elected to Congress. It was never made.

Only for Now. Parker and Glenn Ford were set to co-star as a film star and a diplomat in the American Embassy in Rome. But the film was never made.

The Park Avenue Story. Parker and James Cagney were announced as stars; she as a fashion designer, Cagney as a skyscraper builder. The film was never made.

Madeleine. Parker was to discuss a modern version of Medea with Italian filmmaker Federico Fellini, but it was never made.

Chautauqua. Parker was to have co-starred with Glenn Ford, but the film was never made.

Pontius Pilate. Parker was mentioned for the part of Claudia Procula eventually played by Jeanne Crain when the Italian-made film was released in 1967. The co-director was Irving Rapper, who had directed Parker in The Voice of the Turtle (1947).

Mother Cabrini. Parker expected to play the American saint for Curtis Bernhardt, who had directed her in Interrupted Melody, but the film was never made.

I Was a Spy. Parker was announced for the true story of Marion Miller, a housewife who posed as a Communist while working for the FBI. Instead, in 1962 it became a TV drama with Jeanne Crain and Ronald Reagan entitled My Dark Days.

Mr. Hobbs Takes a Vacation. Parker, columns revealed, was interested in playing James Stewart's wife in this film, but when it was released by 20th Century-Fox, in 1962, Maureen O'Hara had the part.

The Sound You Can't Hear. In June 1961, Hedda Hopper reported, "Eleanor Parker's back from a European vacation. This fall she takes the kids to London, where she'll make The Sound You Can't Hear for Jan Pennington." It was never made.

Kisses for My President. Parker was announced for this comedy about the first woman president of the United States, produced and directed by Curtis Bernhardt, but Polly Bergen got the part in the 1964 release.

Harlow. When Judy Garland bolted the role of Jean Harlow's mother in this Electronovision biography, Eleanor Parker was announced to replace her. Then Parker rejected it, too, and Ginger Rogers wound up co-starring with Carol Lynley in the 1965 release.

High Horse. According to columnist Sheilah Graham, "Three-time Oscar nominee Eleanor Parker has taken an option on High Horse, a screenplay by Tom Wayne. She will film it for her own company." It was never made.

<u>An American Wife</u>. Parker was to play a "Texas millionairess who is also bored, three times a widow and a female Casanova," but Rhonda Fleming enacted the role in the 1966 release re-titled, <u>Run for Your Wife</u>.

<u>The Strange Summer of Signor Fontana</u>. In 1965, columnist Mike Connolly wrote, "[Parker] leaves for Rome to do her first foreign film for actor-turned-director Alberto Sordi entitled <u>The Strange Summer of Signor Fontana</u>." Parker did not make this film.

<u>The Girls of Slender Means</u>. Parker was announced for a British film of that title, from a Muriel Sparks novel; she did not do it.

<u>Something Beginning with M</u>. Parker was supposed to make this film in England, after completing <u>Warning Shot</u> (1967), but did not.

VII. UNREALIZED TELEVISION PROJECTS

A. The 1960s

Of Human Bondage. In April 1961, columnist Jack O'Brian reported, "Eleanor Parker will star in Of Human Bondage on British TV, to be repeated on tape here if the price is right." Parker did not recreate her 1946 film role for TV.

Please Don't Eat the Daisies. Parker was often mentioned to star as the suburban housewife-columnist in the situation comedy based on Jean Kerr's book and Doris Day's M-G-M movie, but when it became a series in 1965, Pat Crowley played the lead.

The Time of My Wife. Parker was asked to co-star with Bob Hope in this Chrysler Theatre book comedy, but did not do it. Eva Marie Saint did.

B. The 1970s

Women in Chains. Parker was offered the part of the sadistic women's prison superintendent in this but turned it down. Ida Lupino made her TV movie debut in the 1972 production.

C. The 1980s

Dynasty. In August 1981, columnist Marilyn Beck announced that "after negotiations collapsed with Eleanor Parker," Joan Collins had been signed to play John Forsythe's former wife, Alexis, in this prime-time soap opera. Sophia Loren also had been mentioned for the continuing role.

A. The 1950s

Tea and Sympathy. It was rumored that Robert Anderson wrote this successful drama for Eleanor Parker. When it opened on Broadway in 1953, Deborah Kerr was starred.

The Girls of Summer. Eleanor Parker was asked to star in this N. Richard Nash Broadway drama, but declined. Shelley Winters opened in the 1956 play that ran for 56 performances.

Women with Red Hair. Parker was offered the lead in this Broadway-bound play, but said no.

B. The 1960s

Cactus Flower. In the late 1960s, columnist Leonard Lyons announced, "Eleanor Parker will play the Lauren Bacall role in the national company of Cactus Flower." Alexis Smith did it.

C. The 1970s

All Through the House. In 1973, Parker was said to be considering making her New York stage debut in this new drama by Tom Scoley, under the production aegis of Joseph Papp, but did not do it.

A Little Night Music. Parker was offered the lead (created by Glynis Johns on Broadway) in the South African company of Stephen Sondheim's 1973 musical, but turned it down.

Marjorie Lawrence
Harmony Hills
Hot Springs, Arkansas

July 4th, 1955

Miss Eleanor Parker
620 Beverly Drive
Beverly Hills
Hollywood, California

Dear Eleanor Parker,

I shall always remember with deep emotion your gracious and generous gesture toward me by appearing on the television program This is Your Life. We all agree that you were terrific.

Words cannot express my deep and grateful thanks to you for your superb portrayal of Marjorie Lawrence in Interrupted Melody. You have captured the many difficult and varied phases of my life with astonishing accuracy and profound understanding.

I realize what an enormous undertaking it was for one so young, but you have proved yourself a magnificent actress by being both dynamic and tender and by your complete at-oneness with the role. You deserve an Academy Award.

Tom and I did enjoy meeting your nice husband. Please give him our warmest regards.

To you, my dear, I can only say God bless you and keep you always.

Affectionately,
Your most ardent fan,

MARJORIE LAWRENCE

INDEX

Powell, Dick 91
Powell, Jane 128
Powers, James 115
Powers, Stephanie 113
Preminger, Otto 17, 88-89
Pride of the Marines 6-7, 13,
   102, 131, 133, 197-98
Prince, William 38
Promises in the Dark 22
Pryor, Thomas M. 32, 39, 53
Punchline 22

Quincy 22
Quinn, Frank 92

Rackin, Martin 66
Rambova, Natacha 66
Rand, Ayn 229
Rapper, Irving 10, 54, 232
Raton Pass 230
Ravetch, Irving 99, 101
Reach, John 94
Reagan, Ronald 10. 52-54, 133,
   229-30, 232
Record World 110
Redbook 87
Reed, Rex 130
Reid, Carl Benton 77
Return to Peyton Place 19, 102-
   103, 216-17
Rey, Alejandro 117
Reynolds, Joyce 30
Rhapsody in Blue 33
Rhodes, Leah 49, 59
Richards, Jeff 82-83
Richardson, Duncan 64
Ridgely, John 42-43
Riordan, Marjorie 229
Risi, Dino 114
Ritter, Thelma 97-98
Roberts, Roy 90
Robinson, Edward G. 97-98
Rodgers, Richard 22, 107
Rogers, Ginger 232
Rogers, Roy 40
Roman, Ric 94
Roman, Ruth 11, 65
Romance of Rosy Ridge, The 84
Roosevelt, Franklin D. 31

Rosay, Francoise 96
Rose, Helen 87, 95
Rose Tattoo, The 87
Rosenstein, Sophie 4
Rosher, Charles 73
Rosing, Vladimir 87-88
Rowland, Roy 84
Rubin, Mann 113
Run for Your Wife 233
Russell, Jane 90, 231

Sachse, Leopold 86
St. Charles, Ill., Free Press
   130
St. John, Howard 103-104
St. John, Jill 109-10
Sakall, S. Z. 49-50
Samson and Delilah 86
Sanders, George 96, 113
Sarafian, Richard C. 117
Sarrazin, Michael 116
Sawyer, Connie 98
Scaramouche 13, 71-74, 205-206
Schallert, Edwin 51
Schary, Dore 12-13
Scheuer, Philip K. 47
Schiffrin, Bill 20
Schmid, Al 41-43
Schoenfeld, Bernard C. 62
Schrock, Raymond L. 37
Scoley, Tom 237
Scott, John L. 11
Screen Album 47
Screen Directors Playhouse 9,
   131
Screen Guide 10
Screen Stars 8, 35
Screenland 14, 63
Sea Hawk, The 35
See You in Hell, Darling 112
Segal, Vivienne 131
Selznick, David O. 38
September Affair 132
Sessions, Almira 68
Set-Up, The 66
Seven Brides for Seven Brothers
   83
Seventh Sin, The 17-18, 95-97,
   213-14
Shain, Percy 20

ABOUT THE AUTHOR ___

DOUG McCLELLAND, a freelance writer-lecturer on film, is the author of nine books: The Unkindest Cuts: The Scissors and the Cinema; Susan Hayward: The Divine Bitch; Down the Yellow Brick Road: The Making of The Wizard of Oz; The Golden Age of "B" Movies; Hollywood on Ronald Reagan: Friends and Enemies Discuss Our President, The Actor; Hollywood on Hollywood: Tinsel Town Talks; StarSpeak: Hollywood on Everything; Blackface to Blacklist: Al Jolson, Larry Parks and "The Jolson Story"; and Eleanor Parker, Woman of a Thousand Faces.

McClelland was an arts editor for The Newark [N.J.] Evening News in the 1950s, and editor of Record World magazine in New York City from 1961 to 1972. His work has appeared in a number of anthologies, including Hollywood Kids, 500 Best American Films to Buy, Rent or Videotape, and The Real Stars (volumes one, two, and three). In addition, he has been published in such periodicals as Films in Review, After Dark, Hollywood Studio Magazine, Films and Filming, Quirk's Reviews, Film Fan Monthly and Filmograph.

Doug McClelland also has been a consultant on many books. Currently, he is a literary critic for The Asbury Park Press and is writing his tenth book, Hollywood Talks Turkey--The Screen's Greatest Flops.